STEP·BY·STEP

# Simple Cookbook

STEP·BY·STEP

# Simple Cookbook

—

*Classic cooking made easy*

*Wordsworth Editions*

This edition published 1993 by Wordsworth Editions Ltd,
Cumberland House, Crib Street, Ware, Hertfordshire.

Copyright © Wordsworth Editions Ltd 1993.

ISBN 1-85326-999-9

Printed and bound in Hong Kong by South China Printing Co.

# *Step-by-Step Simple Cookbook*

The purpose of this book is to show that simple, classic recipes are within everybody's reach. The French language has a gift for making every dish sound mouthwatering by its name alone, yet at the same time, for English speakers at least, making them also sound somewhat daunting to prepare.

The *Step-by-Step Simple Cookbook* shows just *how* simple many of these recipes can be. They are divided into six categories – Hors d'oeuvre, Fish, Beef, Poultry & Game, Vegetables and Desserts – and a starring system grades them as 'Easy' or 'Very easy'. The Table of Contents (which lists all the dishes by their English names) gives both the star rating and the total preparation and cooking times, so that you can easily select recipes to suit your taste and schedule. As an added help, the recipe page itself (which has both the French and English name) gives you the preparation and cooking times separately, and then a numbered, step-by-step list of instructions for preparing and presenting the meal.

The *Step-by-Step Simple Cookbook*, as will be seen from a glance through its colourful pages, covers a very wide variety of dishes to suit all tastes, all levels of skill, and all kinds of occasion: grills, roasts, stews, cold dishes and salads, and everything from the simplest hors d'oeuvre to the most exotic rich desserts. The pages have additional hints, tips and extra recipes sprinkled throughout in the form of footnotes, and there is a page at the back which will help you choose the right wines to accompany each dish. Adventurous, enjoyable, classic cooking couldn't be simpler. *Bon appetit!*

# Table of Contents

## Desserts

---

### Notes: *Getting the Best out of this Book*

1. The preparation times given in the Table of Contents and with each recipe are minimum times: they will vary according to the cook's ability and the equipment available. Certain of the recipes require periods for macerating or chilling. These have not been taken into account in the times given in the table, but are indicated in the recipes.

2. It is best to use double cream for most recipes – it is the nearest equivalent to French cream. Remember also that the French use unsalted butter, and this is assumed in the recipes unless otherwise stated.

3. Certain of the recipes require cooking *au bain-marie*. This consists of placing whatever is to be cooked in a saucepan inside a larger saucepan filled with almost-boiling water. This method is ideal for cooking certain delicate sauces or other dishes which would react badly if exposed to a direct heat.

4. It is always best to use red or white wine vinegar in the recipes where vinegar is required; the result will not be the same if you use malt vinegar. In the same way, freshly ground black pepper should always be used in preference to ready-ground pepper.

5. Oven Temperatures. The following are Gas, Fahrenheit and Centigrade equivalents:

| Gas | ¼ | ½ | 1 | 2 | 3 | 4 | 5 | 6 | 7 | 8 | 9 |
|---|---|---|---|---|---|---|---|---|---|---|---|
| °F | 225 | 250 | 275 | 300 | 325 | 350 | 375 | 400 | 425 | 450 | 475 |
| °C | 110 | 120 | 140 | 160 | 170 | 180 | 190 | 200 | 220 | 230 | 250 |

6. It is important when using these recipes to follow the exact proportions. A set of kitchen scales, measuring jug, glass and spoons are essential. Follow either metric *or* avoirdupois measurements in each recipe.

7. To help you choose the right wine for your meal, see page 160.

# Canapés aux Bouquets

*Serves 3-6. Preparation and cooking: 15 min*

*Prawn Canapés*

★

○ **6 slices white bread, crusts removed**
○ **200g (7 oz) prawns**
○ **60ml (4 tbls) mayonnaise**
○ **6 slices Cheshire cheese**

1. Put aside 12 of the nicest prawns. Shell and finely chop the rest.
2. In a bowl, mix the minced prawns and mayonnaise.
3. Toast the slices of bread on both sides. Spread the prawn mayonnaise on them and cover with a slice of cheese.
4. Place in an ovenproof dish and leave under the grill until the cheese starts to melt. Remove and garnish each canapé with 2 prawns. Serve at once.

# Canapés aux Champignons

*Serves 5-10. Preparation and cooking: 20 min*

*Mushroom Canapés*

★

○ **10 slices white bread, crusts removed**
○ **250g (9 oz) button mushrooms**
○ **100ml (3½ fl oz) double cream**
○ **100g (4 oz) Gruyère cheese**
○ **1 slice smoked ham (Parma or Bayonne style)**
○ **juice of 1 lemon**
○ **15 sprigs chervil, coarsely chopped**
○ **2 pinches grated nutmeg**
○ **salt and pepper**

1. Remove the earthy base of the mushrooms and wash, dry and slice them.
2. Dice the ham and cheese. Place the sliced mushrooms in a bowl and pour the lemon juice over them. Add the cream, ham and cheese, chervil, grated nutmeg, and salt and pepper to taste. Mix well.
3. Toast the bread on both sides. Arrange on a dish and spread the mushroom mixture on each slice while they are still hot. Serve at once.

# Canapés aux Moules

*Serves 5-10. Preparation and cooking: 20 min*

*Mussel Canapés*

★

○ **10 slices white bread, crusts removed**
○ **20 large mussels**
○ **60ml (4 tbls) mayonnaise**
○ **1 onion, chopped**
○ **1 small handful fresh parsley, chervil, tarragon and chives, chopped**
○ **30ml (2 tbls) capers**
○ **pepper**

1. Scrape the mussels and scrub them well. Wash under running water. Put them in a pan over a high heat for 5 minutes or until they open. Drain them, and discard the shells.
2. Mix mayonnaise, chopped onion, herbs and capers, and season with pepper to taste. Mix well.
3. Toast the bread on each side. Leave to cool.
4. Spread the mayonnaise mixture on the bread and garnish each canapé with 2 mussels.

*Smoked fish canapés are delicious. Use eel, herring, salmon or sturgeon, on black or rye bread. With a fork, mix some chopped chervil into some Petit-suisse (soft cream cheese) or fromage blanc (which you can buy in certain good delicatessens). Season with salt and pepper. Spread this on the slices of bread. Garnish with thin slices of smoked eel or smoked herring and a slice of cucumber. Serve with dried fruit (raisins, figs, prunes, etc) to create a pleasant contrast.*

## Canapés au Cresson et aux Radis

*Watercress and Radish Canapés*

*Serves 5-10. Preparation and cooking: 20 min*

★

○ **10 slices bread (from a cottage loaf), crusts removed**
○ **1 bunch watercress**
○ **1 bunch red radishes**
○ **60ml (4 tbls) mayonnaise**
○ **15 sprigs chervil, coarsely chopped**

1. Trim the watercress to just below the point where the leaves join the stems. Wash and drain the leaves, then chop finely.
2. Add the chopped watercress and chervil to the mayonnaise and mix well.
3. Trim the radishes. Wash and slice.
4. Toast the bread on each side and leave to cool. Spread the mayonnaise mixture thickly on each slice. Garnish with slices of radish around the edge of each canapé.

## Canapés au Jambon et aux Cèpes

*Ham and Mushroom Canapés*

*Serves 5-10. Preparation and cooking: 20 min*

★

○ **10 slices white bread, crusts removed**
○ **100g (4 oz) softened butter**
○ **4 slices cooked ham**
○ **4 shallots**
○ **1 tin cèpes (200g/7 oz) or 100g (4 oz) fresh mushrooms**
○ **salt and pepper**

1. Cut one slice of ham into 10 small diamond shaped pieces and mince the remainder.
2. Peel and chop the shallots.
3. Put the butter, shallots and minced ham in a bowl. Season with salt and pepper to taste and mix well with a fork.
4. Drain and slice the cèpes. (Alternatively, sauté the fresh mushrooms lightly in butter.) Toast the slices of bread on both sides. Leave to cool.
5. Spread a thick layer of the ham and butter mixture onto the slices of bread. Garnish each one with slices of cèpe or mushroom and pieces of ham.

## Canapés au Gruyère et au Concombre

*Cucumber and Gruyère Canapés*

*Serves 5-10. Preparation and cooking: 20 min*

★

○ **10 slices bread (from cottage loaf), crusts removed**
○ **1 clove garlic**
○ **200g (7 oz) Gruyère cheese**
○ **30ml (2 tbls) olive oil**
○ **½ cucumber, peeled and seeded**
○ **10 rolled anchovy fillets, drained**

1. Peel the garlic, cut in half and rub on each slice of bread.
2. Heat the oil in a frying pan and fry the bread on both sides. Drain on absorbent paper.
3. Slice the cucumber and grate the cheese.
4. Cover each slice of bread with cheese and grill until the cheese starts to melt.
5. Place the canapés on a serving dish, garnish with cucumber slices and anchovy fillets. Serve at once.

*Canapés are thin slices of fresh, fried or toasted bread covered with a variety of savoury mixtures. To make them look more attractive, the bread may be cut into many different shapes and sizes: round, square, triangular, etc.*

*You can use many kinds of bread: black, wholemeal, rye, brown, white, etc, and these can be spread with butter mixed with a variety of flavourings: butter with lemon, tarragon, tomato, or mustard, for example. Then garnish with any number of mixtures using vegetables, fish, poultry, cold meat, cheese, egg . . . just use your imagination!*

# Brochettes de Pruneaux

*Serves 4. Preparation: 10 min  Cooking: 45 min*

### *Grilled Prunes on Skewers*

★★

○ **500g (18 oz) leeks**
○ **200g (7 oz) prunes, soaked overnight in cold water**
○ **325g (11 oz) smoked bacon**
○ **24 small onions or pickling onions**

*For the sauce:*
○ **15ml (1 tbls) honey**
○ **15 ml (1 tbls) soya sauce**
○ **2 cloves**
○ **30ml (2 tbls) ketchup or tomato sauce**
○ **30ml (2 tbls) white wine**
○ **salt and pepper**

1. Drain and stone the prunes. Put aside.
2. Wash the leeks and discard roots and green tops. Cook in salted water for 20 minutes, or 10 minutes in a pressure cooker. Drain well (press between your hands to remove excess water) and leave to cool, then cut into chunks.
3. Discard the bacon rind, and dice the bacon into about 24 small pieces.
4. Peel the onions.
5. Place the ingredients for the sauce in a saucepan. Cook, uncovered, over a high heat. After about 15 minutes the sauce should be thick. Remove from heat.
6. Thread on skewers alternate pieces of prune, bacon, onion and leek.
7. Cook the kebabs under the grill for at least 10 minutes or until cooked. Turn frequently and baste with the sauce. Serve at once.

# Brochettes d'Escargots

*Serves 4-8. Preparation: 20 min  Cooking: 1 hr 10 min*

### *Grilled Snails on Skewers*

★★

○ **4 dozen snails (in their shells if available, otherwise a tin of 48 snails)**
○ **50g (2 oz) butter**
○ **4 shallots**
○ **small bunch chives, chopped**
○ **200g (7 oz) smoked bacon**
○ **25g (1 oz) breadcrumbs**
○ **45ml (3 tbls) coarse salt**
○ **salt and pepper**

*For the court-bouillon:*
○ **1 bouquet garni consisting of: 1 sprig of thyme, 2 bay leaves, 3 sprigs parsley**
○ **1 clove garlic**
○ **2 small carrots, sliced**
○ **10 whole peppercorns**
○ **coarse salt**

1. If you are using snails in their shells: sprinkle the snails with 3 tbls of coarse salt and leave to soak for 2 hours. Wash well under running water.
2. Prepare the stock: in a large saucepan filled with water, put the bouquet garni, carrots, garlic, salt and peppercorns. Add the snails and cook for 1 hour over medium heat. Remove the snails from the stock and leave to cool. Then remove from their shells and discard the black end.
3. If you are using snails from a tin, cook them in the stock for only 10 minutes. Discard the bacon rind, and cut the bacon into approximately 24 small pieces. Peel the shallots and chop finely. In a bowl, mix the butter, shallots and chives; season.
4. Thread snails onto skewers, alternating with the pieces of bacon.
5. Place the breadcrumbs on a plate. Heat the shallot butter, but do not allow to boil. Dip the kebabs into it, then turn them in the breadcrumbs. Cook under the grill for 5 minutes on each side, basting with the shallot butter. Serve hot.

*Kebabs or brochettes are chunks of meat, fish, fruit or vegetables threaded on skewers, cooked over charcoal or under the grill.*

*Kebabs are an original and amusing way of cooking vegetables: you can use pieces of onion, pepper, tomato, fennel, celery, red cabbage or mushrooms, for example, in whatever combinations you choose. If you like sweet and sour tastes, squares of apple, pineapple or fig make the kebabs even more interesting!*

# Oeufs Farcis aux Cèpes

*Serves 3-6. Preparation: 10 min  Cooking: 30 min*

*Eggs Stuffed with Mushrooms*

★★

○ **3 eggs**
○ **1 tin of cèpes (120g/4½ oz) or 50g (2 oz) fresh mushrooms**
○ **1 clove garlic**
○ **15ml (1 tbls) parsley and chives, chopped**
○ **100ml (3½ fl oz) double cream**
○ **30g (1¼ oz) butter**
○ **salt and pepper**

1. Preheat the oven to 250°C (475°F; gas mark 9).
2. Hard boil the eggs.
3. If using tinned cèpes, drain them and chop finely. Otherwise wash, trim and chop the mushrooms. Peel and crush the garlic. In a frying pan, melt the butter over a low heat; add the mushrooms, garlic, chopped chives and parsley. Season. Cook for 15 minutes, stirring frequently with a wooden spoon. Remove from heat.
4. Shell the eggs. Halve them, keeping the white intact. Remove the yolks and mash with a fork.
5. Blend the cream with the egg yolks; add the mushrooms. Mix once more. Fill the halved egg whites with this mixture and place in the preheated oven for a few minutes until they are just beginning to brown.

# Oeufs Frits au Vin

*Serves 6. Preparation: 25 min  Cooking: 30 min*

*Fried Eggs on Toast with Wine Sauce*

★★

○ **6 eggs**
○ **6 slices white bread**
○ **1 clove garlic**
○ **30ml (2 tbls) oil**
○ **30g (1 oz) butter**
○ **salt and pepper**

*For the sauce:*
○ **240ml (9 fl oz) red wine**
○ **5 small white onions (or pickling onions), minced**
○ **1 slice smoked ham (Parma or Bayonne style), diced**
○ **15ml (1 tbls) flour**
○ **1 sprig thyme**
○ **2 bay leaves**
○ **white part of 1 leek, cut into slices**
○ **20g (¾ oz) butter**
○ **salt and pepper**

1. First prepare the sauce. Pour the wine into a small saucepan, place over a high heat and set alight; when the flame dies down, remove from heat.
2. Melt the butter in a frying pan. Fry the onions and leek. Add the diced ham, thyme and bay leaves. Sprinkle on the flour. When the ingredients start to brown, pour over the wine. Season with salt and pepper and simmer for 20 minutes.
3. Peel the garlic, cut in half and rub it on the slices of bread. Fry the bread in the oil on both sides. Remove from heat, place on a serving dish and keep warm.
4. Fry the eggs in butter, basting the yolks with a spoon to make sure they are well cooked. Season. When the eggs are fried, place them on the slices of bread. Remove the thyme and bay leaves from the sauce and pour around the toast. Serve immediately.

# Oeufs Bonne Femme

*Serves 4. Preparation: 10 min  Cooking: 10 min*

*Baked Eggs with Cream and Tarragon*

★

○ **4 eggs**
○ **1 sprig tarragon**
○ **200ml (7 fl oz) double cream**
○ **20g (¾ oz) butter**
○ **salt and pepper**

1. Wash and dry the tarragon and remove the leaves.
2. Preheat the oven to 200°C (400°F; gas mark 6).
3. Butter the bottom and sides of 4 small ovenproof ramekins or cocotte dishes. Place a few tarragon leaves at the bottom and on the sides of each dish. Pour 15ml (1 tbls) cream in each dish, then break one egg into each dish. Cover with another 15ml (1 tbls) of cream. Season and garnish with more tarragon leaves.
4. Place the ramekins in a large ovenproof dish filled with water and cook for 10 minutes. Serve at once.

*Cornets de Jambon (p16)* ▶

# Cornets de Jambon

*Serves 4. Preparation: 15 min  Cooking: 30 min*

## Ham Cornets Filled with Vegetable Mayonnaise

★★

- ○ **200g (7 oz) rice**
- ○ **100g (4 oz) peas**
- ○ **100g (4 oz) French beans**
- ○ **2 turnips**
- ○ **2 carrots**
- ○ **100g (4 oz) Emmenthal cheese**
- ○ **4 slices cooked ham**
- ○ **90ml (6 tbls) mayonnaise**
- ○ **lettuce leaves**
- ○ **2 tomatoes**
- ○ **10 sprigs parsley**
- ○ **salt and pepper**

1. Cook the rice in boiling water for 15 minutes or until tender. Drain and rinse under hot running water.
2. While the rice is cooking, shell the peas; wash, top, tail and dice the French beans; peel and dice the turnips and carrots. Cook the vegetables for 15 minutes (10 minutes in a pressure cooker) in boiling salted water. They should still be crisp. Drain.
3. Dice the cheese. In a bowl, mix together the vegetables, rice, mayonnaise and cheese. Season to taste.
4. Lay a slice of ham on a dish, spoon a quarter of the vegetable mixture down the centre and roll up. Repeat with the remaining slices of ham. Place some lettuce leaves on a serving dish and top with ham cornets. Garnish with halved tomatoes sprinkled with parsley.

# Pamplemousses Farcis

*Serves 4. Preparation 15 min*

## Stuffed Grapefruit

★

- ○ **2 grapefruit**
- ○ **juice of 1 orange**
- ○ **150g (5 oz) prawns**
- ○ **1 avocado**

*For the sauce:*
- ○ **30ml (2 tbls) ketchup**
- ○ **50ml (3 heaped tbls) mayonnaise**
- ○ **pinch sugar**
- ○ **pinch paprika**

1. Halve the grapefruit. Scoop out the flesh, being careful not to break the skin. Put the shells aside. Remove the white skin from the segments and dice the flesh. Halve the avocado, remove the stone, scoop out the flesh and dice it finely.
2. Mix the grapefruit, avocado and orange juice in a bowl.
3. Shell the prawns and add them to the fruit.
4. Mix together the ingredients for the sauce, add to the grapefruit mixture and fill the shells. Chill in the refrigerator until ready to serve.

# Avocats Piquants

*Serves 4. Preparation: 15 min*

## Avocados Stuffed with Devilled Crab

★★

- ○ **2 large avocados**
- ○ **1 tin (150g/5 oz) crabmeat**
- ○ **100g (4 oz) prawns**
- ○ **4 large mushrooms**
- ○ **30ml (2 tbls) double cream**
- ○ **45ml (3 tbls) mayonnaise**
- ○ **juice of 1 lemon**
- ○ **6 drops Tabasco sauce**
- ○ **4 sprigs parsley, chopped**
- ○ **salt**

1. Halve the avocados and discard the stones. Carefully scoop out the flesh, keeping the skins intact, and dice finely. Reserve the avocado skins.
2. Drain the crabmeat, removing any cartilage, and flake. Shell the prawns. Trim the mushrooms, wash, and slice thinly. Mix with the crabmeat and prawns in a bowl, add the avocado and mix well.
3. In a small bowl, mix the cream with 30ml (2 tbls) mayonnaise. When well blended, add another tablespoon of mayonnaise, the lemon juice and Tabasco sauce. Season with salt and combine with the crabmeat mixture.
4. Fill each avocado skin and garnish with the chopped parsley. Serve chilled.

# Tomates Fourrées au Thon
## *Tomatoes Stuffed with Tuna Fish*

*Serves 4. Preparation: 15 min  Cooking: 6 min*

★ ★

○ **4 large tomatoes**
○ **1 slice tuna weighing 200g (7 oz)**
○ **4 shallots**
○ **100g (4 oz) prawns**
○ **100ml (3½ fl oz) double cream**
○ **30ml (2 tbls) olive oil**
○ **juice of 1 lemon**
○ **15 sprigs chervil, coarsely chopped (or substitute chopped parsley)**
○ **salt and pepper**

1. Slice off the top of each tomato, and carefully take out the seeds with a teaspoon. Place the tomatoes on a dish.
2. Grill the slice of tuna, turning once, for 5 to 6 minutes, brushing it with the olive oil. Then remove the skin and backbone and flake the tuna.
3. Peel the shallots and shell the prawns. Mince the shallots, prawns and tuna together. Put all the ingredients in a bowl, add the chopped chervil, cream and lemon juice. Season and mix well.
4. Fill each tomato with the filling and serve at once.

# Tomates Farcies au Roquefort
## *Tomatoes Stuffed with Roquefort*

*Serves 6. Preparation: 10 min*

★

○ **6 large tomatoes**
○ **100g (4 oz) fromage blanc or cream cheese**
○ **100g (4 oz) Roquefort cheese**
○ **100ml (3½ fl oz) double cream**
○ **10 sprigs parsley, coarsely chopped**
○ **salt and pepper**

1. Slice off the top of each tomato and put aside (these will be used as lids). Scoop out the flesh and seeds with a teaspoon.
2. In a bowl, blend the fromage blanc with the cream and beat with a whisk. Mash the Roquefort with a fork and add to the fromage blanc mixture. Season. Add the parsley, mix well.
3. Place the tomatoes on a serving dish and fill each one with the filling. Cover the lids and serve cold.

# Escargots de Bourgogne
## *Snails with Garlic Butter*

*Serves 4-8. Preparation: 25 min  Cooking: 1 hr 40 min*

★ ★

○ **4 dozen snails (in their shells if available, otherwise 48 tinned snails and shells)**
○ **450g (1 lb) butter**
○ **3 cloves garlic**
○ **1 bunch parsley, chopped**
○ **coarse salt**
○ **salt and pepper**

*For the court-bouillon:*
○ **1 bouquet garni consisting of: 1 sprig thyme, 3 sprigs parsley, 2 bay leaves**
○ **1 clove garlic**
○ **2 small carrots, sliced**
○ **10 peppercorns**
○ **salt**

1. If you are using snails in their shells: cover the snails with 45ml (3 tbls) coarse salt and leave to soak for 2 hours. Wash well under running water.
2. To prepare the stock: in a large saucepan filled with water, place the bouquet garni, carrots, garlic, salt and peppercorns. Cook for 30 minutes. Add the snails, and cook for 1 hour over medium heat. If you are using tinned snails, cook them for only 10 minutes.
3. Preheat the oven to 200°C (400°F; gas mark 6).
4. Leave the snails to cool in the stock, then drain. If they are in their shells, remove them and wash and wipe the shells. Remove the black end of the snails, which is sometimes bitter. Put aside the snails and shells.
5. To prepare the stuffing: peel the garlic and chop finely. In a bowl, cream the butter, garlic and parsley. This should result in a very smooth paste. Season with salt and pepper to taste (use salt sparingly as the snails are salty).
6. Replace the snails in their shells, and fill the shells to the top with the garlic butter.
7. Place the snails in an ovenproof dish, with the holes upwards so that the butter does not leak out of the shells during cooking. Cook for 10 minutes, and serve at once.

# Tomates au Basilic

*Serves 4. Preparation: 10 min  Refrigeration: 30 min*

## Iced Tomato Soup with Basil

★ ★

- ○ 8 red, ripe tomatoes
- ○ 1 cucumber
- ○ 4 sprigs fresh basil
- ○ juice of 1 lemon
- ○ celery salt
- ○ salt and pepper

1. Bring some water to the boil. Wash the tomatoes, plunge them into the boiling water for 10 seconds, then peel and discard the seeds.
2. Peel the cucumber, remove the seeds with a sharp knife, and cut into pieces.
3. Place the cucumber and tomatoes in a liquidizer. Season with salt and pepper. Add the lemon juice. Blend for a few seconds.
4. Pour the mixture into a salad bowl or individual bowls, and leave to chill in the refrigerator for 30 minutes. Sprinkle with the chopped basil leaves before serving. Serve with celery salt.

# Melon au Jambon et aux Figues

*Serves 4-8. Preparation: 10 min*

## Melon with Parma Ham and Fresh Figs

★

- ○ 1 honeydew melon weighing 500g (18 oz)
- ○ 8 very thin slices of Parma ham
- ○ 8 fresh figs
- ○ pepper

1. Cut the melon into 8 slices, scoop out the seeds and cut away the skin.
2. Tail and wash the figs. With a sharp knife, make 4 incisions lengthways in the skin of each fig, without cutting the flesh. Peel back the skin, leaving it attached to the fig, to form 4 petals.
3. Place the melon slices on a serving dish, alternating with the figs and ham. Pepper the melon generously.

# Melon à l'Ananas et au Jambon

*Serves 4. Preparation: 15 min*
*Refrigeration: 1 hr*

## Melon with Pineapple and Smoked Ham

★

- ○ 2 honeydew melons
- ○ 1 thick slice smoked ham
- ○ 1 pineapple slice
- ○ juice of 1 lemon
- ○ 5ml (1 tsp) cognac
- ○ salt and pepper

1. Halve the melons. Scoop out the seeds and flesh with a spoon. Keep the skins.
2. Dice the pineapple and melon.
3. In a bowl, carefully mix the lemon juice, diced pineapple and melon, and add the cognac. Season. Place in the refrigerator for 1 hour.
4. Before serving, dice the slice of ham and add to the melon mixture. Mix well. Fill the melon skins with the mixture. Serve at once.

You can vary this dish by filling the melon shells with diced cheese, ham and pickled onion or raisins.

*Melon with port: Cut a hole in the end of a melon. Remove the seeds through the hole. Pour in 60ml (4 tbls) red port. Leave the melon in the refrigerator for at least 2 hours. Shake the melon from time to time so that the port moistens the flesh of the melon.*

*Melon mousse: In a liquidizer, blend the flesh of 1 melon with 45ml (3 tbls) double cream. Pour this mixture into individual bowls and refrigerate for 1 hour before serving.*

# Salade d'Avocats aux Oranges

*Avocado and Orange Salad*

*Serves 4. Preparation: 20 min*

★

- ○ **3 avocados**
- ○ **2 oranges**
- ○ **2 small onions (or pickling onions)**
- ○ **5ml (1 tsp) parsley, coarsely chopped**
- ○ **1 tomato**
- ○ **10 lettuce leaves**
- ○ **45ml (3 tbls) oil**
- ○ **15ml (1 tbls) vinegar**
- ○ **salt and pepper**

1. Halve 2 avocados, remove the stones and the skin with a sharp knife. Slice the flesh.
2. Peel and segment the oranges. Cut off the stalk end of the tomato, slice and discard the seeds. Peel the onions and slice, separating into rings.
3. Cut off the pointed end of the remaining avocado about one-third of the way down. Remove the stone. With a sharp knife, cut small v shapes around the top.
4. In a bowl, dissolve 3 pinches of salt in the vinegar, add the oil and season with pepper. Stir well.
5. Arrange the lettuce leaves in a serving dish, cover with the sliced tomato, then alternate avocado slices and orange segments on top of the tomato. Garnish with the onion rings, sprinkle with parsley and place the third avocado in the centre of the dish. Pour the vinaigrette into the avocado 'bowl' and serve.

# Caviar d'Aubergine

*Aubergine Purée with Garlic*

*Serves 6. Preparation: 20 min  Cooking: 20 min*
*Refrigeration: 2 hr*
★ ★

- ○ **1.5kg (3¼ lb) aubergines**
- ○ **120ml (8 tbls) olive oil**
- ○ **1 bunch parsley, coarsely chopped**
- ○ **5 cloves garlic**
- ○ **salt and pepper**

1. Place the aubergines under a hot grill and cook, turning to cook all sides, about 20 minutes or until very soft.
2. Peel and finely chop the garlic.
3. When the aubergines have cooled, open them and scoop out the flesh. Place in a bowl and mash with a fork. Mix in the oil a little at a time, then add the garlic and parsley, and salt and pepper to taste. Mix well.
4. Refrigerate for 2 hours. Serve cold.

# Fromage Blanc aux Herbes

*Fromage Blanc with Herbs*

*Serves 6. Preparation: 10 min*

★

- ○ **1 large carton fromage blanc or cream cheese**
- ○ **15ml (1 tbls) olive oil**
- ○ **1 bunch chervil, coarsely chopped**
- ○ **2 cloves garlic**
- ○ **salt and pepper**

1. Peel the garlic and chop finely.
2. In a bowl, mash the cheese with a fork, add the oil and garlic. Season with salt and generously with pepper. Mix carefully with a wooden spoon so that the oil and garlic blend well into the cheese. Finish off with a whisk. Add the chervil. Mix again and serve cold.

Serve this with toast. Instead of chervil, you can use chives, parsley, tarragon or fresh mint. If you use any of these herbs, do not add garlic. Refrigerate for at least 1 hour before serving.

# Asperges en Salade

*Serves 4-8. Preparation: 15 min  Cooking: 30 min*

*Asparagus Salad*

★ ★

○ **2kg (4½ lb) asparagus**
○ **2 tins asparagus tips weighing 200g (7 oz) each**
○ **90ml (6 tbls) mayonnaise made with lemon juice**
○ **coarse salt**

1. Add 15ml (1 tbls) of coarse salt to 1 litre (1¾ pints) water and bring to the boil.
2. Remove the base of the stems from the asparagus. Using a knife, scrape the white part of the stems downwards, to remove the hard skin. Wash well and tie them in a bundle.
3. Plunge the asparagus into the boiling water. Reduce heat, and simmer, uncovered, for 30 minutes.
4. Prepare some mayonnaise using the juice of half a lemon instead of vinegar.
5. Open the tins of asparagus, drain and rinse under running water.
6. In a liquidizer, purée the asparagus tips. Fold this into the mayonnaise and mix well.
7. Remove the asparagus from the water, drain and untie them. Serve the sauce separately.

# Purée de Pois Chiches

*Serves 6. Preparation: 15 min*

*Purée of Chick Peas*

★

○ **1 tin (500g/18 oz) chick peas**
○ **120ml (8 tbls) olive oil**
○ **3 cloves garlic**
○ **5 sprigs parsley, coarsely chopped**
○ **1 lemon**
○ **salt**

1. In a large saucepan, bring some salted water to the boil. Open the tin of chick peas and drain. Plunge the chick peas into the water, cook for 2 minutes and drain.
2. Peel and crush the garlic. Mash the chick peas with a fork or purée them in a liquidizer. Place them in a bowl and add the olive oil, a little at a time, using a whisk. Add the garlic, mix well and leave to cool.
3. Before serving, sprinkle with the parsley and garnish with lemon wedges.

This purée is delicious spread on toast.

# Salade d'Oronges aux Fruits

*Serves 4. Preparation: 20 min*

*Mushroom Salad with Fruit*

★

○ **400g (14 oz) mushrooms**
○ **100g (4 oz) Tomme de Savoie cheese (or substitute any mild, medium-soft cheese)**
○ **1 tart apple**
○ **1 orange**
○ **60ml (4 tbls) oil**
○ **juice of 1 lemon**
○ **salt and pepper**
○ **1 small celeriac**

1. Trim the earthy base off the mushroom stalks, and wash them under running water. Wash and peel the celeriac. Peel the apple and remove the core. Cut the mushrooms, celeriac and apple into julienne strips. Place them in a salad bowl and sprinkle with a little of the lemon juice.
2. Remove the crust from the cheese, and dice. Peel the orange and remove the white skin from the segments. Chop the flesh finely. Add to the ingredients in the bowl.
3. In a small bowl, dissolve a few pinches of salt in the remaining lemon juice, add the oil and season with pepper. Mix well. Pour this sauce over the salad and serve at once.

*As a cold hors d'oeuvre, you can serve vegetables cut into strips or small pieces, to be dipped into a variety of sauces: mustard, anchovy and tartare, for example.*

# Cocktail Marin

*Seafood Cocktail*

*Serves 4. Preparation and cooking: 50 min*
*Refrigeration: 2 hr*
★★

○ **500g (18 oz) mussels**
○ **500g (18 oz) cockles**
○ **200g (7 oz) small cuttlefish**
○ **200g (7 oz) octopus**
○ **200g (7 oz) prawns**
○ **2 red peppers**
○ **150g (5 oz) green and black olives**
○ **30g (1¼ oz) small gherkins**
○ **2 cloves garlic**
○ **15ml (1 tbls) vinegar**
○ **100ml (3½ fl oz) oil**
○ **juice of 1 lemon**
○ **1 bunch parsley**
○ **salt and pepper**

1. Wash and dry the peppers. Grill them on all sides for about 15 minutes or until the skin turns black and becomes shrivelled. Leave to cool.
2. Scrub the mussels well, scrape away their beards, wash well under running water and drain. Wash the cockles in water with a little vinegar added, rubbing them between your hands. Rinse well and drain.
3. Place the mussels and cockles in a large saucepan with 1½cm (½ in) water, and cook, uncovered, over a high heat until they open. Drain and remove them from their shells. Put aside.
4. Clean the octopus and cuttlefish by removing their ink sacs, mouths, eyes and inner bones. Skin and wash repeatedly under cold running water. Cook in boiling salted water for 10 minutes. Drain and put aside.
5. Shell the prawns.
6. Roughly chop the octopus, and place in a large bowl with the whole cuttlefish, prawns, mussels and cockles.
7. Remove the skin and seeds from the peppers with a sharp knife. Cut into thin strips. Stone and halve the olives. Cut the gherkins into small pieces. Place all the ingredients in the bowl.
8. To prepare the sauce: peel the garlic and crush it into a bowl. Dissolve the salt in the lemon juice and add, along with the oil; season with pepper. Pour the sauce over the salad, mix carefully and refrigerate for 2 hours. Just before serving, wash the parsley, remove the stalks, chop and garnish the salad with the leaves.

# Crevettes et Crabe en Pamplemousse

*Shrimp and Crab Cocktail in Grapefruit*

*Serves 4. Preparation: 20 min*
★★

○ **2 large grapefruit**
○ **200g (7 oz) shrimps**
○ **1 tin (200g/7 oz) crabmeat**
○ **1 small mango**

*For the sauce:*
○ **60ml (4 tbls) mayonnaise**
○ **15ml (1 tbls) cognac**
○ **200ml (7 fl oz) double cream**
○ **1 pinch cayenne pepper**

1. Halve the grapefruit. Gently scoop out the flesh with a teaspoon and dice. Place in a salad bowl. Reserve the skins.
2. Shell the shrimps. Open the tin of crabmeat, rinse under running water, and drain. Flake the crabmeat, removing any cartilage which might have been left in. Add to the diced grapefruit.
3. Peel the mango and dice the flesh, discarding the stone. Add the mango to the bowl.
4. In a small bowl, beat the cream lightly with a whisk and fold into the mayonnaise with the cognac and cayenne pepper. Blend well.
5. Pour the sauce over the salad and mix gently. Fill the grapefruit skins with the salad and serve.

*Shellfish do not take long to cook when grilled or cooked over a high heat.*

*Shellfish such as clams or mussels should open after cooking for a short time. If they remain closed, this indicates that they are no longer fresh and should be discarded.*

*Salade d' Avocats aux Oranges (p20)* ▶

# Salade de Crevettes aux Fruits

*Shrimp and Fruit Salad*

*Serves 4. Preparation: 15 min*

★

○ **250g (9 oz) prawns**
○ **1 small mango**
○ **2 bananas**
○ **juice of 1 lemon**
○ **60ml (4 tbls) mayonnaise**
○ **45ml (3 tbls) double cream**
○ **5ml (1 tsp) mango chutney**
○ **1 pinch sugar**
○ **15ml (1 tbls) cognac**
○ **1 drop Tabasco sauce**
○ **10 lettuce leaves**

1. Shell the prawns and place them in a salad bowl. Peel and dice the mango and add to the prawns. Peel and slice the bananas and sprinkle with the lemon juice to prevent discoloration.
2. Add to the mayonnaise the mango chutney, sugar, cognac and Tabasco. Whisk the cream lightly and add. Blend all the ingredients well.
3. Mix the sauce gently into the fruit and prawns.
4. Place the lettuce leaves in a dish, and top with the salad mixture. Refrigerate until ready to serve.

# Salade de Saumon et de Gambas

*Salmon and Giant Prawn Salad*

*Serves 4. Preparation and cooking: 20 min*

★★

○ **150g (5 oz) giant prawns**
○ **2 slices smoked salmon**
○ **1 tin (200g/7 oz) crabmeat**
○ **1 tin (50g/2 oz) anchovies in oil**
○ **1 red pepper**

*For the sauce:*
○ **100ml (3½ fl oz) oil**
○ **100ml (3½ fl oz) double cream**
○ **juice of 1 lemon**
○ **1 pinch paprika**
○ **salt and pepper**

1. Drain the crabmeat, removing any cartilage which might have been left in. Flake and place in a salad bowl. Drain off the oil from the anchovies and add them to the crab.
2. Cut the salmon into small pieces. Cut the pepper into strips. Put aside.
3. Grill the prawns for 2 minutes on each side. Leave to cool slightly.
4. In a liquidizer, place the salmon, lemon juice, cream, oil and salt and pepper. Blend until you obtain a smooth sauce. Add to the salad mixture. Sprinkle with paprika.
5. Shell the prawns while still warm and add them to the salad. Gently mix all the ingredients together. Garnish with pepper strips. Serve at once.

# Salade de Moules et Pommes de Terre

*Mussel and Potato Salad*

*Serves 4-6. Preparation: 20 min  Cooking: 30 min*

★★

○ **1kg (2¼ lb) potatoes**
○ **3 litres (approx 6½ lb) mussels**
○ **200ml (7 fl oz) double cream**
○ **1 onion**
○ **juice of 1 lemon**
○ **1 bouquet garni consisting of: 1 sprig thyme, 2 bay leaves, 3 sprigs parsley**
○ **60ml (4 tbls) olive oil**
○ **5 finely chopped gherkins**
○ **5 chive leaves, coarsely chopped**
○ **5 sprigs chervil, coarsely chopped**
○ **240ml (9 fl oz) white wine**
○ **salt and pepper**

1. Scrub the mussels, scrape away their beards, and wash well under running water. Place in a saucepan over a high heat, with the onion and bouquet garni. Shake from time to time, and remove from the heat when the mussels have opened. Drain and remove the shells. Put aside.
2. Cook the potatoes, in their jackets, in boiling salted water for 20 to 25 minutes. Peel and slice them while still hot, and pour the wine over them.
3. To prepare the sauce: in a bowl, dissolve the salt in the lemon juice and add the cream. Stir in the oil, add the herbs and chopped gherkins. Season with pepper. Mix well.
4. In a salad bowl, place alternate layers of potatoes, mussels and sauce.

# Acras de Morue

*Cod Croquettes*

*Serves 6. Preparation: 20 min  Cooking: 20 min*

★★

- ○ **400g (14 oz) salt cod fillets**
- ○ **2 cloves garlic**
- ○ **1 bunch parsley, coarsely chopped**
- ○ **10ml (2 tsp) paprika, mild or hot**
- ○ **30g (1¼ oz) breadcrumbs**
- ○ **30g (1¼ oz) flour**
- ○ **1 egg**
- ○ **240ml (9 fl oz) oil**

1. Soak the cod fillets in water overnight. Drain and rinse thoroughly under running water.
2. Bring some water to the boil. Poach the cod in boiling water for 5 minutes. Drain and remove bones and skin. Flake the fish as finely as possible.
3. Peel the garlic and chop finely. Mix the flour with half a glass of water, and whisk in the egg. In a bowl, mix this sauce with the fish, add the paprika and the parsley. Mix well.
4. Form the mixture into small balls. Place the breadcrumbs on a plate and roll the fish balls in them.
5. Heat the oil in a frying pan. Fry the fish balls in hot oil for 2 minutes on each side, or until brown.

Acras are a delicious West Indian speciality. You can serve them with a sauce of pepper, lemon mayonnaise and half an avocado, reduced to a smooth paste in a liquidizer.

# Harengs Fumés aux Poireaux

*Smoked Herrings with Leeks*

*Serves 4. Preparation: 10 min Cooking: 20 min  Marinade: 48 hr*

★

- ○ **400g (14 oz) smoked herrings**
- ○ **250g (9 oz) carrots**
- ○ **2 large onions**
- ○ **1 sprig thyme**
- ○ **½ litre (18 fl oz) oil**
- ○ **2 bay leaves**
- ○ **cloves**
- ○ **1kg (2¼ lb) leeks**
- ○ **1 lemon**
- ○ **salt and pepper**

1. Prepare a marinade for the herrings: peel the carrots and cut into thin slices. Peel and slice the onions. In a deep dish, place a layer of herrings, some carrots and then some onions and 3 cloves. Repeat until there are no ingredients left. Add the oil, and make sure it runs to the bottom of the dish. Add the bay leaves and thyme. Marinate for 48 hours at the bottom of the refrigerator.
2. Trim and wash the leeks. Tie the white parts in a bundle and cook in salted water for 20 minutes (or for 10 minutes in a pressure cooker).
3. Meanwhile, drain the herrings and some of the carrots and onions. Serve 1 or 2 herrings per person. Place them on a serving dish, garnish with carrots and onions and surround with the drained but still warm leeks. Season with salt and pepper. Serve with lemon wedges.

*Fish can be eaten raw: large sardines, for example. Remove the scales and head, cut them in half and discard the backbone, then cut the flesh into thin strips. Marinate with olive oil, lemon slices, pepper and thyme for 4 hours in the refrigerator. Drain and eat them with bread and butter: they are delicious. You can also prepare a variety of fish fillets in the same way. The marinade can be altered slightly, for example: oil, ground ginger and pepper, or oil, white wine, green pepper and onions.*

# Coquilles Saint-Jacques à la Ciboulette
## *Scallops with Chives*

*Serves 6. Preparation: 20 min*
*Marinade: 30 min*
★

- 18 scallops
- juice of 4 lemons
- 1 bunch chives
- 100ml (3½ fl oz) olive oil
- 100ml (3½ fl oz) groundnut oil
- 5 shallots
- 45ml (3 tbls) chopped green pepper

1. Place the scallops under a grill until they open. Detach the shells with a sharp knife and keep 6. Remove the beard-like fringe and black intestinal thread. Keep only the white flesh with the coral. Rinse well and cut into pieces.
2. Peel and chop the shallots. Wash the chives and chop them roughly.
3. Place the flesh of the scallops in a dish. Add the 2 kinds of oil, lemon juice, shallots, green pepper and chives. Mix well and marinate for 30 minutes in the refrigerator.
4. Fill the shells with the strained scallop mixture, and pour over each shell a little of the marinade. Serve the rest of the marinade separately in a sauceboat. Accompany with lemon quarters.

# Coquilles Saint-Jacques aux Poireaux
## *Scallops with Leeks*

*Serves 6. Preparation: 20 min*
*Cooking: 35 min*
★★

- 18 scallops
- 1.5kg (3¼ lb) leeks
- 400ml (14 fl oz) double cream
- 25g (1 oz) butter
- 1 pinch grated nutmeg
- 1 pinch cayenne pepper
- salt and pepper

1. Place the scallops under the grill until they open. Detach the shells with a sharp knife and discard. Remove the beard-like fringe and the intestinal black thread. Keep only the white flesh and coral. Rinse under running water.
2. Preheat the oven to 200°C (400°F; gas mark 6).
3. Clean the leeks, keeping only the white part. Tie them in a bundle and cook in salted boiling water for 20 minutes. When they are tender, remove and rinse in cold water, then drain by pressing carefully in your hands.
4. Butter an ovenproof dish, make a nest of the leeks and top with the scallops. Season with salt and pepper and a pinch of cayenne pepper. Pour over the cream, and sprinkle with grated nutmeg.
5. Bake for 10 to 15 minutes.

# Vénus Sauce Moutarde
## *Clams in Mustard Sauce*

*Serves 4. Preparation: 10 min Cooking: 10 min*
★

- 1kg (2¼ lb) clams
- 200ml (7 fl oz) double cream
- 15ml (1 tbls) French mustard
- 1 bunch parsley, roughly chopped
- 15ml (1 tbls) vinegar
- salt and pepper

1. Scrub the clams in water and a little vinegar, rubbing between your hands to remove any grit. Rinse well in cold water and drain.
2. Place them in a saucepan over a medium heat until they open, shaking from time to time.
3. Meanwhile, prepare the sauce: in a bowl, mix the cream and mustard, add the parsley, season with salt and pepper. This will result in a light yellow paste. Remove the clams from the heat, keeping some of their juice to add to the sauce. Place the clams in a dish and cover with the sauce. Mix well and serve warm.

*Huîtes Gratinées (p28)* ▶

# Huîtres Gratinées

*Oysters au Gratin*

*Serves 4. Preparation: 20 min Cooking: 10 min*

★★

- ○ **18 oysters**
- ○ **1 small clove garlic**
- ○ **100g (4 oz) softened butter**
- ○ **10 sprigs parsley, roughly chopped**
- ○ **juice of half a lemon**
- ○ **20g (¾ oz) breadcrumbs**
- ○ **pepper**

1. Preheat the oven to 250°C (475°F; gas mark 9).
2. Open the oysters, but leave them in their shells. Drain off their juice and set aside. Peel and crush the garlic.
3. In a bowl, place the softened butter, lemon juice, garlic, chopped parsley and a little of the juice from the oysters. Season with pepper. Mix well.
4. Place a little of this mixture on top of each oyster. Sprinkle with breadcrumbs and cook in the oven for 10 minutes, until brown.

# Coques aux Echalotes

*Cockles with Shallots*

*Serves 4. Preparation: 10 min Cooking: 15 min*

★★

- ○ **3 litres (6½ lb) cockles**
- ○ **6 shallots**
- ○ **50ml (3 large tbls) double cream**
- ○ **45ml (3 tbls) wine vinegar**
- ○ **10 sprigs parsley, roughly chopped**
- ○ **10g (½ oz) butter**
- ○ **pepper**

1. Wash the cockles in water mixed with 30ml (2 tbls) vinegar, then rinse in water, rubbing them together in your hands. Drain.
2. Peel the shallots and chop roughly. Melt the butter in a saucepan and gently fry the shallots, moistening with a little hot water. Cook over a low heat for 10 minutes.
3. Meanwhile, place the cockles in a saucepan over a high heat for approximately 10 minutes until they open, shaking the pan from time to time. Remove from heat. Keep 45ml (3 tbls) of the juice.
4. Add 15ml (1 tbls) vinegar to the shallots. Cook for 1 minute, add the cream, season with pepper, and leave the sauce to boil for a few minutes, then add the cockle juice. Mix well and remove from the heat.
5. Place the cockles in a dish, pour the sauce over them and sprinkle with parsley. Serve at once.

# Gratin de Fruits de Mer

*Shellfish au Gratin*

*Serves 4. Preparation: 30 min Cooking: 45 min*

★★

- ○ **200g (7 oz) cod fillets**
- ○ **1kg (2¼ lb) mussels**
- ○ **150g (5 oz) prawns**
- ○ **1kg (2¼ lb) fresh spinach**
- ○ **50g (2 oz) Gruyère cheese, grated**
- ○ **60g (2¼ oz) butter**
- ○ **15ml (1 tbls) flour**
- ○ **200ml (7 fl oz) double cream**
- ○ **salt and pepper**

1. Poach the cod fillets for 5 minutes in boiling water. Flake the flesh. Scrub and wash the mussels. Place them in a saucepan over a high heat until they open. Drain and remove them from their shells. Shell the prawns.
2. Clean and prepare the spinach. Cook in boiling salted water for 15 minutes. Drain thoroughly and chop roughly.
3. Prepare the sauce: melt 50g (2 oz) butter in a saucepan over a low heat. Add the flour, stir well, then add the cream. Season. Cook for 10 minutes until it thickens; remove from the heat.
4. Heat the grill. Mix together the spinach, mussels, prawns, cod fillets and sauce. Butter an ovenproof dish with the remaining butter and pour in the shellfish mixture. Sprinkle with Gruyère and cook until brown, 10 to 15 minutes.

*A useful method for checking whether live shellfish are fresh is to squeeze the juice of a lemon over them. If they are fresh it will cause them to contract.*

# Soufflé aux Épinards

*Spinach Soufflé*

*Serves 5. Preparation: 15 min Cooking: 1 hr*

★★

○ **400g (14 oz) fresh spinach**
○ **50g (2 oz) grated Gruyère cheese**
○ **5 eggs**
○ **10g (½ oz) butter**
○ **salt and pepper**

*For the white sauce (béchamel):*
○ **50g (2 oz) butter**
○ **30g (1¼ oz) flour**
○ **240ml (9 fl oz) milk**
○ **15ml (1 tbls) double cream**
○ **1 pinch grated nutmeg**
○ **salt and pepper**

1. Preheat the oven to 140°C (275°F; gas mark 1).
2. Cut off the stalks of the spinach. Wash the leaves well. Plunge them into a saucepan filled with salted water and cook for 20 minutes.
3. Prepare a béchamel: melt the butter in a saucepan over a low heat, blend in the flour, stir well and cook until the flour and butter start to froth without colouring. Add the cold milk, a little at a time, stirring constantly with a wooden spoon, and cook for 15 minutes. Season, add the nutmeg and double cream. Stir and put aside.
4. Drain the spinach, and press it with a spoon to remove all the water. Chop roughly.
5. Separate the eggs. Beat the whites until stiff.
6. Mix the spinach with the béchamel, then add the egg yolks and grated Gruyère. Season to taste. Fold in the egg whites as gently as possible.
7. Butter a soufflé dish or mould, and fill with the spinach mixture. The dish should be almost three-quarters full. Place in the oven for 15 minutes at 140°C, then turn the heat up to 200°C (400°F; gas mark 6) and cook for a further 10 minutes. Serve at once.

# Soufflé aux Blettes

*Chard Soufflé*

*Serves 4. Preparation: 20 min Cooking: 1 hr 10 min*

★★

○ **1 bundle chard**
○ **150g (5 oz) smoked bacon**
○ **4 eggs**
○ **50g (2 oz) grated Gruyère cheese**
○ **20g (¾ oz) butter**
○ **salt and pepper**

*For the white sauce (béchamel):*
○ **50g (2 oz) butter**
○ **30g (1¼ oz) flour**
○ **240ml (9 fl oz) milk**
○ **15ml (1 tbls) double cream**
○ **1 pinch grated nutmeg**
○ **salt and pepper**

1. Preheat the oven to 140°C (275°F; gas mark 1).
2. Clean and prepare the chard by removing the threads and wash under running water. Cook for 20 minutes in salted water.
3. Prepare the white sauce: melt the butter in a saucepan over a low heat, and add the flour, stirring. Do not let it colour. Add the cold milk a little at a time, stirring constantly with a wooden spoon and cook for 15 minutes. Season, add the nutmeg and double cream. Stir well and put aside.
4. Dice the bacon, having removed the rind. Melt 10g (½ oz) butter in a frying pan over a medium heat, and fry the bacon for 10 minutes.
5. When the chard is cooked, drain well and chop roughly.
6. Separate the eggs. Beat the whites until stiff.
7. Mix the chard into the egg yolks, diced bacon, cheese and béchamel. Season. Gently fold in the egg whites.
8. Butter a soufflé dish or mould. Turn the chard mixture into it and cook in the oven for 15 minutes at 140°C, then turn the heat up to 200°C (400°F; gas mark 6) and cook for a further 10 minutes. Serve at once.

*Egg whites, beaten until stiff, make a soufflé expand and attain its lightness. The success of the soufflé will depend on how stiffly the whites have been beaten, and also how lightly they have been folded into the body of the soufflé. When folding in the egg whites, make sure they retain as much of their volume as possible by cutting quickly into the soufflé mixture, from top to bottom, with a wooden spatula.*

# Mousse de Tomates

*Tomato Mousse*

*Serves 4. Preparation: 15 min*

★

○ **2kg (4½ lb) red, ripe tomatoes**
○ **1 small clove garlic**
○ **200ml (7 fl oz) double cream**
○ **2 sprigs fresh basil or parsley**
○ **salt and pepper**

1. Bring some water to the boil and immerse the tomatoes for 10 seconds. Drain, peel and remove the seeds. Mash with a fork and pour away any excess juice.
2. Peel and chop the garlic. Pass the tomatoes and garlic through the fine mesh of a vegetable mill (or use a liquidizer). Season.
3. Place some ice cubes in a deep dish. Place a smaller bowl inside. Pour the cream into the bowl and whip. Fold the cream gently into the tomato purée. Pour the mousse into 4 ramekins and refrigerate. Just before serving, sprinkle with the basil leaves or chopped parsley.

# Mousse de Jambon

*Ham Mousse*

*Serves 4. Preparation: 20 min  Cooking: 45 min*

★★

○ **500g (18 oz) cooked ham**
○ **200ml (7 fl oz) double cream**
○ **2 pinches paprika**
○ **2 egg whites**
○ **10g (½ oz) butter**
○ **salt and pepper**

1. Preheat the oven to 200°C (400°F; gas mark 6).
2. Pass the ham through a vegetable mill or an electric mincer. Beat the egg whites until stiff.
3. Whip the cream. In a bowl, gently mix the cream with the minced ham. Add 2 pinches paprika and season lightly with salt and pepper. Fold in the egg whites gently.
4. Butter a charlotte or similar mould and pour in the ham mixture. Place the mould in an ovenproof dish filled with water and cook for 40 to 45 minutes. When the contents of the mould begin to rise and puff up, the mousse is cooked. Remove from the oven. Wait a few minutes while the mousse sinks slightly, then turn onto a serving dish. Wait 2 to 3 minutes, then unmould.

# Mousse de Cervelle à l'Oseille

*Mousse of Brains and Sorrel*

*Serves 6. Preparation and cooking: 1 hr 30 min*
*Refrigeration: 1 hr*

★★

○ **4 lamb's brains**
○ **400g (14 oz) sorrel**
○ **100g (4 oz) butter**
○ **200ml (7 fl oz) double cream**
○ **1 jar (50g/2 oz) stuffed olives**
○ **juice of ½ lemon**

*For the court-bouillon:*
○ **½ litre (18 fl oz) dry white wine**
○ **2 peeled onions**
○ **4 cloves**
○ **2 peeled carrots**
○ **2 peeled cloves garlic**
○ **bouquet garni consisting of: thyme, bay leaves, parsley**
○ **salt and pepper**

1. Prepare the stock: add all the ingredients for the court-bouillon to ½ litre (18 fl oz) water and bring to the boil. Simmer for 30 minutes. Meanwhile, soak the brains in cold water for approximately 30 minutes.
2. When the court-bouillon is ready, strain it through a sieve and put aside to cool. Remove the fibres and all traces of blood from the brains. Drain and place them in the court-bouillon. Poach over a low heat for 20 minutes.
3. Wash the sorrel and cut off the stalks. Melt 50g (2 oz) butter in a frying pan and cook the sorrel leaves for 10 minutes. Remove the brains from the stock and drain. Fry them gently in another frying pan with the remaining butter for 5 minutes. Do not allow to brown.
4. Mince the brains and sorrel in a liquidizer or mincer, or push them through a sieve. Mix well and add the lemon juice. Whip the cream until stiff and then fold, a little at a time, into the brain and sorrel mixture. Pour the mousse into ramekins and garnish with olives. Refrigerate for 1 hour before serving.

*Boulettes de Fromage Blanc (p32)* ▶

# Boulettes de Jambon

*Ham Croquettes*

*Serves 4. Preparation: 10 min Cooking: 10 min*

★★

- ○ **250g (9 oz) white bread, crusts removed**
- ○ **240ml (9 fl oz) milk**
- ○ **150g (5 oz) ham (Parma or Bayonne style)**
- ○ **15ml (1 tbls) roughly chopped herbs: chervil, parsley, chives**
- ○ **2 eggs**
- ○ **50g (2 oz) butter**
- ○ **30g (1¼ oz) breadcrumbs**
- ○ **20g (¾ oz) flour**
- ○ **salt and pepper**

1. Soak the bread in the milk. Mash with a fork, then drain. In a bowl, mix the bread with the eggs until it becomes paste-like.
2. Mince the ham finely. Fry in 30g (1¼ oz) butter over a low heat. Add the chopped herbs. Mix with the bread paste and season to taste.
3. Bring some salted water to the boil in a large saucepan.
4. Form walnut-sized balls with the ham mixture and roll them in the flour. Plunge them in boiling water for 5 minutes. Drain. Fry the breadcrumbs in the remaining butter, then roll the croquettes in them.

You can serve these croquettes with grated Parmesan or Gruyère cheese.

# Boulettes de Viande au Concombre

*Meatballs with Cucumber*

*Serves 4. Preparation: 15 min Cooking: 15 min*

★

- ○ **250g (9 oz) minced beef (steak preferably)**
- ○ **1 egg**
- ○ **15ml (1 tbls) cornflour**
- ○ **15ml (1 tbls) dry white wine**
- ○ **half a cucumber**
- ○ **10 button mushrooms**
- ○ **salt and pepper**
- ○ **240ml (9 fl oz) oil for deep frying**

1. Peel the cucumber, remove the seeds and chop. Bring some water to the boil, blanch the cucumber pieces for 10 minutes and drain. Cut the earthy base off the mushrooms, wash and chop finely.
2. In a bowl mix the minced beef, egg, white wine, cornflour, chopped mushrooms and cucumber. Season, and mash all the ingredients well.
3. Form small balls with the mixture. Heat the oil, fry the balls for 5 minutes and drain on absorbent paper.

# Boulettes de Fromage Blanc

*Cream Cheese Croquettes*

*Serves 5. Preparation: 15 min Cooking: 15 min*

★★

- ○ **500g (18 oz) fromage blanc or cream cheese**
- ○ **150g (5 oz) butter**
- ○ **50g (2 oz) flour**
- ○ **50g (2 oz) breadcrumbs**
- ○ **3 eggs**
- ○ **salt**

1. Drain the fromage blanc, if used. Melt 50g (2 oz) butter.
2. In a bowl, mix the flour, salt, eggs and melted butter and mix well to obtain a smooth paste.
3. Bring some salted water to the boil in a large saucepan. Drop tablespoonfuls of the mixture into the boiling water.
4. As soon as they come to the surface of the water, remove the croquettes and drain in a colander. Separate them if they stick together.
5. Place the breadcrumbs on a plate and roll each croquette in them. Heat the remaining butter in a frying pan over a medium heat. Fry the croquettes for 3 minutes. They must be firm on the outside and soft inside.

# Galettes de Fromage
*Cream Cheese Cakes*

*Serves 6. Preparation: 10 min  Cooking: 30 min*

★★

- ○ **500g (18 oz) fromage blanc or cream cheese**
- ○ **4 eggs**
- ○ **1 bunch chives**
- ○ **200g (7 oz) flour**
- ○ **salt and pepper**
- ○ **200ml (7 fl oz) oil for deep frying**

1. Drain the fromage blanc, if used. Separate the eggs. Beat the whites until stiff.
2. Chop the chives finely. In a bowl, whisk gently together the fromage blanc, egg yolks, flour and chives. Season with salt and pepper.
3. Heat the oil in a frying pan. Meanwhile, fold the egg whites into the ingredients in the bowl.
4. Form the mixture into small balls and flatten with a fork. Fry them, a few at a time, in hot oil for 5 minutes on each side. As soon as each batch is cooked, drain and keep warm in a low oven.

# Allumettes au Roquefort
*Roquefort Sticks*

*Serves 4. Preparation: 10 min  Cooking: 15 min*

★★

- ○ **200g (7 oz) flour**
- ○ **150g (5 oz) Roquefort cheese**
- ○ **50g (2 oz) butter**
- ○ **200ml (7 fl oz) milk**
- ○ **salt and pepper**

1. Preheat the oven to 250°C (475°F; gas mark 9).
2. In a saucepan over a low heat, melt the butter and cheese. Stir well with a wooden spoon until the ingredients become paste-like.
3. Place the flour, milk and butter and Roquefort paste in a bowl. Season and knead into a ball. Roll out the dough on a flour-covered board to a thickness of ½cm (¼ inch).
4. With a knife, cut the dough into rectangles 4cm (1½ inches) wide and 10cm (4 inches) long. Butter a baking sheet.
5. Place the sticks on the baking sheet and bake for 15 minutes. Check from time to time. Do not allow them to get too brown. You can serve these Roquefort sticks hot or cold.

In the same way, you can prepare ham, almond or cumin sticks: mix the flour, milk, butter, salt and pepper. Then add either minced ham, fried flaked almonds or a few pinches of cumin to the paste. These sticks are delicious when served with an apéritif, accompanied by black or green olives.

# Éperlans Frits
*Deep-fried Smelts*

*Serves 6. Preparation and cooking: 10 min*

★

- ○ **500g (18oz) smelts**
- ○ **juice of 1 lemon**
- ○ **5ml (1 tsp) parsley, roughly chopped**
- ○ **30g (1¼ oz) flour**
- ○ **1 litre (1¾ pints) oil for deep frying**

1. Heat the oil.
2. Wash and dry the smelts. Place the flour on a plate and roll the smelts in it. Then plunge them into hot oil and cook for 2 minutes. Drain well.
3. Mix the lemon juice with the parsley. Serve this sauce with the smelts.

# Pâtés aux Épinards

*Serves 6. Preparation: 30 min Cooking: 40 min*

## Spinach Pasties

★★

**For the pastry:**
- ○ **250g (9 oz) flour**
- ○ **30ml (2 tbls) olive oil**
- ○ **5ml (1 tsp) salt**
- ○ **1 egg**

**For the filling:**
- ○ **1kg (2¼ lb) fresh spinach**
- ○ **10g (½ oz) butter**
- ○ **2 eggs**
- ○ **1 carton fromage blanc or cream cheese**
- ○ **15ml (1 tbls) parsley, coarsely chopped**
- ○ **30g (1¼ oz) pistachio nuts, ground**
- ○ **salt and pepper**

**For the glaze:**
- ○ **1 egg yolk**

1. Prepare the pastry: beat the egg with a little water. Sift the flour and salt into a bowl. Fold in the oil and add the beaten egg, a little at a time, working with your hands. Knead the dough on a floured surface until it is firm and springy. If necessary, add a little flour. Cover the dough and let rest for 30 minutes.
2. Meanwhile, prepare the filling: remove the stalks from the spinach, wash and drain. Fry gently in the butter for 10 minutes, turning with a wooden spatula.
3. Drain the cheese, if necessary, and beat the 2 eggs.
4. On a board, place the drained spinach, parsley and pistachio nuts. Season and chop roughly.
5. Place these ingredients in a bowl, add the beaten eggs and cheese and mix well.
6. Preheat the oven to 200°C (400°F; gas mark 6).
7. Divide the dough equally into 4 balls and roll them out, one at a time, to a thickness of 3mm (⅛ inch). Cut the dough into small rectangles. You should get 12 of them. Place a small amount of the filling in the centre of each rectangle. Dampen the edges with a little water and fold over to enclose the filling. Press to seal. For the glaze, brush each pasty with the beaten egg mixed with a little water.
8. Place the pasties onto a baking sheet sprinkled with a little water. Bake for 30 minutes, checking from time to time. Serve at once.

# Pâtés à la Viande et aux Pignons

*Serves 6. Preparation: 20 min Cooking: 1 hr*

## Meat and Pine Nut Pasties

★★

**For the pastry:**
- ○ **200g (7 oz) flour**
- ○ **15ml (1 tbls) wine vinegar**
- ○ **30ml (2 tbls) olive oil**
- ○ **5ml (1 tsp) salt**
- ○ **1 egg**

**For the filling:**
- ○ **500g (18 oz) minced steak**
- ○ **5 fresh mint leaves**
- ○ **1 small onion**
- ○ **20g (¾ oz) pine nuts**
- ○ **10g (½ oz) currants**
- ○ **20g (¾ oz) butter**
- ○ **salt and pepper**

**For the glaze:**
- ○ **1 egg yolk**

1. In a bowl, mix the flour, egg, vinegar, oil and salt. The dough should be firm. Cover and let rest for 1 hour.
2. Prepare the filling: peel and chop the onion. Fry in butter for 10 minutes over a low heat. Add the minced steak, currants, mint leaves and pine nuts. Season. Stir with a wooden spoon and cook for 15 minutes over a low heat.
3. Preheat the oven to 200°C (400°F; gas mark 6).
4. Roll out the dough to a thickness of 3mm (⅛ inch) and divide it into squares of approximately 10cm (4 inches). Place 30-45ml (2-3 tbls) filling in the centre of each square. Wet the edges with a little water, and fold the 4 corners towards the centre. Press to seal and brush with a mixture of beaten egg yolk and a little water.
5. Sprinkle a little water on a baking sheet and place the pasties onto it. Bake for 35 minutes.

*As a change, why not serve a selection of assorted small pasties with an apéritif or as the first course of a meal? Very simple to prepare, they can be filled with vegetables, meat or cheese and look attractive when glazed with an egg yolk and decorated using the blade of a knife.*

*Friands aux Foies de Volaille (p36)* ▶

# Friands aux Foies de Volaille

*Chicken Liver Puffs*

*Serves 6. Preparation: 20 min*
*Cooking: 35 min*
★★

○ **400g (14 oz) frozen puff pastry**
○ **150g (5 oz) chicken livers**
○ **150g (5 oz) pork sausagemeat**
○ **5ml (1 tbls) cognac**
○ **15 sprigs parsley, coarsely chopped**
○ **1 clove garlic**
○ **30g (1¼ oz) butter**
○ **salt and pepper**

*For the glaze:*
○ **1 egg yolk**

1. Thaw the pastry.
2. Prepare the filling: peel and chop the garlic finely. Coarsely chop the chicken livers. Melt the butter in a frying pan over a medium heat and fry the livers gently. Add the sausagemeat and garlic. Season and stir with a wooden spoon. Cook for 15 minutes. Pour over the cognac and set alight. Remove from the heat and add the parsley.
3. Preheat the oven to 230°C (450°F; gas mark 8).
4. Roll out the pastry to a thickness of 5mm (¼ inch) and cut it into 12 squares. Place a small amount of the filling in the centre of each square and fold the corners towards the middle. Brush the puffs with a mixture of beaten egg yolk and a little water.
5. Sprinkle a baking sheet with water and place the chicken liver puffs onto it. Bake for 20 minutes, checking occasionally, to make sure they do not get too brown.

# Friands au Jambon

*Ham Puffs*

*Serves 4. Preparation: 20 min  Cooking: 30 min*
★★

○ **400g (14 oz) frozen puff pastry**
○ **1 onion**
○ **150g (5 oz) cooked ham**
○ **25g (1 oz) butter**
○ **60ml (4 tbls) double cream**
○ **100g (4 oz) Tomme de Savoie cheese**
○ **salt and pepper**

*For the glaze:*
○ **1 egg yolk**

1. Thaw the pastry. Peel and chop the onion. Chop the ham. Melt the butter in a frying pan and gently fry the onion and ham over a low heat, stirring occasionally. Add the cream and cook, uncovered, for 5 minutes. Season, remove from the heat and leave to cool.
2. Dice the cheese and add it to the mixture in the frying pan.
3. Preheat the oven to 230°C (450°F; gas mark 8).
4. On a floured surface, roll out the pastry to a thickness of 3mm (⅛ inch). Divide it into 8 squares and place one-quarter of the filling in the centre of each of 4 squares. Wet the edges with a little water and cover each with one of the 4 remaining squares. Press the edges firmly together. Brush with the egg yolk beaten with a little water to glaze.
5. Sprinkle a baking sheet with water and place the puffs on it. Bake for 20 minutes, checking from time to time to make sure they do not get too brown. Serve hot.

# Vol-au-Vent Breton

*Vol-au-Vent Breton Style*

*Serves 4. Preparation and cooking: 50 min*
★★

○ **1 large vol-au-vent**
○ **200g (7 oz) cushion of veal**
○ **200g (7 oz) chicken breasts**
○ **120ml (4 fl oz) white wine**
○ **30g (1¼ oz) flour**
○ **1 chicken stock cube**
○ **200ml (7 fl oz) double cream**
○ **150g (5 oz) button mushrooms, cut into strips**
○ **90g (3¾ oz) butter**
○ **salt and pepper**

1. Thaw and bake the vol-au-vent, if frozen. Dice the veal and chicken, and gently fry with the mushrooms in 30g (1¼ oz) butter over a low heat, until brown. Season and add the white wine, and cook for 15 minutes.
2. Preheat the oven to 200°C (400°F; gas mark 6).
3. Dissolve the stock cube in 240ml (9 fl oz) water. In a saucepan, melt 60g (2½ oz) butter. Add the flour and stir with a wooden spoon. Add the chicken stock, a little at a time, stirring constantly. Add the cream, season, and cook for 10 minutes, stirring constantly to ensure that the sauce thickens properly. Add the sauce to the meat, mix gently and fill the vol-au-vent case with the mixture. Bake for 15 minutes.

# Crêpes au Fromage

*Cheese Pancakes*

*Serves 4-6. Preparation: 10 min Cooking: 40 min*

★★

*For the pancake batter:*
○ **200g (7 oz) flour**
○ **½ litre (18 fl oz) milk**
○ **2 eggs**
○ **15ml (1 tbls) oil**
○ **1 pinch salt**

*For the filling:*
○ **300g (11 oz) Comté cheese (or substitute Gruyère)**
○ **200ml (7 fl oz) double cream**
○ **4 pinches grated nutmeg**
○ **15ml (1 tbls) oil**
○ **salt and pepper**

1. Prepare the pancake batter: sift the flour into a bowl. Make a well in the centre and break the eggs into it, then add the oil, pinch of salt and 60ml (2 fl oz) milk. Beat vigorously with a wooden spoon until smooth. Stir in the remaining milk a little at a time. Let rest for 1 hour.
2. Remove the crust of the cheese and cut it into strips.
3. Preheat the oven to 140°C (275°F; gas mark 1).
4. Cook the pancakes: heat the oil in a frying pan, and, when the pan is very hot, pour in just enough batter to cover the base of the pan thinly. Cook each pancake, turning to cook both sides, for 3 minutes. Rub the frying pan with oil when necessary. Fill the pancakes with the strips of cheese and fold them over to form a triangle. Leave them on the heat for a few seconds so that the cheese melts. As soon as each pancake is ready, place in an ovenproof dish and keep warm in the oven, leaving the door ajar.
5. Beat the cream with a whisk, add the grated nutmeg. Season and place in the freezer for 2 minutes. Serve the very cold cream with the hot pancakes.

# Crêpes au Fromage et aux Épinards

*Cheese and Spinach Pancakes*

*Serves 5. Preparation: 15 min Cooking: 30 min*

★★

*For the pancake batter:*
○ **200g (7 oz) flour**
○ **½ litre (18 fl oz) milk**
○ **2 eggs**
○ **15ml (1 tbls) oil**
○ **1 pinch salt**

*For the filling:*
○ **500g (18 oz) fromage blanc or cream cheese**
○ **200g (7 oz) fresh spinach**
○ **15ml (1 tbls) coarsely chopped herbs: tarragon, parsley, chervil and chives**
○ **1 lemon**
○ **15ml (1 tbls) oil**
○ **20g (¾ oz) butter**
○ **salt and pepper**

1. Prepare the pancake batter: sift the flour into a bowl, make a well in the centre and break the eggs into the middle. Add the oil, pinch of salt and 60ml (2 fl oz) milk. Beat vigorously with a wooden spoon until smooth. Add the remaining milk a little at a time. Let rest for 1 hour.
2. Bring some salted water to the boil. Remove the stalks from the spinach, wash and drain the leaves, and plunge them into the boiling water. Cook for 10 minutes. Drain well.
3. Chop the spinach. Beat the fromage blanc with a whisk, then mix in the chopped spinach and herbs. Season.
4. Preheat the oven to 200°C (400°F; gas mark 6).
5. Cook the pancakes: heat the oil in a frying pan. When the oil is hot, pour in just enough batter to cover the base of the pan thinly. Turn or toss the pancake when brown. Repeat, rubbing the pan with oil whenever necessary.
6. Place the pancakes on a plate, spread each one with the fromage blanc mixture and roll them up. Place them in an ovenproof dish. Dot with knobs of butter and cook in the oven for 3 to 5 minutes. Serve with lemon slices.

*Stuffed pancakes can be a pleasant surprise: there are so many fillings to choose from. Here are just a few examples for you to try: chopped chicken livers fried with shallots and mushrooms in white wine; diced ham sautéed with black olives, parsley and a beaten egg; fish or shellfish bound with a béchamel. Just cook the pancakes and stuff with your favourite filling.*

# Alose à l'Oseille

*Shad with Sorrel*

*Serves 4. Preparation: 20 min Cooking: 1 hr 35 min*

★

○ **1.2kg (2½ lb) shad**
○ **500g (18 oz) fresh sorrel**
○ **1 slice raw ham**
○ **2 onions, finely chopped**
○ **30ml (2 tbls) oil**
○ **100ml (3½ fl oz) brandy**
○ **salt and pepper**

1. Scale, clean and wash the fish under cold running water and dry thoroughly. Remove the stalks from the sorrel, wash and drain. Chop the ham finely.
2. Heat the oil and fry the chopped onions and ham gently for 5 minutes.
3. Set the oven to 190°C (375°F; gas mark 5). Pour the contents of the frying pan into an ovenproof dish, add salt and pepper, cover with one-third of the sorrel, lay the shad on top and season; add the rest of the sorrel and sprinkle with brandy. Cover the dish with buttered paper or foil and bake for 1½ hours.
4. Serve immediately.

Sorrel and brandy are both noted for dissolving the numerous bones of the shad.

# Anchois en Tourte

*Anchovies Tourtière*

*Serves 4. Preparation: 20 min Cooking: 30 min*

★

○ **1kg (2¼ lb) fresh anchovies**
○ **150g (5 oz) breadcrumbs**
○ **80g (3 oz) grated Parmesan**
○ **2 eggs**
○ **30ml (2 tbls) parsley, coarsely chopped**
○ **5ml (1 tsp) basil, coarsely chopped**
○ **5ml (1 tsp) powdered oregano**
○ **60ml (4 tbls) oil**
○ **salt and pepper**

1. Cut the heads off the anchovies, clean and wash under cold running water and dry on kitchen paper.
2. Mix the breadcrumbs, grated cheese and herbs in a bowl. Beat the eggs in another bowl with a tablespoon of oil, salt and pepper.
3. Set the oven to 220°C (425°F; gas mark 7). Grease an ovenproof dish and place in it a layer of anchovies, each curled in a circle, with the tail tucked inside. Sprinkle with oil, cover with half of the breadcrumb mixture and season. Proceed with the second layer, using the remaining anchovies, sprinkle with oil and add the rest of the mixture, salt and pepper. Pour over the beaten eggs and bake for 30 minutes.
4. Serve hot.

Instead of Parmesan, this delicious Italian speciality may be prepared with grated Pecorino or goat's milk cheese from the Pyrenees.

*A good fish is above all a fresh fish, whether it is the humble whiting, sardine or mackerel, or the noble and expensive turbot, sea-perch or salmon. Never buy a fish whose freshness is in doubt; no subtle dressing or delicate sauce will ever disguise its lack of freshness.*

*Those lucky enough to buy fish straight from the fishing boats will recognise a fresh fish and its signs: bright eyes, red gills, body rigid and arched; the colours are bright and the scales shining; the flesh is firm and springy and does not give under pressure of a finger; the smell is that of the sea and not of ammonia.*

*The shad has very delicate flesh in spite of its numerous bones, but deteriorates rapidly. It inhabits the estuaries of large rivers in France and can weigh several pounds.*

*Anchois en Tourte* ▶

# Matelote d'Anguilles

*Eels in Red Wine*

*Serves 6. Preparation: 20 min  Cooking: 50 min*

★ ★

○ **1.6kg (3½ lb) medium-sized eels**
○ **24 small peeled onions**
○ **24 button mushrooms**
○ **1 bottle red wine**
○ **2 cloves garlic**
○ **1 sprig thyme**
○ **1 small bay leaf**
○ **½ oz (1 tbls) flour**
○ **80g (3 oz) butter**
○ **2.5ml (½ tsp) sugar**
○ **salt and pepper**

1. Clean and skin the eels, wash and cut into 5cm (2 inch) lengths. Melt half the butter in a saucepan and gently sauté the onions for about 10 minutes, then lift from the pan with a slotted spoon and reserve.
2. Stir in the flour with a wooden spoon, and add the wine, stirring continuously, then add the cloves of garlic, unpeeled and crushed in the palm of the hand, together with the sugar, salt, pepper, thyme, bay leaf and onions. Allow to simmer for 15 minutes.
3. Meanwhile, remove the mushroom stalks, wash and dry the mushrooms and place in the saucepan.
4. When the wine sauce has cooked for 15 minutes, add the eels and simmer for 20 minutes. Because their flesh is firm and oily eels can be plunged into a boiling sauce and then allowed to cook gently.
5. When the eels are cooked, lift out the pieces with a slotted spoon and place on a serving dish. Keep warm. Reduce the sauce for 5 minutes over a high heat; then remove the thyme, bay leaf and garlic. Turn off the heat and add the remaining butter, allowing it to melt slowly in the sauce by gently moving the saucepan. Pour the sauce over the eels and serve immediately.

You can serve this with croûtons fried in butter. This dish cooked in wine is sometimes called 'meurette'. If you add 150g (5 oz) of lean bacon cut into thin strips and fried with the onions it will become a 'pochouse', to which you can add 2 tablespoons of cream at the last minute.

Carp, pike, tench or bream can be prepared in the same way, separately or together.

# Anguilles au Four

*Baked Eels*

*Serves 4. Preparation: 10 min  Cooking: 30 min*

★

○ **1kg (2¼ lb) medium-sized eels**
○ **100g (4 oz) butter**
○ **100ml (½ cup) oil**
○ **3 cloves garlic, peeled**
○ **30ml (2 tbls) water**
○ **60ml (4 tbls) flour**
○ **60ml (4 tbls) coarse salt**
○ **salt and pepper**

1. Sprinkle the flour on a plate. Skin the eels, cut off the heads, clean and wash. Cut into 5cm (2 inch) lengths, roll in the flour, shake to remove excess and put aside on a plate.
2. Heat the oil in a frying pan and sauté the pieces of eel for 5 minutes until golden brown, turning continuously; drain well.
3. Set the oven to 220°C (425°F; gas mark 7). Melt the butter in a frying pan and fry the cloves of garlic gently, without browning. Place the pieces of eel in an ovenproof dish and spoon over the butter, garlic and water. Season with salt and pepper. Bake for 20 minutes, and serve immediately.

*Eel is appreciated for its rich, firm flesh which can be cooked in many different ways: fried, grilled, boiled (*au bleu*), with spinach (*au vert*), in red wine, in pâté or even pickled. Smoked eel is delicious, cut into elegant fillets and served on canapés with a slice of lemon.*

# Bar au Vin Blanc

*Serves 4. Preparation: 10 min Cooking: 40 min*

*Bass in White Wine*

★ ★

○ **1.2kg (2½ lb) bass**
○ **250ml (9 fl oz) dry white wine**
○ **100g (4 oz) butter**
○ **1 sprig thyme**
○ **1 bay leaf**
○ **30ml (2 tbls) parsley**
○ **1 small onion**
○ **2 cloves**
○ **salt and pepper**
○ **nutmeg**

1. Scale, clean and rinse the fish under cold running water. Butter an ovenproof dish.
2. Set oven to 200°C (400°F; gas mark 6). Peel and slice the onion in thin rounds and lay in the dish, covering the base. Lay the fish on top, pour in the wine and add the thyme, bay leaf, parsley and cloves. Season with salt, pepper and nutmeg. Cover with foil or buttered paper and bake for 30 minutes.
3. When the fish is cooked, lift it out and place on a serving dish. Strain the cooking liquid into a saucepan and place over a high heat. Reduce to approximately 45ml (3 tbls), then lower the heat and whisk in the remaining butter, cut into small knobs, until the sauce is smooth. Pour the sauce over the fish and serve immediately.

Serve with boiled potatoes, leeks julienne or fresh spinach.

# Barbue à la Rhubarbe

*Serves 4. Preparation and cooking: 1 hr*

*Brill with Rhubarb*

★ ★

○ **1.5kg (3¼ lb) brill**
○ **1 onion**
○ **2 shallots**
○ **1 carrot**
○ **30ml (2 tbls) parsley**
○ **250ml (9 fl oz) white wine**
○ **6 rhubarb sticks**
○ **200g (7 oz) cream**
○ **20g (1 oz) butter**
○ **salt and pepper**

1. Fillet the fish and skin it. Put aside the head and bones to make stock.
2. Prepare the stock: wash the head and bones of the brill and put in a pan with white wine and a pint of water; add the peeled onion and carrot cut into slices, together with the parsley. Season slightly with salt; bring to the boil and simmer for 20 minutes on low heat.
3. Meanwhile, peel and cut the rhubarb into 3cm (1 inch) pieces. Blanch in boiling water for 10 minutes, then drain and pass through the fine mesh of a vegetable mill. Put aside.
4. When the stock is ready, strain and put aside. Set the oven to 200°C (400°F; gas mark 6). Peel and finely chop the shallot. Butter an ovenproof dish large enough to contain the brill fillets without overlapping, sprinkle with shallots and lay the fillets on top. Pour over the stock, cover with foil and bake for 15 minutes.
5. When cooked, turn off the oven. Lift out the fillets and arrange them on a serving dish, cover with the rhubarb purée and place the dish in the oven with the door ajar.
6. Set the cooking dish over a high heat and reduce the sauce to 250ml (½ pint) of liquid. Add the cream and reduce further for 1 minute. Season to taste with salt and pepper and strain to remove the shallots. Spoon the sauce over the fish and serve immediately.

The tart, fragrant rhubarb adds delicacy to this dish, and today is used more often than sorrel. This recipe is also suitable for turbot, dab and bass.

# Baudroie Gratinée à la Crème

## *Angler Gratin with Cream*

*Serves 4.*
*Preparation and cooking: 45 min approximately*
★

○ **8 slices of angler**
○ **50g (2 oz) butter**
○ **3 onions**
○ **1 clove garlic**
○ **2 eggs**
○ **200ml (7 fl oz) milk**
○ **100ml (4 fl oz) cream**
○ **salt and pepper**
○ **nutmeg**

1. Rinse the fish under cold running water and dry on kitchen paper. Peel the garlic and onion and chop finely.
2. Melt the butter in a frying pan, sauté the fish for 1 minute on each side, then place in an ovenproof dish large enough to contain the fish without overlapping. Season with salt and pepper; add the nutmeg and cover with the chopped garlic and onion.
3. Set the oven to 190°C (375°F; gas mark 5). Beat the eggs in a bowl and stir in the cream and milk. Pour the mixture over the fish and bake for 30 minutes. Serve at once in the same dish.

Serve with small grilled tomatoes or green beans in butter.

# Gigot de Lotte à l'Ail Rose

## *Tail of Angler with Pink Garlic*

*Serves 4.*
*Preparation: 15 min Cooking: 25 min*
★

○ **1 tail of angler, weighing approximately 1.2kg (2½ lb)**
○ **1 head of pink garlic**
○ **2.5ml (½ tsp) thyme**
○ **1 bay leaf**
○ **2.5ml (½ tsp) fennel seeds**
○ **100ml (3½ fl oz) oil**
○ **1 lemon**
○ **salt and pepper**

1. Set the oven to 220°C (425°F; gas mark 7). Skin the fish, wash and dry it, and tie it up as for a leg of lamb.
2. Peel two cloves of garlic and chop in thin slices. Insert into the flesh of the fish, as for a leg of lamb.
3. Heat the oil in a flameproof dish, sauté the fish gently for 5 minutes, letting it colour evenly on all sides, then remove from the heat.
4. Squeeze the lemon juice onto the fish, dust with thyme and fennel, and season with salt and pepper. Place the rest of the cloves of garlic around the fish, add the bay leaf and bake for 20 minutes. Baste frequently.
5. Once cooked, arrange the fish on a serving dish, remove the string, place the roasted garlic around the fish for everyone to help themselves, pour on the cooking liquid and serve immediately.

A suggested way of serving *gigot de lotte* is with fresh spinach, grilled tomatoes, *lace* potatoes, or braised fennel. Pink garlic comes from Provence and has the most delicate and perfumed of flavours, it is also much more easily digested. Try preparing this dish with fresh garlic, you will be pleasantly surprised at its fine flavour.

*Always make sure that you buy angler fish with its skin intact – its delicate soft flesh is damaged by contact with ice, destroying its fine taste and consistency which is similar to that of lobster. It is better to skin the fish yourself or to ask the fishmonger to do it for you.*

*There is another type of angler, a freshwater fish whose latin name lota lota is easy to remember, and which inhabits still waters in Central Europe and Eastern France. Its tender, oily, succulent flesh and white liver are highly praised. Like the sea fish it must be skinned before being prepared, whether baked in the oven, cooked in red wine, with cream or simply fried.*

*With fish sold headless like the angler or the* roussette, *it is easy to check freshness: the flesh should be pale pink and pearly, never blotched red or yellow.*

# Cabillaud aux Câpres

*Cod with Capers*

*Serves 4. Preparation: 10 min Cooking: 8 min*

★

○ **4 cod steaks, weighing approximately 200g (7 oz) each**
○ **80g (3 oz) capers**
○ **50g (2 oz) black olives**
○ **250g (9 oz) ripe tomatoes**
○ **15ml (1 tbls) basil, coarsely chopped**
○ **90ml (6 tbls) olive oil**
○ **salt and pepper**

1. Rinse the cod steaks under cold water and dry on kitchen paper. Stone the olives and chop finely.
2. Scald the tomatoes in boiling water for 10 seconds. Drain, refresh in cold water and peel. Cut into halves, remove the seeds and mash roughly with a fork.
3. Set the oven to 220°C (425°F; gas mark 7). Oil an ovenproof dish with 30ml (2 tbls) olive oil, lay the steaks in the dish and dust with basil, then add the olives, capers and tomatoes. Season with salt and pepper. Sprinkle over the rest of the oil and bake for 20 minutes.
4. Serve hot in the cooking dish.

Basil can be replaced by parsley, oregano, savory or rosemary.

# Cabillaud aux Légumes Nouveaux

*Cod with Fresh Vegetables*

*Serves 4. Preparation: 25 min Cooking: 30 min*

★

○ **2 cod steaks, 400g (14 oz) each**
○ **250g (9 oz) fresh peas**
○ **250g (9 oz) new carrots**
○ **12 small fresh onions (or pickling onions)**
○ **300g (11 oz) ripe tomatoes**
○ **60ml (4 tbls) oil**
○ **salt and pepper**

1. Rinse the steaks and dry on kitchen paper. Season with salt and pepper. Peel, wash and finely chop the onions and carrots and shell the peas.
2. Scald the tomatoes in boiling water for 10 seconds, peel and cut into halves. Remove seeds and crush roughly. Put aside.
3. Oil a deep saucepan with 15ml (1 tbls) oil. Arrange the fish in the pan, covered by a layer of onions, a layer of carrots, a layer of peas and finally a layer of tomatoes. Season and sprinkle over the rest of the oil. Cover tightly and simmer over moderate heat for 30 minutes without lifting the lid.
4. At the end of the cooking time, carefully mix together the vegetables and the fish and cook for a further 5 minutes with the lid off. Serve immediately.

Tuna or hake could be substituted for cod.

*Fresh cod is excellent and can be prepared in many ways. Salted, it becomes* morue; *salted and dried,* morue sèche.

*Cod is appreciated for its famous liver, its roe, which can be salted and smoked, and its tongue. Fishermen are traditionally given the right to remove the cod tongues themselves, which is apparently the best part of the fish. These tongues can be eaten fresh, fried or pickled.*

*In international gastronomy carp has quite a reputation. Very popular in the Middle Ages it seems to be less so today, although it is a fish of exquisite taste with a delicate roe which can be prepared* à la meunière *(fried in butter), baked in the oven with* beurre blanc, *sautéed with red wine and mushrooms, cooked Jewish style (sweet and sour) or stuffed.*

# Haddock au Lait

*Haddock in Milk*

*Serves 4. Preparation: 5 min  Cooking: 15 min*

★

○ **800g (2 lb) haddock**
○ **1 litre (1¾ pints) milk**

*For the sauce:*
○ **100g (4 oz) butter**
○ **juice of 1 lemon**
○ **45ml (3 tbls) capers**
○ **salt and pepper**

1. Rinse the haddock and dry on kitchen paper.
2. Place the fish in a saucepan and cover with the milk. Set on medium heat, bring to the boil, and reduce heat at once to simmer for 10 minutes.
3. Meanwhile, prepare the butter with capers: melt the butter, remove from the heat and add the lemon juice, capers, salt and pepper. Keep warm.
4. When the haddock is cooked, lift it out with a fish slice and place in a serving dish. Serve immediately, handing round the sauce separately.

# Haddock au Citron

*Haddock with Lemon*

*Serves 4. Preparation: 5 min  Cooking: 20 min*

○ **800g (2 lb) haddock**
○ **125g (4 oz) butter**
○ **juice of 4 lemons**
○ **salt and pepper**

1. Rinse the fish under cold water and dry on kitchen paper.
2. Place the fish in a saucepan, cover with cold water and bring to the boil. The minute it comes to the boil, remove from the heat and lift out the fish.
3. Meanwhile, set the oven at 170°C (325°F; gas mark 3).
4. Place the fish in an ovenproof dish. Cut the butter into large knobs, dot over the fish and squeeze over the lemon juice. Bake for about 10 minutes. The butter and lemon must be hot, but should not be allowed to boil.
5. Serve the fish very hot, in its cooking dish.

Serve with small steamed potatoes or fresh spinach poached for 3 minutes in boiling water.

The haddock, with its grey sides and white front, has a characteristic black spot near the first back fin. It is also called black cod. Fresh, it is prepared like cod; salted and smoked, it becomes the fish beloved of the English.

The true smoked haddock should be pale yellow, the colour that comes naturally from smoking over a wood fire; if it is darker, more orange, it has been smoked artificially. Often, fillets of ling are sold as haddock. Always ask for real haddock.

The smelt, a small silver fish, is never longer than 25cm (10 inches) and can be deep fried, whole if small, or in fillets when larger. It must not be mistaken for the sand eel which is also tasty but more bland. The smelt, when fresh, has a faint aroma of cucumber, or if less fresh, violet. Always choose the smallest. Clean through the gills, dust with flour, tie up in small bunches and deep fry in hot oil (but not smoking); season with salt, pepper and lemon.

The sturgeon, famous mostly for its roe – caviar – has an extremely succulent flesh when smoked, but it is also excellent braised, grilled or fried. It is found in France in the Rhone and Garonne regions.

The féra, which inhabits Lake Geneva and Lake Constance, tastes much like trout and can be prepared in the same way. In Geneva, féras are served deep fried, the bigger ones in fillets.

# Harengs au Bacon

*Herrings with Bacon*

*Serves 4. Preparation: 20 min Cooking: 15 min*

★ ★

○ **8 fresh herrings, each about 150g (5 oz)**
○ **16 slices of bacon**
○ **30ml (2 tbls) mustard**
○ **juice of 1 lemon**
○ **100ml (3½ fl oz) oil**
○ **salt**

1. Scale, clean and rinse the fish under cold running water and dry. Remove the heads, separate into fillets and remove the backbone. Place the fillets on a large plate, sprinkle with lemon juice and season with a little salt. Coat each fillet with mustard, reshape the fish and put 2 slices of bacon around each herring, securing with string or cocktail sticks.
2. Heat the oil in a large frying pan and fry the fish for 5 to 7 minutes on each side. When cooked, drain on kitchen paper before arranging on a serving dish. Serve immediately.

Serve with a green or mixed salad: tomato and cucumber, mushroom and fennel, or red and white cabbage. Small mackerel called *lisettes* can be prepared in the same way.

# Harengs Salés au Vin Blanc

*Salted Herring with White Wine*

*Serves 4. Preparation: 10 min Marinade: 2 hr*
*Cooking: 25 min*

★ ★

○ **8 salted herrings**
○ **250ml (9 fl oz)) dry white wine**
○ **250ml (½ pint) milk**
○ **100ml (3½ fl oz) alcohol vinegar**
○ **60g (2 oz) butter**
○ **1 medium-sized onion**
○ **1 clove garlic**
○ **2.5ml (½ tsp) chopped thyme**
○ **2.5ml (½ tsp) rosemary**
○ **3 sage leaves**
○ **1 bay leaf**
○ **1 celery stick**
○ **10 sprigs parsley**

1. The day before: put the fish to soak in milk for 12 hours.
2. The next day: peel the garlic and onion and chop finely together with the bay leaf, sage, parsley and celery. Drain the fish and dry with kitchen paper to remove all the milk from the marinade.
3. Melt the butter in a frying pan, add the herbs, garlic, onion and celery and fry for 5 minutes. Add the wine and vinegar and boil down to a third of the liquid. Reduce the heat, add the fish and allow to simmer for 10 minutes.
4. Serve hot or cold.

*Flounder resembles plaice, except that its yellow spots are not as obvious. It is slightly longer and can live up to 40 years of age. Its flesh is rather oily and is best prepared in fillets and fried in butter (*à la meunière*).*

*Halibut is the largest flat fish. It looks like an enormous plaice and can weigh up to 200kg (440 lb). It is found in northern waters and its firm white flesh is greatly valued and very delicate. It can be prepared in escalopes and baked in the oven, fried, poached or cooked* au gratin. *In Northern countries it is often salted or smoked and in Great Britain most fish restaurants offer halibut on their menu.*

*Gurnet, often called red mullet, is mistakenly sold as the real mullet but it is quite different to look at and to taste. Although its flesh is quite delicate, this fish with its huge head and many bones is best used in* bouillabaisses *and fish soup. Beware of these bones, they can be dangerous. You can tell a gurnet is fresh from its bright colours: red back and white front. If it is pink, don't buy it.*

*Gudgeon is a small fish which is to be found in all the lakes and rivers of Europe and is best deep fried. It is delicious.*

# Maquereaux Marinés à la Cannelle

*Marinated Mackerel with Cinnamon*

*Serves 4. Preparation: 10 min*
*Marinade: 5 hr Cooking: 20 min*
★

- ○ **1.2kg (2½ lb) small mackerel**
- ○ **½ litre (18 fl oz) dry white wine**
- ○ **4 medium-sized onions**
- ○ **2 cloves**
- ○ **1 small stick cinnamon**
- ○ **15ml (1 tbls) parsley, coarsely chopped**
- ○ **45ml (3 tbls) olive oil**
- ○ **2.5ml (½ tsp) peppercorns**
- ○ **salt**

1. Clean and rinse the fish under cold running water and dry on kitchen paper. Remove the heads. Peel and chop the onions. Place the mackerel in a salad bowl with the cloves, pepper, chopped onions, parsley and cinnamon. Season with salt and moisten with white wine. Cover and marinate for 5 hours, preferably in the fridge.
2. After 5 hours, peel and chop two more onions. Heat the oil in a saucepan and sauté the onions gently for approximately 5 minutes without browning.
3. Lift out and drain the mackerel and strain the marinade to remove the onions, parsley, pepper, cloves and cinnamon.
4. Place the fish on the bed of onions, add the marinade and enough water to cover. Cover and leave to cook gently for 15 minutes, without boiling.
5. Serve hot in the same dish.

# Maquereaux au Vin Blanc

*Mackerel in White Wine*

*Serves 4. Preparation: 20 min Cooking: 10 min*
★

- ○ **1.2kg (2½ lb) small mackerel**
- ○ **½ litre (18 fl oz) dry white wine**
- ○ **¼ litre (9 fl oz) water**
- ○ **100ml (3½ fl oz) wine vinegar**
- ○ **2 medium-sized onions**
- ○ **2 carrots**
- ○ **1 lemon**
- ○ **1 bay leaf**
- ○ **1 sprig thyme**
- ○ **2 cloves**
- ○ **2.5ml (½ tsp) peppercorns**
- ○ **salt**

1. Peel and chop the onions and carrots. Place half of the vegetables at the bottom of a flameproof dish large enough to contain the fish. Rinse and cut the lemon in thin slices. Remove the pips.
2. Clean, rinse and dry the mackerel. Place on the vegetables, add the pepper, thyme, bay leaf and cloves. Season with salt, cover with the rest of the onions and carrots and add the wine and vinegar. The fish must be covered; add water if necessary.
3. Place the dish over a medium heat and when the liquid starts to simmer, cook for 5 minutes and then draw off the heat. Leave to cool in the dish and when it is completely cold, place in the fridge.

These mackerel can be kept in the fridge for 3 days: they are an excellent starter.

*Mackerel is found everywhere; it is a migrating fish perfectly designed to swim fast, and can reach up to 60cm (2¼ ft) in length. Its flesh, similar to that of the tuna, is oily and savoury whether it is grilled, marinated, smoked, cooked in stock or in wine, hot or cold. Small mackerel, called* liselettes, *are delicious, especially in a marinade.*

*Unlike other fish, mackerel can be put into boiling stock; it makes the flesh firmer.*

*Never buy ready-prepared fillets; it may be the wrong fish. Buy it whole and ask your fishmonger to cut it into fillets.*

# Maquereaux aux Oignons

*Serves 4. Preparation: 15 min Cooking: 30 min*

## Mackerel with Onions

★

- ○ **1.2kg (2½ lb) small mackerel**
- ○ **400ml (14 fl oz) dry white wine**
- ○ **3 onions, chopped finely**
- ○ **3 bay leaves**
- ○ **30ml (2 tbls) olive oil**
- ○ **salt and pepper**

1. Clean the fish, remove the heads and separate into fillets. Rinse and dry on kitchen paper. Crumble the bay leaves.
2. Place a layer of onions in a deep saucepan, add the fish, cover with the rest of the onions and sprinkle with bay leaves. Season with salt and pepper. Sprinkle with the oil and white wine. Cover, and allow to simmer for 30 minutes.
3. Serve hot in the same dish, with lemon quarters.

# Merlans Farcis

*Serves 4. Preparation: 20 min Cooking: 15 min*

## Stuffed Whiting

★★

- ○ **4 whiting, about 250g (9 oz) each**
- ○ **300g (10 oz) whiting fillets**
- ○ **50g (2 oz) white bread, with the crusts cut off**
- ○ **30ml (2 tbls) cream**
- ○ **1 egg**
- ○ **1 egg white**
- ○ **100g (4 oz) butter**
- ○ **30ml (2 tbls) breadcrumbs**
- ○ **the juice of 1 lemon**
- ○ **salt and pepper**
- ○ **nutmeg**

1. Scale, clean and rinse the fish under cold water. Remove the backbone without separating the fillets.
2. Put the whiting fillets, bread and cream in a blender. Put the mixture in a bowl and add the egg and the egg white. Season with salt, pepper and nutmeg, and stuff each whiting with the mixture. Secure with cocktail sticks.
3. Set the oven to 230°C (450°F; gas mark 8). Melt half of the butter in an ovenproof dish; lay in the fish, dust with breadcrumbs and add the rest of the butter. Bake for 15 minutes. Add the lemon juice 5 minutes before you take the fish out of the oven.

Serve hot with lemon quarters and a salad.

# Merlans Poêlés en Persillade

*Serves 4. Preparation: 10 min Cooking: 12 min*

## Fried Whiting with Parsley

★

- ○ **4 whiting, about 300g (11 oz) each**
- ○ **1 onion**
- ○ **2 cloves garlic**
- ○ **30ml (2 tbls) parsley, roughly chopped**
- ○ **100ml (3½ fl oz) dry white wine**
- ○ **50g (2 oz) butter**
- ○ **1 lemon**
- ○ **100ml (3½ fl oz) oil**
- ○ **salt and pepper**

1. Scale and clean the fish; remove the heads and rinse under cold water. Dry on kitchen paper. Peel the garlic and onions and chop finely.
2. Place the oil, onion and garlic, parsley and fish in a frying pan. Season with salt and pepper. Leave the whitings to cook gently for 3 minutes on each side, then add the wine. Allow to simmer for another 3-4 minutes, until the wine has reduced, then add the butter.
3. When the butter has melted, remove from heat, arrange the fish on a serving dish, pour over the cooking liquid and garnish with slices of lemon. Serve at once.

Serve this dish with baked tomatoes or salad.

*Although not very exotic, boiled potatoes go very well with fried or poached fish. But all fresh vegetables are suitable: green beans, peas, grilled tomatoes, spinach, celery hearts, braised fennel, mushrooms and leeks fried in butter, boiled or steamed cauliflower. Try dried vegetables: dried white beans with angler, chick peas with tuna . . . Fresh pasta goes well with white fish cooked in sauce: brill or sole fillets, stewed cod, roast angler, etc.*

# Merlu aux Oignons

*Hake with Onions*

*Serves 4. Preparation and cooking: 55 min*

★

○ **4 hake steaks, about 200g (7 oz) each**
○ **1kg (2¼ lb) onions**
○ **1 red pepper**
○ **100ml (3½ fl oz) vinegar**
○ **1 clove garlic**
○ **5ml (1 tsp) sugar**
○ **30ml (2 tbls) flour**
○ **120ml (8 tbls) ground nut oil**
○ **salt and pepper**
○ **nutmeg**

*Serve with:*
○ **1 hard-boiled egg**
○ **15ml (1 tbls) capers**
○ **10 green olives**

1. Peel and chop the onions finely. Wash the pepper, cut into quarters and remove the middle and the seeds. Cut into thin strips.
2. Heat 60ml (4 tbls) of oil and sauté the garlic, onions and pepper for 10 minutes. When the onions are golden brown, add the vinegar and sugar. Season with salt, pepper and nutmeg. Cover and cook gently for 20 minutes, stirring occasionally. Pour the mixture into a bowl and reserve.
3. Sprinkle the flour on a plate. Rinse and dry the fish steaks, dip in the flour and shake to remove excess.
4. Heat 60ml (4 tbls) of oil in a frying pan and fry the fish for 3 minutes on each side, until they are golden brown. Lift out, drain and arrange on a serving dish.
5. Pour the sauce over the steaks, allow to cool and add slices of hard-boiled egg, olives and capers.

Serve the same day or, even better, the following day.

# Merlu Gratiné à la Tomme Fraîche

*Hake Gratin*

*Serves 4. Preparation: 10 min
Cooking: 25 min Marinade: 30 min*

★

○ **4 hake steaks, about 200g (7 oz) each**
○ **200g (7 oz) tomme de Savoie, if available, or another soft cheese**
○ **100g (4 oz) cream**
○ **250g (9 oz) ripe tomatoes**
○ **30ml (2 tbls) oil**
○ **juice of 1 lemon**
○ **salt and pepper**
○ **nutmeg**

1. Wash and dry the fish. Put in a dish, sprinkle with lemon juice, and leave to marinate for 30 minutes.
2. Meanwhile, scald the tomatoes in boiling water for 10 seconds, drain and refresh in cold water, then peel and cut into halves; press to remove seeds and crush to a pulp. Cut the cheese into thin slices.
3. Set the oven to 220°C (425°F; gas mark 7). Oil an ovenproof dish, arrange the fish in it and season with salt, pepper and nutmeg. Add the tomatoes, cover with slices of cheese and sprinkle the cream over. Bake for 25 minutes.
4. Serve hot in the same cooking dish.

*Hake, called* colin *in the Paris region, is often referred to as whiting in the South of France. Its firm white flesh, as lean as that of the sole, is very delicate. Although it can be found all year round, it is at its best in June.*

*Small hake are delicious deep fried; large ones can be either baked or fried in butter. The largest, weighing up to 10kg (22 lb) are often sold in steaks and can be fried, or stewed with vegetables or tomatoes.*

*Hake is very fragile: it is fresh when its scales are still in place and when its three colours – black back, white front, and grey sides – are still visible. Its black eye should be very bright, like a pearl. If sold in steaks, its flesh should be milky white.*

*Mulet aux Fines Herbes (p53)* ▶

# Gratin de Morue à l'Origan

*Serves 4. Preparation and cooking: 1 hr 15 min*

### Salt Cod Gratin with Oregano

★ ★

○ **800g (2 lb) salt cod, soaked**
○ **500g (1 lb) ripe tomatoes**
○ **3 medium-sized potatoes**
○ **2 red or green peppers**
○ **1 onion, finely chopped**
○ **1 clove garlic**
○ **30ml (2 tbls) parsley, coarsely chopped**
○ **2.5ml (½ tsp) oregano**
○ **30ml (2 tbls) breadcrumbs**
○ **90ml (6 tbls) oil**
○ **salt and pepper**

1. Remove the skin and bones and cut the salt cod into 5cm (2 inch) pieces. Wash the peppers and cut into four, lengthwise. Remove the seeds and middle and slice each quarter. Peel the potatoes and slice into thin rounds.
2. Heat 30ml (2 tbls) of oil in a frying pan and sauté the onion gently for 5 minutes, then add the peppers and cook slowly for 10 minutes over low heat. Season with salt and pepper.
3. Scald the tomatoes (except for two) in boiling water for 10 seconds, drain and refresh in cold water; peel, cut into halves, remove the seeds and crush to a pulp.
4. Set the oven to 200°C (400°F; gas mark 6). Peel and chop the garlic finely. Slice the two remaining tomatoes.
5. Oil an ovenproof dish with 30ml (2 tbls) of oil. Put in first the crushed tomatoes, then the potatoes and sprinkle with the garlic and parsley. Pour over the onion and pepper mixture and add the salt cod. Cover with slices of tomato and season.
6. Dust with oregano, the rest of the garlic, parsley and breadcrumbs. Sprinkle with the oil and bake for 30 minutes. Serve hot.

# Morue aux Raisins de Corinthe

*Serves 4. Preparation: 15 min*
*Cooking: 30 min*

### Salt Cod with Currants

★

○ **800g (2 lb) salt cod, soaked**
○ **50g (2 oz) currants**
○ **2 onions, finely chopped**
○ **15ml (1 tbls) tomato purée**
○ **30ml (2 tbls) flour**
○ **60ml (4 tbls) oil**
○ **salt**

1. Soak the currants in warm water.
2. Remove the skin and bones and cut the salt cod into 8cm (3 inch) pieces. Dip in flour and shake to remove excess.
3. Heat the oil in a frying pan and sauté the onions gently for 5 minutes. Add the salt cod and sauté gently for 2 minutes on each side. Add the tomato purée diluted in 200ml (7 fl oz) water and bring to the boil. Drain the currants and place in the frying pan. Season with salt and simmer for 15 minutes, without boiling.
4. When ready, arrange the salt cod on a serving dish, pour the sauce over and serve immediately.

*When using a* court-bouillon *you must ensure that it is cold before immersing and cooking the fish. In this way the fish can cook gradually without disintegrating.*

*Moreover, it should not be allowed to boil, but only simmer. Count 25 minutes for a 3 lb fish to be served hot. If the fish is to be served cold, place it in cold stock; when it starts to boil remove from the heat, cover and allow the fish to cool in the stock.*

# Mulets aux Fines Herbes

*Serves 4. Preparation: 20 min Cooking: 15 min*

*Grey Mullet with Herbs*

★

○ **4 grey mullet, about 300g (11 oz) each**
○ **100ml (3½ fl oz) oil**
○ **100ml (3½ fl oz) dry white wine**
○ **juice of 1 lemon**
○ **1 small pimento**
○ **3 anchovy fillets, in oil**
○ **1 basil leaf**
○ **6 sage leaves**
○ **20 sprigs parsley**
○ **1 bay leaf (fresh)**
○ **15ml (1 tbls) vinegar**
○ **salt and pepper**

1. Scale, clean and wash the mullet and dry on kitchen paper. Arrange in an ovenproof dish and season with salt and pepper.
2. Beat together the oil and lemon juice and reserve. Set the oven to 220°C (425°F; gas mark 7).
3. Finely chop the anchovies, pimento, basil, sage, parsley and bay leaf. Add the vinegar and 15ml (1 tbls) of the oil-lemon mixture. Coat the fish with this thick paste and sprinkle with the rest of the oil-lemon mixture and white wine.
4. Bake for 15 minutes and serve hot.

Serve with tomatoes 'Provençal-style' or a mixed salad: endive and fennel, for instance.

# Mulet à la Crème et aux Poivrons

*Serves 4. Preparation: 20 min*
*Cooking: 30 min*

*Grey Mullet with Cream and Peppers*

★

○ **1 mullet, 1.2kg (2½ lb)**
○ **juice of 1 lemon**
○ **50g (2 oz) bacon**
○ **2 peppers**
○ **50g (2 oz) butter**
○ **1 large onion**
○ **4 ripe tomatoes**
○ **100g (4 oz) cream**
○ **15ml (1 tbls) mustard, (Dijon preferably)**
○ **salt**

1. Scale, clean and wash the mullet under cold running water and dry on kitchen paper. Sprinkle with lemon juice and season with salt both inside and out.
2. Set the oven to 220°C (425°F; gas mark 7). Cut the bacon into small pieces. Wash the peppers, remove the seeds, chop into quarters, then slice each quarter finely. Peel the onion and chop finely. Scald the tomatoes for 10 seconds in boiling water, drain and refresh in cold water. Peel, cut into halves and press to remove the seeds. Crush to a pulp with a fork.
3. Butter an ovenproof dish with 20g (¾ oz) of the butter and lay in the mullet. Cover with the bacon and half of the peppers and surround with the rest of the peppers, onion and tomatoes. Melt the remaining butter and pour over the fish. Bake for 20 minutes, basting from time to time with the cooking juices.
4. Meanwhile, mix the cream and mustard and season with salt. Pour this sauce over the fish and cook for a further 10 minutes. Serve hot.

Serve with pilau rice.

*The mostelle, a fish of the gade family, is found mainly in the Mediterranean. This fish is very delicately flavoured and must be eaten fresh on the spot, as it does not travel well.*

*The best way to prepare it is to slit it open along the back, remove the backbone, season with salt and dot with butter. Bake in the oven, basting frequently. Serve with a squeeze of lemon.*

# Raie au Beurre Noir

*Serves 4. Preparation and cooking: 45 min*

*Skate with Black Butter*

★

○ 1kg (2½ lb) skate, cut in
   4 pieces
○ 180g (6 oz) butter
○ 30ml (2 tbls) parsley, coarsely
   chopped
○ 45ml (3 tbls) capers
○ 30ml (2 tbls) wine vinegar

*For the court-bouillon:*
○ 100ml (3½ fl oz) vinegar
○ 1 onion
○ 1 carrot
○ 1 bouquet garni, consisting of:
   bay leaf, sprig thyme, 5 sprigs
   parsley
○ 6 peppercorns
○ 15ml (1 tbls) coarse salt

1. Remove the skin and wash the skate under running water. Peel the onion and carrot and chop finely.
2. Place the pieces of skate in a large saucepan, cover with cold water, and add the carrot, onion, bouquet garni, peppercorns, salt and vinegar. Put on a low heat; the minute it comes to the boil, reduce the heat and barely simmer for 20 minutes – it must not boil. Skim the top when it first begins to boil.
3. After 20 minutes drain the skate and arrange the pieces on a serving dish; sprinkle with capers and parsley and keep warm.
4. Melt the butter in a frying pan and heat until it turns a caramel colour (not black, in spite of the name!), and pour over the fish. Add the wine vinegar to the pan, heat for 2 seconds, then pour it over the fish.

Serve hot on its own or with small steamed potatoes.

# Rougets en Papillotes

*Serves 4. Preparation: 15 min Cooking: 12 min*

*Red Mullet in Foil*

★

○ 8 red mullet, about 180g
   (6 oz) each
○ 4 stems fresh fennel (or
   rosemary, basil or fresh
   savory)
○ 30ml (2 tbls) olive oil
○ salt and pepper
○ foil

1. Scale and wash the fish under cold running water. Clean through the gills, remove the liver and replace with a few fennel leaves. Dry on kitchen paper.
2. Set the oven to 220°C (425°F; gas mark 7). Cut 8 rectangles of aluminium foil, each large enough to contain a fish.
3. Oil each red mullet and place in the foil with salt, pepper and fennel; close each packet by twisting both ends.
4. Place the packets on a baking sheet and bake for 12 minutes.

Serve the red mullets in their foil with lemon quarters and anchovy butter prepared as follows: mix 15ml (1 tbls) of anchovy paste with 100g (4 oz) soft butter and add a few drops of garlic juice.

*Char is a highly sought after delicacy. It can be prepared like salmon when small and like trout when larger, and is found in the deep lakes and rivers of Switzerland, the Auvergne and the Pyrenees.*

*There are many types of skate, but the best can be recognised by the large bony marks under the skin. As your fishmonger will only sell you the wings, you will have to trust him!*

*The small skate is best fried. First clean and skin it (having scalded it beforehand), cut off the head and keep the liver, much prized by connoisseurs.*

*The best recipe for skate is with* beurre noir, *but it is worth trying others: with white sauce, or baked with a cheese* béchamel *on a bed of thinly sliced potato rounds.*

*Filets de Sole Poêlés au Citron (p58)* ▶

# Sardines au Laurier

*Sardines with Bay Leaves*

*Serves 4. Preparation: 25 min Cooking: 20 min*

★

- 1.2kg (2½ lb) sardines
- 30 bay leaves
- 100g (4 oz) breadcrumbs
- 150ml (5 fl oz) olive oil
- salt and pepper

1. Clean the sardines, cut the heads off, rinse quickly and dry on kitchen paper. Split them open, press gently and remove the backbone, then close the fish again.
2. Oil an ovenproof dish with 30ml (2 tbls) of oil and arrange the fish in a single layer. Season. Scatter on the bay leaves and sprinkle with vinegar.
3. Set the oven to 220°C (425°F; gas mark 7). Mix the breadcrumbs and the rest of the oil together with a fork. If the paste is too thick, add a drop more oil. Coat the sardines with this paste and bake for 20 minutes until the fish is crisp and golden.
4. Serve at once.

Serve with a mixed salad, spring onions and lemon quarters.

# Sardines Froides au Fenouil

*Chilled Sardines with Fennel*

*Serves 6. Preparation and cooking: 1¾ hr*

★ ★

- 1.5kg (3¼ lb) sardines
- 15ml (1 tbls) fennel seeds
- 60ml (4 tbls) breadcrumbs
- 45ml (3 tbls) olive oil
- salt

*For the sauce:*
- 2 tins peeled tomatoes, 750g (1½ lb) each
- 4 onions
- 100ml (3½ fl oz) vinegar
- 100ml (3½ fl oz) white vermouth
- 15ml (1 tbls) tomato purée
- 45ml (3 tbls) olive oil
- 1 pinch sugar
- 1 small pimento
- salt and pepper

1. Peel and finely chop the onions. Open the tins of tomatoes, reserve the juice and roughly chop the tomatoes.
2. To prepare the sauce: gently sauté the onions in 45ml (3 tbls) of oil for 5 minutes. When they are a nice golden colour, add the vinegar and reduce over a high heat. Add the vermouth, leave to evaporate, and then pour in the crushed tomatoes and their juice. Season, and add the tomato purée, sugar and the crushed pimento. Cook gently for 30 minutes, stirring from time to time with a wooden spoon.
3. Meanwhile, clean the sardines and cut off the heads. Rinse under cold water and dry. Oil a baking dish and set the oven to 230°C (450°F; gas mark 8).
4. When the sauce is cooked, pour into the dish and spread out with a spatula. Place the sardines on top in a single layer. Season with salt, sprinkle with fennel seeds, breadcrumbs and the rest of the oil. Bake for 25 minutes.
5. When ready, arrange the fish on a serving dish and leave to cool.

The sardines will be even better if you prepare them the day before serving.

*The pike-perch, much prized by the Hungarians who call it* fogash, *has left its birth-place – Lake Balaton – to inhabit the Rhine and Rhone valleys. It is as delicious as pike, but without the bones, and may be prepared in the same way as bass, pike, trout or salmon.*

*Blood appearing at the gills of fish like sardines, herring, red mullet or anchovy is a sign of decomposition, whereas with other fish, such as the bass or dorado, it is a sign of freshness.*

# Saumon Cru au Poivre Vert

*Serves 4. Preparation: 15 min, 15 min before serving*

*Raw Salmon with Green Pepper*

★

○ **800g (2 lb) fresh salmon**
○ **24 green peppercorns**
○ **30ml (2 tbls) olive oil**
○ **1 green lemon**

1. Ask your fishmonger to give you a piece of salmon near the head, and to remove the skin and cut it into fillets, removing the backbone.
2. Check that no bones are left. Use a tweezer if necessary.
3. Slice the fillets of salmon finely (so thin they are transparent) and arrange on decorated plates. Brush with olive oil and place on a plate in the fridge for 15 minutes.
4. Crush the peppercorns in a mortar. Just before serving, sprinkle the fish with pepper and garnish with lemon quarters.

Serve with hot toast. No need for butter or salt. It is easier to cut the salmon into thin slices if you put it in the fridge beforehand: its flesh will then be firmer.

# Saumon à l'Unilatérale

*Serves 4. Preparation: 10 min Cooking: 30 sec*

*One-way Salmon*

★

○ **800g (2 lb) fresh salmon**
○ **10ml (2 tsp) oil**

*To serve:*
○ **100g (4 oz) butter**
○ **1 lemon**
○ **salt and pepper**

1. Ask your fishmonger for a piece of salmon near the head. Ask him to remove the skin and cut it into two fillets, removing the backbone.
2. Light the grill. Check that no bones are left, using a pair of tweezers if necessary.
3. Cut each fillet in half and brush with oil.
4. Gently melt the butter in a saucepan. Cut the lemon into quarters.
5. Grill the fillets for 30 seconds on one side only. The salmon scallops should be golden on one side, opaque in the middle and transparent on top, hence its name 'one-way'.
6. Arrange the slices on individual plates and pour the melted butter into a sauceboat.
7. Serve at once, garnished with lemon, salt and pepper. Hand the butter separately.

This Scandinavian-style salmon is delicious simply served with melted butter, but you can add leaf spinach or steamed potatoes. This kind of cooking can also be done in a non-stick frying pan, without fat.

*Nowadays many restaurants serve lightly cooked or even raw fish: salmon in thin scallops, diced bass, dorado in thin slices, salted small sardines. If you want to try it at home, make sure the fish is absolutely fresh, caught less than 48 hours before.*

# Filets de Sole Poêlés au Citron

*Serves 4. Preparation: 5 min  Cooking: 10 min*

## Fillets of Sole Fried with Lemon

★

○ **4 soles, 300g (11 oz) each**
○ **120g (4 oz) butter**
○ **45ml (3 tbls) flour**
○ **45ml (3 tbls) parsley, coarsely chopped**
○ **juice of 1 lemon**
○ **salt and pepper**

1. Skin the sole, clean and cut off the heads. Cut into fillets. All this can be done by your fishmonger. Rinse quickly under cold water, dry and season with salt and pepper. Roll in flour and shake to remove excess.
2. Heat 80g (3 oz) of butter in a frying pan and gently fry the fillets for 4 minutes on each side: the butter must not burn and should keep its golden colour. Lift out the fish and arrange on a serving dish. Keep the dish warm.
3. Add the lemon juice to the butter used for frying, remove from the heat and put in the last of the butter. Stir with a wooden spoon and pour this butter over the fillets. Sprinkle with parsley and serve at once.

# Soles Colbert

*Serves 4. Preparation and cooking: 35 min*

## Sole Colbert

★★

○ **4 soles, 300g (11 oz) each**
○ **45ml (3 tbls) flour**
○ **45ml (3 tbls) breadcrumbs**
○ **2 eggs**
○ **30ml (2 tbls) oil**
○ **30ml (2 tbls) water**
○ **125g (4 oz) soft butter**
○ **30ml (2 tbls) parsley, coarsely chopped**
○ **30ml (2 tbls) lemon juice**
○ **oil for frying**
○ **salt and pepper**

1. Skin the sole, clean through the gills, rinse under cold water and dry on kitchen paper. Make a cut down the centre of each sole, along the backbone. Slide the knife in so that the flesh is eased away from the bone, without removing the fillet. Snip the backbone at each end, this makes it easily removable when the fish is cooked. Roll back the cut edges to make an opening in the fish.
2. Place the flour in a soup dish, breadcrumbs in another and in a third the eggs beaten with water and oil. Season with salt and pepper.
3. Season the soles with salt and pepper both inside and out. Dip them in the flour, then in the egg and finally in the breadcrumbs.
4. Heat the oil for frying and gently fry the sole for 4 minutes on each side over a low heat. Lift out and remove the backbone with a small knife.
5. Arrange the fish on a serving dish and keep warm while you prepare the butter *maître d'hôtel*: mash the soft butter with the parsley and lemon juice. Season with salt and pepper. Stuff each sole with the butter *maître d'hôtel* and serve immediately.

Serve with lemon quarters and small boiled or steamed potatoes.

*The fresher a sole is, the more difficult it is to skin. Generally the fishmonger does it, but if you want to do it yourself, lay the fish on a board dark side up; cut off the tail, loosen the black skin at the cut where the fish was cleaned, grasp the tail end of the skin with the corner of a tea towel and pull it off.*

*If the sole is prepared in fillets, the white skin should be removed in the same way. To cut into fillets, trim the fins with scissors. Run the point of the knife down the backbone between the fillets and the backbone, until the fillet is detached.*

*Entrecôte à la Florentine (p61)* ▶

# Thon à la Livournaise

*Tuna Italian-Style*

*Serves 4. Preparation: 15 min  Cooking: 15 min*

★

- ○ **4 slices of tuna, 200g (7 oz) each**
- ○ **1 400g (14 oz) tin peeled tomatoes**
- ○ **150ml (5 fl oz) oil**
- ○ **100g (4 oz) black olives**
- ○ **50g (2 oz) capers**
- ○ **2 cloves garlic**
- ○ **salt and pepper**

1. Rinse the fish under cold running water and dry on kitchen paper.
2. Crush the tomatoes to a fine purée. Stone and roughly chop the olives. Peel and finely chop the garlic.
3. Pour the oil into a large frying pan, add the tomatoes, capers, olives, garlic and the fish. Season. Place the frying pan on a strong flame and cook the tuna for 5 to 6 minutes on each side, depending on its thickness. Serve hot with a mixed salad.

Red mullet can be prepared in the same way.

# Truites au Beurre Rouge

*Trout with Butter and Wine*

*Serves 4. Preparation: 10 min  Marinade: 2 hr*
*Cooking: 20 min*
★ ★

- ○ **4 good-sized trout**
- ○ **½ litre (18 fl oz) red wine**
- ○ **2 shallots**
- ○ **1 sprig thyme**
- ○ **4 sprigs parsley**
- ○ **125g (4 oz) butter**
- ○ **1 pinch sugar**
- ○ **salt and pepper**

1. Clean and rinse the fish under cold running water and dry. Season with salt.
2. Butter a flameproof dish large enough to contain the fish without overlapping. Peel and finely chop the shallots, scatter in the bottom of the dish and place the trout on top. Sprinkle with thyme and parsley and cover with the red wine. Leave to marinate in the fridge for 2 hours.
3. After 2 hours, place the dish over a low heat. At the first sign of boiling, reduce the heat, season with salt and cover the dish with aluminium foil. Allow to simmer for 12 minutes then remove from the heat.
4. Arrange the trout on a serving dish, cover with foil and keep warm over a saucepan full of hot water.
5. Return the cooking dish to a high heat, add the sugar, remove the thyme and parsley and boil down until you have roughly 30ml (2 tbls) of liquid left. Remove from the heat. Cut the butter into small knobs, add to the dish and allow the butter to melt slowly while mixing with a wooden spoon. Season with pepper and pour over the trout. Serve at once.

Thin slices of apple fried in butter or potatoes boiled in their jackets go very well with this recipe. Choose a full-bodied wine to cook this dish and serve it with the same.

Small bass or two soles can be prepared in the same way without marinating.

# Filet aux Cèpes à la Braise

*Serves 4. Preparation: 3 min Cooking: 10 min*

## Grilled Fillet with Mushrooms

★

- ○ 4 fillet steaks, 200g (7 oz) each
- ○ 4 large mushrooms
- ○ 15ml (1 tbls) oil
- ○ salt

1. Remove the stalks from the mushrooms (save them and use them for stuffing, sauces or omelettes). Wipe the mushrooms with a damp cloth. Brush the mushrooms and steaks with oil.
2. Cook under a grill or on a barbecue. Start cooking the mushrooms first: place them hollow side up on the grill and cook for 10 minutes. Cook the steaks for 4 minutes (rare) to 7 minutes (well done). Add salt after 5 minutes.
3. When the meat and mushrooms are cooked, place the steaks on a dish and decorate each with a mushroom. Serve at once.

These steaks can be served with a dash of olive oil or a knob of butter, seasoned with a little garlic, anchovy paste and herbs.

# Tournedos Maître d'Hôtel

*Serves 4. Preparation: 10 min Cooking: 8 min*

## Grilled Tournedos with Parsley Butter Sauce

★

- ○ 4 tournedos, 150g (5 oz) each
- ○ 100g (4 oz) butter
- ○ 30ml (2 tbls) roughly chopped parsley or mixed herbs
- ○ 15ml (1 tbls) lemon juice
- ○ 15ml (1 tbls) strong French mustard
- ○ salt and pepper

1. Heat the grill or barbecue.
2. Cut the butter into small cubes and place in a small saucepan over a low heat. Whip with a whisk or fork till it acquires a creamy consistency. Remove from the heat and add the lemon juice and mustard, beating constantly. Add salt, pepper and parsley. Mix again and pour into a sauceboat.
3. Place the tournedos on the hot grill. Cook for 5 minutes (rare) to 8 minutes (well done). Place them on a serving dish. Salt them and serve at once. Each person tops his or her tournedos with a spoonful of parsley butter sauce which will melt on contact.

# Entrecôte à la Florentine

*Serves 2. Preparation and cooking: 15 min*

## Rib Steak Florentine Style

★

- ○ 1 rib steak
- ○ olive oil
- ○ salt and pepper

1. Place the meat on a large dish. Sprinkle with oil, season with plenty of freshly ground pepper and leave to marinate for 10 minutes.
2. Heat the grill (for best results cook over a wood fire). Add the meat and cook for 3-4 minutes on each side. Salt just before removing from the heat and serve immediately, on a hot dish.

# Araignée Mignonnette

*Serves 2. Preparation: 5 min Cooking: 3-4 min*

## Steak Mignonnette

★

- ○ 2 steaks
- ○ 10ml (2 tsp) coarsely ground pepper
- ○ 5ml (1 tsp) olive oil
- ○ salt

1. Preheat the grill. Brush the steaks with oil. Press the pepper well into the meat, making sure it sticks.
2. When the grill is very hot, cook the steak for 1½ to 2 minutes each side, depending on whether you like your meat rare or well done.
3. When the steaks are cooked, season and serve immediately.

The steaks may be basted with a little olive oil whilst cooking. Serve with grilled tomatoes and pommes frites. Alternatively serve with a knob of butter and garnish with cress.

# Hampe au Persil

*Flank with Parsley Sauce*

*Serves 4. Preparation: 10 min Cooking: 2-4 min*

★

○ **2 pieces of flank, 350g (12 oz) each**
○ **60ml (4 tbls) roughly chopped parsley**
○ **60ml (4 tbls) double cream**
○ **10ml (2 tsp) French mustard**
○ **5ml (1 tsp) crushed peppercorns**
○ **nutmeg**
○ **salt**

1. Heat the grill. Place the mustard in a small saucepan. Add the cream, salt, nutmeg to taste, pepper and parsley. Mix well.
2. When the grill is very hot, place the meat on it and cook for 1 minute (rare) to 2 minutes (well done). (This cut of meat is very flat and therefore cooks very quickly, hence the necessity for a very hot grill.)
3. While the meat is cooking, place the saucepan on a very low heat and heat the sauce, without allowing it to boil.
4. When the meat is cooked, cut each steak into two. Arrange them on a serving dish and cover with parsley sauce. Serve immediately.

This dish can be served with jacket potatoes: they are delicious with the parsley sauce.

# Bavette à la Vinaigrette Verte

*Top of Sirloin with Green Vinaigrette*

*Serves 4. Preparation: 15 min Cooking: 4-7 min*

★

○ **4 top of sirloin steaks, 150 to 200g (5-7 oz) each**
○ **60ml (4 tbls) olive oil**
○ **15ml (1 tbls) sherry vinegar (if available, otherwise substitute white wine vinegar)**
○ **1 clove garlic**
○ **1 small onion**
○ **30ml (2 tbls) chopped parsley**
○ **15ml (1 tbls) chopped herbs: chervil or chives**
○ **cayenne pepper**
○ **salt and freshly ground pepper**

1. Peel the garlic and onion. Chop the onion as finely as possible. Put the garlic through a press and collect the juice in a bowl. Add the oil and vinegar, salt, pepper and cayenne to taste. Whip until the mixture is creamy, then add the parsley, chervil or chives and onion. Mix again. Allow the sauce to stand for 1 hour before serving.
2. Heat a grill or barbecue. Grill the steaks for 4 minutes (rare) to 7 minutes (well done), according to their thickness. Arrange them on individual plates or on one dish and serve immediately. Serve the parsley sauce separately.

A small spoonful of anchovy paste may be added to the sauce and a small fresh chopped red pepper may be substituted for the cayenne.

# Pavés au Jus d'Ail

*Rump Steak with Garlic*

*Serves 4. Preparation: 10 min Cooking: 6-8 min*

★

○ **4 rump steaks, 180g (6 oz) each**
○ **6 cloves garlic**
○ **6 drops Tabasco sauce**
○ **45ml (3 tbls) olive oil**
○ **salt and pepper**

1. Ask your butcher to cut 4 steaks from one slice of meat. You will get thick pieces with right angles – 'slabs'.
2. Pour the oil into a small bowl. Add plenty of pepper and the Tabasco sauce. Peel the garlic cloves and put them through a garlic press. Add to the oil and beat with a fork until creamy.
3. Heat a grill or a barbecue. Brush the steaks with the oil mixture and place them on the grill. Cook the steaks for 3 minutes (rare) to 4 minutes (well done) on each side.
4. When the steaks are cooked, add salt, arrange them on individual plates and serve immediately.

*Escalopes à la Pizzaiola (p69)* ▶

# Côte Marinée aux Oignons Dorés

*Marinated Rib of Beef with Golden Onions*

*Serves 4. Preparation and cooking: 50 min*
*Marinade: 4-6 hr*
★

○ **1kg (2¼ lb) rib of beef**
○ **30ml (2 tbls) vinegar**
○ **60ml (4 tbls) olive oil**
○ **2 bay leaves, crumbled**
○ **5ml (1 tsp) thyme**
○ **5ml (1 tsp) freshly ground pepper**
○ **6 large onions**
○ **15ml (1 tbls) strong French mustard**
○ **100g (4 oz) double cream**
○ **2.5ml (½ tsp) curry powder**
○ **50g (2 oz) butter**
○ **salt**

1. 4-6 hours in advance, prepare the marinade. Place the vinegar, oil, thyme, bay leaf and pepper in a bowl. Beat with a fork until the mixture is creamy.
2. Place the meat in a dish and pour over half the marinade. Turn the meat over and coat the other side with the remaining marinade. Put the dish in the refrigerator for 4-6 hours, turning it over once or twice during this time.
3. Take the meat out of the refrigerator 1 hour before cooking. 45 minutes before serving, peel the onions and mince them. Put them into a frying pan and allow them to 'sweat', turning them continuously for 5 minutes over a low heat. Then add the butter and cook over a low heat for 15 minutes. Add the cream and the curry powder and allow to simmer for 5 minutes.
4. Meanwhile, prepare the coals of a barbecue or heat the grill. Wipe the beef, then grill it for 12 minutes (rare) to 15 minutes (well done) on each side. Turn it over halfway through cooking. Do not place the meat too close to the heat.
5. When the meat is cooked, arrange on a serving dish. Pour the contents of the frying pan into a sauceboat and serve immediately.

Serve this dish with salads or vegetables in season: buttered green beans, baked tomatoes, grilled mushrooms.

# Brochettes Sauce Piquante

*Kebabs with Piquant Sauce*

*Serves 4. Préparation: 10 min Cooking: 15 min*
★

○ **500g (18 oz) rump steak or fillet**
○ **200g (7 oz) smoked bacon**
○ **3 medium-sized onions**
○ **100ml (3½ fl oz) wine vinegar**
○ **30ml (2 tbls) tomato purée**
○ **2.5ml (½ tsp) freshly ground pepper**
○ **2.5ml (½ tsp) cayenne pepper**
○ **60g (2¼ oz) butter**
○ **2.5ml (½ tsp) sugar**
○ **5ml (1 tsp) salt**

1. Cut the bacon into strips ½cm (¼ inch) wide. Cut the meat into cubes 3cm (1¼ inches) square. Peel the onions and chop them as finely as possible.
2. Put the onions into a small saucepan with the vinegar, salt, sugar and pepper. Place the saucepan on a low heat and allow to simmer until the vinegar is reduced by half (about 5 minutes).
3. Add the tomato purée, 30ml (2 tbls) water and the cayenne pepper and allow to simmer for 5 minutes over a low heat.
4. Meanwhile, heat the grill or prepare a barbecue. Thread the cubes of meat and the strips of bacon onto skewers.
5. When the grill is hot, cook the kebabs for 5-6 minutes, turning often.
6. When the sauce is ready, add the butter, cut in small pieces. Whip the mixture until it is creamy. Pour the sauce into a sauceboat.
7. When the kebabs are cooked, arrange them on a serving dish and serve immediately with the sauce separately.

Serve with creole rice or with a green salad, grilled peppers or chips. Chopped herbs may be added to the sauce.

# Rosbif à l'Anglaise

*Roast Beef English Style*

★

○ **800g (1¾ lb) fillet (for roasting)**
○ **100g (4 oz) butter**
○ **salt and pepper**

1. Trim the fat from the meat and bind with kitchen thread so that it will hold its shape.
2. Melt the butter in a stewpan and when it browns add the meat. Cook over a high flame for exactly 30 minutes: the meat should brown evenly all over. Turn the meat with a spatula to avoid piercing it. If you wish, baste with a little brandy and add a little water if necessary.
3. 5 minutes before the meat is cooked, salt and pepper it lightly, then place on a plate, cover with a second plate, and place a weight on the top. Collect the blood extracted from the meat, add to the cooking juices and heat, adding a little water if necessary, then pour into a heated sauceboat.
4. Slice the beef thinly (it should be lukewarm and red at the centre), place on a serving dish and serve the hot gravy separately. If you wish, surround with green vegetables.

The 'classic' English way to prepare roast beef allows a maximum of 40 minutes cooking time per kilo (2¼ lb) meat. If you don't like very rare meat, it can be cooked for a longer period.

# Rosbif au Sel

*Roast Beef Cooked in Salt*

○ **800g (1¾ lb) rib of beef**
○ **6kg (13½ lb) coarse salt**

1. Preheat the oven to 300°C (550°F; gas mark 12). Trim the fat from the meat. Fill an oval flameproof dish with salt. Place the meat in the centre. Cover the meat completely with the remaining salt and place in the oven. During cooking, the salt will first melt and then form a crust.
2. Cook for 1 hour 30 minutes. Then remove the dish from the oven, break the crust with a knife so that it comes away from the edges of the dish and remove the salt from the meat with a pounder. Cut the meat into thick slices and serve.

This method is a variation of clay-baked roast. You may keep the salt and use for other dishes, but remember that it retains the flavour of the meat.

*Meat of good quality is recognizable by its bright red colour and its layer of covering fat which should be thick and white or pale yellow. The older the animal, the darker the meat. Good meat looks smooth and has a slight sheen. It is criss-crossed by little veins of fat (when it is said to be 'marbled'). It should be slightly elastic and firm to the touch. Meat that is too lean or flabby, too light or too dark is not good-quality meat.*

# Faux-Filet Poivre et Sel

*Serves 6. Preparation: 5 min Cooking: 30 min*

*Sirloin Steak with Salt and Pepper* ★

○ 1 slice sirloin steak, 1.3kg
  (2¾ lb)
○ 30ml (2 tbls) green peppercorns
○ 15ml (1 tbls) thyme
○ 15ml (1 tbls) olive oil
○ 500g (18 oz) coarse sea salt

1. Ask the butcher to tie up the meat. Preheat the oven to 250°C (475°F; gas mark 9). Crush the peppercorns in a mortar with a pestle.
2. Oil the meat and press the pepper onto both sides with the palm of your hand to make it stick.
3. Mix the salt and thyme. Pour this into an ovenproof pan just large enough to hold the meat and put it in the oven. You will notice the delicious smell of thyme almost immediately.
4. Wait for 10 minutes, until the salt is fairly hot, then place the meat on it and cook for 15 minutes, first on one side and then the other – having turned it over without piercing it – and then for another 15 minutes to obtain well-done meat. If you like it rare, cook for 3 minutes less each side.
5. When the meat is cooked, turn off the oven and remove the meat. Place the meat on a rack over the dripping in the pan, and put it back in the oven. Allow the meat to rest for 10-15 minutes in the turned-off oven, turning it once during this time.
6. Serve thinly sliced, hot or cold.

This roast can be accompanied by sautéed mushrooms or tomatoes stuffed with garlic and breadcrumbs, and with various butter mixtures: garlic butter, mustard butter, anchovy butter, etc.

# Rôti Enrobé de Moutarde

*Serves 6. Preparation: 5 min Cooking: 35 min*

*Roast Beef with Mustard Sauce* ★

○ 1 piece of rump for roasting,
  1.2kg (2½ lb), bound
○ 45ml (3 tbls) strong French
  mustard
○ 15ml (1 tbls) freeze-dried green
  peppercorns
○ 200g (7 oz) double cream
○ 1 sprig tarragon
○ 60ml (4 tbls) port
○ 15ml (1 tbls) oil
○ salt

1. Preheat the oven to 250°C (475°F; gas mark 9). Crush the peppercorns in a mortar with a pestle. Add the mustard and 15ml (1 tbls) cream. Mix well.
2. Oil an ovenproof dish which is just big enough to hold the roast. Spread the pepper mixture all over the roast, place it in the dish and place in the oven. Cook for 30 minutes (rare) to 35 minutes (well done). After 10 minutes of cooking, add half the port to the base of the dish; add the remainder 15 minutes later.
3. When the roast is cooked, turn the oven off and leave the meat to rest in the oven for 10 minutes, then place on a serving dish. Remove the string and place the dish in the lukewarm oven to keep it warm while the sauce is being prepared.
4. Pour the rest of the cream into the ovenproof dish and place the dish over a gentle heat. Mix well with a spatula, scraping up the crusty bits on the bottom, and allow the sauce to reduce by one-third. Meanwhile, wash the tarragon, dry it and roughly chop the leaves.
5. When the sauce is ready add salt to taste and the tarragon, pour it into a sauceboat and serve with the roast.

*Tournedos à la Crème (p72)*

# Filet à la Broche aux Trois Poivres

*Fillet Steak with Three Peppers on a Spit*

*Serves 6. Preparation: 10 min*
*Cooking: 30 min* ★

- ○ **1.2kg (2½ lb) beef fillet, bound**
- ○ **10ml (2 tsp) black peppercorns**
- ○ **10ml (2 tsp) white peppercorns**
- ○ **10ml (2 tsp) green peppercorns**
- ○ **15ml (1 tbls) oil**
- ○ **50ml (1¾ fl oz) armagnac**
- ○ **2 shallots**
- ○ **15ml (1 tbls) French mustard**
- ○ **150g (5 oz) double cream**
- ○ **50g (2 oz) butter**
- ○ **salt**

1. Crush the 3 kinds of peppercorn together with a pestle and mortar. Oil the roast and roll it in the pepper, pressing with the palm of your hand.
2. Heat the rotisserie. Put the roast on the spit above a roasting pan and cook for 30 minutes for medium-cooked meat.
3. Meanwhile, prepare the sauce: peel the shallots, chop very finely, and place in a small saucepan over a low heat with 20g (¾ oz) butter. When the shallots are transparent (about 5 minutes), add the cream and, as soon as it begins to boil, add the mustard. Salt to taste and keep the sauce warm.
4. When the roast is cooked, sprinkle with armagnac, using a ladle with a long handle. On contact with the heat, the alcohol will burst into flames.
5. Turn off the heat. Place the roast on a cutting board. Add 5ml (1 tsp) water to the drippings in the pan and bring to the boil, scraping up the crusty bits with a spoon. Add to the sauce.
6. Slice the roast and arrange on a hot serving dish. Heat the sauce until it bubbles and turn off the heat. Add the remaining butter while beating with a fork. Pour the sauce into a sauceboat through a fine strainer and add the juice drained from the meat while cutting. Serve immediately.

Serve this roast with Yorkshire pudding, gratinéed potatoes or cheese fritters.

# Rôti à l'Ail en Chemise

*Rump Roast with Garlic*

*Serves 8. Preparation: 5 min Cooking: 50 min*
★

- ○ **1.5kg (3¼ lb) rump steak**
- ○ **1 head garlic**
- ○ **2 sprigs rosemary**
- ○ **45ml (3 tbls) oil**
- ○ **salt and pepper**

1. Ask the butcher to cut the rump steak in one piece and to bind it round to obtain a slab about 6cm (2½ inches) thick.
2. Separate the cloves from the head of garlic, remove the fine external skin but do not peel them. Make a small cut along the length of each clove with a small pointed knife.
3. Heat the oil in a sauté pan and lightly brown the meat for 5 minutes on each side, over a high heat. Then lower the heat as much as possible, salt the meat, surround it with cloves of garlic and sprigs of rosemary and cook for 25 minutes (rare) to 40 minutes (medium), turning every 10 minutes. Use two spatulas to turn the meat without piercing it.
4. When the roast is cooked, arrange on a serving dish. Untie the string and place the garlic cloves around the meat. Discard three-quarters of the cooking fat, add 100ml (3½ fl oz) water to the remainder of the fat in the pan and bring to the boil quickly, scraping up the crusty bits on the bottom of the pan. Pour this juice into a sauceboat. Serve immediately.

Serve with vegetables in season, either sautéed or braised.

# Escalopes à la Pizzaiola

*Escalopes with Wine and Anchovies*

*Serves 4. Preparation and cooking: 40 min*

★★

○ **500g (18 oz) chuck steak or thin flank, sliced**
○ **flour**
○ **40g (1¾ oz) butter**
○ **salt and pepper**
○ **75ml (2½ fl oz) white wine**
○ **75ml (2½ fl oz) beef stock**
○ **15ml (1 tbls) tomato purée**
○ **30g (1¼ oz) anchovy fillets**
○ **30g (1¼ oz) pickled onions**
○ **30g (1¼ oz) pickled gherkins**
○ **small handful of dried oregano**

1. Lightly flatten the slices of beef with a meat pounder and sprinkle with flour.
2. Melt the butter in a large pan and place the escalopes in it. Season. Add the white wine and cook over a low heat until the wine evaporates. Add the hot stock and tomato purée and cook for 15 to 20 minutes.
3. Meanwhile, finely chop the anchovy fillets, onions, capers and gherkins and add this mixture to the meat halfway through cooking.
4. When cooked, sprinkle with the oregano and transfer the escalopes and their sauce to a serving dish. Serve immediately.

# Onglet aux Échalotes Grises

*Skirt Steak with Grey Shallots*

*Serves 4. Preparation: 20 min  Cooking: 20 min*

★

○ **4 top of skirt steaks, 180g (6 oz) each**
○ **16 grey shallots**
○ **15ml (1 tbls) oil**
○ **60g (2¼ oz) butter**
○ **salt and pepper**

1. Peel the shallots and chop finely.
2. Place a small frying pan over a gentle heat, add the shallots and sweat them for 5 minutes, turning them constantly with a spatula. Add 40g (1¾ oz) butter and brown them very gently for at least 10 minutes, turning them constantly. Add salt halfway through cooking.
3. When the shallots are cooked and lightly browned, turn off the heat and cover the pan to keep them warm.
4. Heat the oil in a large pan; add 20g (¾ oz) butter and cook the steaks over a medium heat for 3-5 minutes, depending on thickness and taste, turning them often. Arrange them on a serving dish. Discard the fat. Add 100ml (3½ fl oz) water to the dish and, scraping the bottom with a spatula, cook over a high heat until the juice is reduced to half its quantity (about 1 minute). Pour this over the steaks.
5. Spread the steaks with the shallots and the butter they were cooked in, and serve immediately.

# Escalopes en Béchamel

*Escalopes in White Sauce*

*Serves 4. Preparation: 40 min  Cooking: 20 min*

★

○ **500g (1 lb 2 oz) fillet or sirloin**
○ **salt and pepper**
○ **200ml (7 fl oz) milk**
○ **25g (1 oz) flour**
○ **80g (3¼ oz) butter**
○ **50g (2 oz) Parmesan cheese**
○ **1 truffle**

1. Slice the meat very thin, preferably using an electric slicer. Place it in a flat dish, season with salt and pepper, and sprinkle the milk over. Leave to marinate for 20 minutes, turning frequently.
2. At the end of this time, drain the slices of meat and dip them in flour several times.
3. Melt the butter in a large frying pan and add the meat. Brown lightly on both sides, then add the milk from the marinade and allow to boil until the gravy has thickened.
4. Transfer the meat slices onto a serving dish. Sprinkle with the grated Parmesan and top with very thin slices of truffle.

# Entrecôtes à la Confiture d'Oignons
*Rib Steaks with Onion Sauce*

*Serves 4. Preparation: 20 min*
*Cooking: 45 min*
★

○ **2 rib steaks, 500g (18 oz) each**
○ **700g (1½ lb) onions**
○ **80g (3½ oz) butter**
○ **30ml (2 tbls) granulated sugar**
○ **15ml (1 tbls) vinegar**
○ **15ml (1 tbls) oil**
○ **salt and pepper**

1. Peel the onions and mince finely. Place them in a sauté pan, sprinkle with sugar, add 60g (2¼ oz) butter, cut up, and 100ml (3½ fl oz) cold water. Heat the pan over a medium flame to boiling point. Mix, then lower the heat and cook, turning often with a spatula, until the onions are caramelized (40-45 minutes). Halfway through the cooking, add the vinegar and season to taste.
2. When the onions are cooked, cover the pan and keep warm. Heat the oil in a frying pan, add 20g (¼ oz) butter and cook the steaks for 2 minutes (rare) to 4 minutes (well done). Salt halfway through cooking.
3. Arrange the steaks on a serving dish, cover with the onion mixture and serve immediately.

# Petit Sauté aux Olives de Nyons
*Sautéed Steak with Black Olives*

*Serves 2. Preparation: 15 min*
*Cooking: 15 min*
★

○ **500g (18 oz) sirloin or rump steak**
○ **24 black olives**
○ **20 peeled cloves of garlic**
○ **15ml (1 tbls) dried breadcrumbs**
○ **5ml (1 tsp) herbs of Provence or mixed herbs**
○ **45ml (3 tbls) olive oil**
○ **salt and pepper**

1. Cut the meat into small cubes 1.5cm (¾ inch) square.
2. Heat the oil in a small saucepan. Add the cloves of garlic and allow to cook over a low heat for about 10 minutes, until they are tender and just golden. Pour the contents of the saucepan into a frying pan large enough to hold the meat cubes without any overlapping.
3. Place the frying pan over a medium heat. As soon as the oil is hot, add the meat cubes, stirring continuously for 2 minutes, until the meat is golden brown. Then add the olives and sprinkle with herbs and breadcrumbs. Cook for 1 minute and remove from the heat. Arrange the sauté on two individual plates and serve immediately.

This Mediterranean dish may be served with *tomates à la provençale*, tomatoes stuffed with breadcrumbs, herbs and garlic, or with small potato rissoles.

# Capilotade à l'Ail Nouveau
*Beef with Fresh Garlic*

*Serves 4. Preparation: 20 min Cooking: 3½-4 hr*
★

○ **1kg (2¼ lb) silverside or cheek**
○ **500g (1 lb 2 oz) ripe tomatoes**
○ **2 heads fresh garlic**
○ **2 pinches each rosemary, thyme or oregano**
○ **30ml (2 tbls) olive oil**
○ **2.5ml (½ tsp) sugar**
○ **salt and pepper**

1. Cut the meat into 2cm (¾ inch) cubes, and sprinkle with salt. Peel the garlic. Cut the tomatoes into quarters and put through a sieve or blender.
2. Heat the oil in a flameproof dish and turn the meat in it without allowing it to colour for 5 minutes. Then add the rosemary and other herbs, the cloves of garlic and the tomatoes. Season with sugar and salt. Cover the dish and leave to simmer over a low heat. Or place in the oven at 180°C (350°F; gas mark 4) for between 3 and 4 hours depending on the piece of meat chosen: cheek, which is more tender, will cook in 2½ to 3 hours.
3. The dish is ready when the meat is tender enough to fall apart easily, the cloves of garlic can be reduced to purée and the sauce has thickened up nicely. Add pepper and serve immediately.

*Boeuf à la Mode (p76)* ▶

# Tournedos à la Crème

*Serves 4. Preparation and cooking: 20 min*

## Tournedos with Cream Sauce

★

○ **handful black peppercorns**
○ **salt**
○ **4 tournedos, 150g (5 oz) each**
○ **50g (2 oz) butter**
○ **100ml (3½ fl oz) brandy**
○ **120ml (4 fl oz) double cream**
○ **15ml (1 tbls) French mustard**

1. Pound the peppercorns roughly in a mortar, mix with a pinch of salt and press with the palms of your hands onto both sides of each tournedos.
2. Melt the butter in a frying pan and add the tournedos, letting them brown on both sides over a high flame for 2-3 minutes. Place on a dish and keep warm. Pour the brandy into the pan, allow to get hot, then set alight. As soon as the flame dies, add the cream mixed with the mustard, stir well and bring to the boil.
3. Return the tournedos to the pan, cook for a minute, then remove from the heat, place on a serving dish and serve immediately.

# Entrecôtes au Vinaigre

*Serves 2. Preparation: 5 min Cooking: 5 min*

## Rib Steaks with Vinegar

★

○ **2 rib steaks, 200g (7 oz) each**
○ **2 small sprigs rosemary**
○ **6 cloves garlic**
○ **30ml (2 tbls) wine vinegar**
○ **30ml (2 tbls) olive oil**
○ **salt and pepper**

1. Peel the garlic. Heat the oil in a pan large enough to contain both steaks.
2. When the oil is hot, place the steaks in the pan with the garlic and rosemary sprigs and cook over a medium heat, for 1-2 minutes on each side, depending on whether you want the meat rare or well done. Don't forget to turn the garlic cloves as well.
3. When the steaks are done, arrange them on individual plates and pour the vinegar into the pan, scraping the bottom with a spatula to deglaze it. When the vinegar boils, put the steaks back in the pan, salt and pepper them, turn them after 10 seconds, season the other side, and after another 10 seconds remove the pan from the heat.
4. Put the steaks back on the plates, pour the sauce over them, surround them with the browned garlic cloves and rosemary sprigs and serve immediately.

Here is another version of this recipe: substitute 3 finely chopped shallots for the garlic cloves; substitute thyme for the rosemary, and replace the olive oil with 40g (1¾ oz) butter. Accompany these delicious steaks with gratinéed potatoes, cauliflower or courgettes.

# Steak Mariné

*Serves 4. Preparation: 30 min Cooking: 10 min*

## Marinated Steak

★

○ **8 100g (4 oz) slices sirloin or fillet steak**
○ **90ml (6 tbls) oil**
○ **juice of 1 lemon**
○ **salt and pepper**
○ **marjoram**

1. Pour the oil into a dish. Add the lemon juice, a pinch of salt and a dash of pepper. Beat this mixture with a fork and put the meat into it. Leave to marinate for about 20 to 30 minutes (during this time, turn the meat frequently to make sure it absorbs as much marinade as possible).
2. Heat the grill and cook the slices of meat on both sides under a high heat. Then arrange on a serving dish. Pour a little of the marinade over, and garnish with a handful of marjoram. Serve at once.

This dish should be eaten very hot.

# Alouettes sans Tête

*Beef Olives in Tomato Sauce*

*Serves 6. Preparation: 30 min Cooking: 2 hr 15 min*

★★

○ **12 top of sirloin or round steaks, 100g (4 oz) each**
○ **120g (4½ oz) mild-cure bacon**
○ **2 cloves garlic**
○ **45ml (3 tbls) chopped parsley**
○ **1kg (2¼ lb) red, ripe tomatoes**
○ **150ml (5 fl oz) dry white wine**
○ **45ml (3 tbls) oil**
○ **2 medium-sized onions**
○ **nutmeg**
○ **salt and pepper**

1. Peel and chop onions finely. Wash the tomatoes, cut into 4, pass through a mincer and put the purée aside.
2. Peel the garlic and chop finely. Discard the rind of the bacon; chop the remainder as finely as possible. Mix the bacon, garlic and parsley. Pepper generously.
3. Spread the centre of each steak with this mixture and roll up. Bind each end with white thread.
4. Heat the oil in a stewpan and seal the beef olives for about 5 minutes over a high flame without allowing them to brown. Then add the onions, lightly brown for 2 minutes, and add the white wine. Lower the heat and allow the wine to evaporate completely while turning the meat rolls constantly. Then add the purée of tomatoes, salt, pepper and nutmeg to taste, cover the stewpan and allow to simmer for at least 2 hours, until meat is tender and sauce syrupy. Correct seasoning, untie the meat rolls and serve.

Serve this dish with noodles with butter and grated cheese.

# Carbonades Flamandes

*Beef and Onions Braised in Beer*

*Serves 4. Preparation: 25 min Cooking: 3 hr*

★

○ **1.2kg (2½ lb) beef: chuck, rump or blade**
○ **400g (14 oz) onions**
○ **1 slice white bread, crusts removed**
○ **15ml (1 tbls) strong Dijon mustard**
○ **300ml (10 fl oz) beer, brown preferably**
○ **1 clove garlic**
○ **5ml (1 tsp) sugar**
○ **30ml (2 tbls) wine vinegar**
○ **45ml (3 tbls) oil**
○ **1 bay leaf**
○ **salt and pepper**

1. Ask the butcher to cut the meat into slices 1cm (½ inch) thick. Cut these into strips 4cm (1½ inches) by 6cm (2½ inches). Salt and pepper them. Peel and finely chop the onions. Peel the garlic and chop very finely.
2. Preheat the oven to 120°C (250°F; gas mark ½). Heat the oil in a sauté pan and seal the meat slices over a high flame without browning. Remove from the pan and reserve. Add the onions to the pan and cook over a medium heat until transparent, about 5 minutes, then sprinkle with sugar, add the vinegar, mix and remove from the heat.
3. Place alternate layers of meat and onions in a stewpan or earthenware ovenproof dish. Place in the centre a slice of bread spread with the mustard. Break the bay leaf in half and put half on each side of the bread. Push the bread down well.
4. Heat the beer in the sauté pan and then pour over the meat and onions. It should not cover the meat. Cover the dish and cook in the oven for 3 hours. When the meat is tender, remove from the stewpan or dish, arrange the slices in a deep serving dish, cover and keep warm in the turned-off oven. Purée the sauce, bread and onions in a vegetable mill, and pour over the meat. Serve immediately.

Accompany this stew with chipped or steamed potatoes. This dish can also be cooked on top of the stove over a low heat for 4 hours. In this case, crumble the bread and cut the meat into large cubes.

# Compote de Gîte-Gîte au Poivre

*Brisket Stew with Pepper*

*Serves 6. Preparation: 10 min*
*Cooking: 5 hr*
★

○ **1.5kg (3¼ lb) brisket**
○ **750ml (1 bottle) red wine**
○ **20g (¾ oz) coarsely ground pepper**
○ **3 ripe tomatoes, peeled, seeded and crushed**
○ **2 cloves garlic**
○ **50g (2 oz) butter**
○ **salt**

1. It is important to use this gelatinous part of the beef which will become, after long, gentle cooking, tender and succulent. Cut the meat into cubes 2cm (¾ inch) square. Put them in a stewpan and add salt to taste and the crushed tomatoes.
2. Peel the garlic cloves, crush them with the palm of your hand on a board, and add to the meat. Barely cover with water, and add the butter cut into small pieces. Cover with the lid and allow to simmer over a very low heat.
3. After 2 hours, remove the lid, add 150ml (5 fl oz) wine and 15ml (1 tbls) pepper to the stewpan. Repeat this five times – every 30 minutes – until no wine or pepper remains, then cook for a further 30 minutes or longer until the stew is done. When cooked, allow to cool slightly before serving for even better results.

Accompany this dish with buttered noodles or with roughly mashed potatoes, with butter and grated cheese.

# Compote aux Pommes de Terre

*Beef Stew with Potatoes*

*Serves 6. Preparation: 25 min Cooking: 3 hr*
★

○ **1kg (2¼ lb) chuck or cheek**
○ **1kg (2¼ lb) floury potatoes**
○ **1kg (2¼ lb) ripe tomatoes**
○ **45ml (3 tbls) olive oil**
○ **salt and pepper**

1. Cut the meat into 2cm (¾ inch) cubes and season with salt. Peel and dice the potatoes into 2cm (¾ inch) pieces. Wash and quarter the tomatoes, put them through a sieve or blender.
2. Preheat the oven to 195°C (375°F; gas mark 5). Grease an ovenproof dish with 15ml (1 tbls) of oil. Put in the meat, potatoes and tomato purée. Mix together well and season to taste. Pour in 15ml (1 tbls) of oil, cover the dish and place in the oven for 3 hours.
3. At the end of this time, the meat should be tender enough to part easily, and the potatoes reduced to a purée. If not, leave to cook for a further 30 minutes. Add a generous seasoning of pepper and the last 15ml (1 tbls) of oil before serving.

*To seal a stewpan with luting: work 200g (7 oz) flour with 100ml (3½ fl oz) water. Form the paste into a sausage shape and press this around the edge of the lid of the stewpan, then place the lid on the pan and press together. It is a good idea to do this when you are cooking a stew for several hours.*

*Boeuf à la Moelle (p77)* ▶

# Boeuf à la Mode

*Beef in Wine Marinade*

*Serves 6. Preparation and cooking: 3 hr 15 min Marinade: 12 hr*

★ ★

○ **1kg (2¼ lb) rump steak**
○ **100g (4 oz) butter**
○ **50g (2 oz) bacon**
○ **75ml (2½ fl oz) brandy**
○ **1 calf's foot**
○ **1 tomato**
○ **1 small leek**
○ **beef stock**
○ **300g (10 oz) small onions**
○ **300g (10 oz) new carrots**
○ **5ml (1 tsp) flour**
○ **salt and pepper**

*For the marinade:*
○ **450ml (15 fl oz) red wine**
○ **1 onion**
○ **1 carrot, cut into rounds**
○ **1 clove garlic**
○ **2 bay leaves**
○ **sprig parsley**
○ **150ml (5 fl oz) water**

1. Bind the meat so that it will keep its shape. Sprinkle with salt and pepper and place in a bowl. Mix all the ingredients for the marinade and leave the meat in this for 12 hours, turning from time to time.
2. After 12 hours, heat 50g (2 oz) butter in a stewpan and add the chopped bacon. Remove the meat from the marinade and brown it on all sides. Then sprinkle with the brandy and set alight. Let the flames die out.
3. Immerse the tomato in boiling water for 10 seconds, then peel.
4. Add to the meat the calf's foot, halved tomato, bay leaf, chopped leek, 200ml (7 fl oz) hot beef stock, 150ml (5 fl oz) strained marinade, and salt to taste. Cover the pan and cook over a very low heat for about 2 hours, adding a little strained marinade if necessary.
5. In a saucepan, melt the remaining butter, add the new carrots and small onions and salt to taste. Cook over a low heat for 30 minutes, basting with a little stock.
6. Remove the meat from the stewpan and keep warm. Sieve the contents left in the pan and add the flour mixed with a little stock. Cook the sauce until it thickens slightly, then pour some over the carrots and onions to glaze them.
7. Slice the meat, having removed the binding thread. Surround with the vegetables and pour the sauce over. Serve immediately.

# Daube de Boeuf aux Haricots

*Beef Stew with Haricot Beans*

*Serves 4. Preparation and cooking 2 hr 15 min*

★ ★

○ **300g (10 oz) haricot beans**
○ **300g (10 oz) chuck**
○ **100g (4 oz) smoked ham**
○ **300g (10 oz) gherkins**
○ **75ml (2½ fl oz) oil**
○ **20g (¾ oz) capers**
○ **150g (5 oz) pearl barley**
○ **salt and pepper**

1. Soak the beans and barley separately for 12 hours or overnight, then drain and rinse them. Reserve the barley. Bring to the boil 2 litres (3½ pints) water in a large pan, add the beans, lower the heat and simmer, partially covered, for about 1 hour, or until the beans are almost tender.
2. Cut the beef into small chunks, then, when the beans are tender, add the beef and cook for another hour.
3. Lightly brown the ham in a sauté pan, then add the gherkins, capers and oil. Mix well. Then add to the beans and beef, along with the barley. Continue cooking until the beef, beans and barley are all tender. Season and serve immediately.

This is a very ancient dish from the Mediterranean region. You can substitute rice for the barley – in this case you don't need to soak it, of course, and you would add it about 20 minutes before the meat and beans are ready.

# Daube aux Petits Pois

*Serves 4. Preparation and cooking: 1 hr 45 min*

*Beef Stew with Peas*

★★

○ **800g (1¾ lb) rump steak, in one piece**
○ **200g (8 oz) cooked ham, in one slice**
○ **300g (10 oz) fresh peas (petits pois, if available)**
○ **1 onion**
○ **2 cloves**
○ **150ml (5 fl oz) dry white wine**
○ **150ml (5 fl oz) mushroom broth (made with stock cubes)**
○ **1 pinch curry powder**
○ **salt and pepper**

1. Place the beef in a stewpan. Cube the ham, shell the peas and add to the beef. Spike the onion with the cloves and add. Pour over the wine.
2. Cook over a medium heat for 1½ hours, turning the meat every now and then, and basting with the stock.
3. Add the curry powder and season with salt and pepper. Place on a hot serving dish, slice and serve very hot. This dish is best when eaten the day after it is prepared.

# Boeuf à la Moelle

*Serves 4. Preparation and cooking: 2 hr*

*Shin of Beef Peasant Style*

★★

○ **4 pieces of shin on the bone, 200g (7 oz) each**
○ **flour**
○ **1 onion**
○ **1 clove garlic**
○ **1 carrot**
○ **1 stick celery**
○ **50g (2 oz) bacon**
○ **40g (1¾ oz) butter**
○ **45ml (3 tbls) oil**
○ **salt and pepper**
○ **150ml (5 fl oz) dry white wine**
○ **150ml (5 fl oz) beef stock**
○ **45ml (3 tbls) tomato purée**
○ **250g (9 oz) petits pois**

1. Place some flour on a plate and dip the pieces of meat into it, then tie them up so that they don't lose their shape during cooking.
2. Finely chop the onion, garlic, carrot, celery and bacon. Heat the oil and butter in a stewpan, add the chopped mixture and fry lightly. Add the beef and brown on all sides. Add the wine and salt and pepper to taste.
3. When the wine has completely evaporated, add the hot stock mixed with the tomato purée. Turn the heat down very low and allow the meat to cook, covered, for about 1 hour 20 minutes, turning often and basting with the sauce.
4. Three-quarters of the way through cooking, add the peas which have been drained and rinsed. When cooked, place the meat with its sauce on a hot serving dish and serve immediately.

# Boeuf en Cocotte aux Oignons

*Serves 4. Preparation: 20 min*
*Cooking: 5 hr 10 min*

*Beef Stew with Onions*

★

○ **1kg (2¼ lb) rump or flank, larded and bound by the butcher**
○ **1kg (2¼ lb) large onions**
○ **7 cloves**
○ **400g (14 oz) medium spaghetti**
○ **50g (2 oz) grated Parmesan cheese**
○ **salt and pepper**

1. Preheat the oven to 120°C (250°F; gas mark ½). Peel the onions and cut them into rounds 1cm (½ inch) thick. Cover the base of an earthenware dish with them and add salt. Spike the meat with the cloves, add salt and pepper and place on the bed of onions. Cover and cook in the oven for 5 hours. Turn the meat over once or twice during this time.
2. Remove the meat from the pot and arrange on a hot serving dish. Remove the string. Decorate with half the onions separated into rings (they will have remained whole despite their long cooking). Cover the dish with aluminium foil and keep warm in the turned-off oven.
3. Bring some water to the boil in a large saucepan, add salt and then the spaghetti. Pass the rest of the onions and the remaining cooking juices through a vegetable mill into a saucepan. When the spaghetti is just tender (*al dente*), drain it and add to the saucepan. Cook on a very low heat for 1 minute, stirring, then pour into a hot serving dish. Serve the spaghetti together with the meat, which you slice at table. Serve with grated Parmesan cheese and freshly ground black pepper.

# Boeuf à la Ficelle
## *Boiled Beef on a String*

*Serves 4. Preparation: 15 min Cooking: 40 min*

★★

○ **800g (1¾ lb) fillet or rump, bound but not barded**
○ **8 new carrots, peeled**
○ **8 small leeks, peeled**
○ **8 small turnips, peeled**
○ **2 celery hearts, quartered**
○ **4 small onions**
○ **4 sprigs chervil**
○ **2 sprigs parsley**
○ **1 sprig tarragon**
○ **2 cloves**
○ **12 peppercorns**
○ **15ml (1 tbls) sea salt**

1. Bring to the boil 2.5 litres (4½ pints) water in a large saucepan, add salt, peppercorns and cloves and then the prepared vegetables. Tie together the parsley, chervil and tarragon to make a bouquet garni. Add to the water and simmer for 10 minutes.
2. Meanwhile, tie a string at each end of the piece of beef, long enough to be able to tie to the handles of the saucepan so you can remove the meat easily.
3. When the vegetables have cooked for 15 minutes, plunge the meat into the pan, keeping it barely immersed, and tie the string to the handles of the pan. Allow it to cook for 25 minutes at a gentle boil for medium beef, pink at the centre. Skim as necessary.
4. When the meat is cooked, remove it from the pan by the strings and place it on a board. Remove the strings and cut the meat into 4 thick slices. Arrange on a hot serving dish. Remove the vegetables with the skimmer, garnish the meat with them and serve immediately. Accompany with mustard, coarse sea salt and gherkins, with *sauce verte* (mayonnaise, to which a purée of green herbs has been added) or cold tomato sauce with capers.

The meat can also be sliced before cooking for 10 to 15 minutes. You can serve the cooking liquid as a soup if, instead of using water for cooking, you use beef stock.

# Pot-au-Feu à la Provençale
## *Boiled Beef Provence Style*

*Serves 8. Preparation and cooking: 4 hr*

★★

○ **800g (1¾ lb) silverside**
○ **500g (18 oz) topside on the bone**
○ **500g (18 oz) shoulder of beef**
○ **600g (21 oz) shoulder of lamb**
○ **600g (21 oz) leg of veal**
○ **200g (7 oz) lean bacon**
○ **1 onion spiked with 3 cloves**
○ **3 turnips**
○ **8 leeks**
○ **8 carrots**
○ **2 tomatoes**
○ **3 cloves garlic**
○ **1 sprig thyme**
○ **1 bay leaf**
○ **2 celery sticks**
○ **6 juniper berries**
○ **6 black peppercorns**
○ **200ml (7 fl oz) dry white wine**
○ **salt**

1. Pour 4 litres (7 pints) cold water into a large saucepan and add the topside on the bone and shoulder of beef. Bring to the boil slowly, over a low heat. Skim, then add the silverside, lamb, veal and bacon. Bring back to the boil and skim carefully, then add salt and wine. Tie together the thyme, bay leaf and celery and add this bouquet garni to the pan along with the spiked onion, unpeeled garlic, juniper berries and peppercorns.
2. When the water boils, lower the heat so that it simmers gently for 1½ hours.
3. At the end of this time, peel and wash the turnips, carrots and leeks. Remove most of the green of the leeks and tie together the white parts. Plunge these vegetables into the pan along with the unpeeled, washed tomatoes. Continue to cook for 1½ to 2 hours, until all the meat is tender.
4. When the *pot-au-feu* is ready, sieve the liquid, skim off the fat and serve in a soup bowl. Put the meats – except the topside and the shoulder, which will be served after the other meats – on a hot serving dish. Surround with the vegetables and serve immediately.

Traditionally, this is served with a salad of chickpeas dressed with wine vinegar and olive oil, capers, gherkins and black olives and served lukewarm, and with a tomato sauce. Or you could cook some thin spaghetti in the stock to accompany the meat and vegetables.

*Soupe Lombarde (p81)*

# Queue en Hochepot

*Serves 6. Preparation: 10 min Cooking: 4 hr*

## Oxtail Hot Pot

★★

○ **1 oxtail in 4cm (1½ inch) segments**
○ **2 pig trotters**
○ **1 pig's ear**
○ **1 small cabbage**
○ **6 carrots**
○ **6 turnips**
○ **salt**

1. Place the oxtail, trotters and pig's ear in a large pan. Cover with water and bring to the boil over a moderate heat, removing the scum as it appears. Once it has boiled, lower the heat and leave to simmer for 2 hours.
2. Peel the vegetables; quarter the cabbage, removing the hard centre. Leave them to stand in a basin of cold water.
3. After 2 hours, salt the stockpot and add the vegetables to it. If there is not enough liquid, add some hot water but make sure you do not cover the vegetables. Bring back to the boil on a higher heat, then lower again and simmer for a further 2 hours until the meat and vegetables are tender.
4. When all is ready remove from the heat. Slice the ear thinly, bone the trotters and cut into small pieces. Arrange the meat and vegetables on a serving dish. The stock can be kept to be used for another dish, or it can be poured into a gravyboat and served, but be sure you skim off the fat first.

Accompany this springtime dish with new potatoes and grilled chipolata sausages.

# Pot-au-Feu à la Flamande

*Serves 4-6. Preparation and cooking: 4 hr*

## Flemish Hot Pot

★★

○ **1.5kg (3¼ lb) flank or brisket, in one piece**
○ **1kg (2¼ lb) carrots**
○ **1kg (2¼ lb) floury potatoes**
○ **4 medium onions**
○ **salt and pepper**

1. Bring 2 litres (72 fl oz) of water to the boil in a large pan, place the piece of beef in it and wait until it boils again. Remove the scum, then add salt, lower the heat and simmer for 1 hour.
2. Now peel the onions, chop them into rough pieces and add to the pan. Peel the carrots, slice across in thick chunks and leave to stand in a basin of cold water. Peel and quarter the potatoes and do the same. After the onions have cooked for an hour drain the carrots and add to the pan. Continue cooking over a low heat. One hour later add the potatoes and cook for another hour. By then the meat should be tender and the stock almost entirely have evaporated. If not, cook for a little longer.
3. When everything is ready, remove the meat from the pot and slice finely, removing the bone and the fatty pieces. Arrange on a serving dish and cover with an aluminium lid to keep hot. If there is some stock left reduce it over a high heat, stirring the vegetables to prevent them from sticking, then mash them with a fork. Season if necessary. Surround the meat with the mashed vegetables and serve.

# Soupe Lombarde
*Soup Lombardy Style*

*Serves 4. Preparation and cooking: 1 hr 15 min*

★★

○ **1 small savoy cabbage**
○ **400g (14 oz) flank**
○ **1 clove garlic**
○ **1 onion**
○ **1 stick celery**
○ **1 beef stock cube**
○ **150g (5 oz) rice**
○ **handful parsley**
○ **freshly grated Parmesan cheese**
○ **salt and pepper**

1. Trim the cabbage and remove the outer leaves. Wash and cut up. Cut the flank into chunks. Chop the garlic and onion. Cut the celery into chunks.
2. Put everything into a stewpan with 1½ litres (2¾ pints) water and the stock cube and bring to a boil, then lower the heat and simmer for about 40 minutes. Then add the rice and parsley and continue cooking until the rice is tender. Add the grated Parmesan.
3. Allow the soup to stand for a few minutes, then serve very hot. This is an ideal winter soup.

# Anneaux de Courgettes à la Coriandre
*Courgette Rings with Coriander*

*Serves 4-5.*
*Preparation and cooking: 1 hr*
★

○ **400g (14 oz) steak minced with 50g (2 oz) beef kidney fat**
○ **5 medium-sized courgettes: approx 1.2kg (2½ lb)**
○ **30ml (2 tbls) chopped fresh coriander**
○ **15ml (1 tbls) chopped parsley**
○ **3 medium-sized onions**
○ **50g (2 oz) butter**
○ **1 pinch cayenne pepper**
○ **salt and pepper**

1. Ask your butcher to mince together the beef and the kidney fat.
2. Put the meat in a bowl, add salt, pepper generously, and add 15ml (1 tbls) chopped coriander and the parsley. Mix well with your fingertips.
3. Peel the onions and grate them finely. Add one-third to the mince and mix again.
4. Place the remainder of the onions in a large saucepan 25cm (10 inches) across and add the butter and ½ litre (18 fl oz) water, the cayenne and salt and pepper to taste. Bring to the boil, cover and leave to cook over a low heat for 15 minutes.
5. Meanwhile, prepare the courgette rings: wash the courgettes, wipe them dry, cut off the ends and cut into slices 2.5cm (1 inch) thick. Depending on the size of the courgettes, you should obtain about 25 rounds. With a small spoon, scoop out the seeds so that only the pulp and the skin remain.
6. Fill the rings with the beef mixture. When the onions have cooked for 15 minutes, add the stuffed courgettes and salt. Cover and cook for 15 minutes on a low heat.
7. Turn the rings and cook, covered, for a further 15 minutes then remove the lid, increase the heat and cook for 8-10 minutes, until the sauce has reduced to one-third of its original volume and has a syrupy consistency.
8. Turn the rings once during the reduction of the sauce, then remove them from the pan with a skimmer, and arrange on a hot serving dish.
9. Add the remaining coriander to the sauce, stir well and pour over the courgette rings. Serve immediately.

# Saucisses aux Quatre-Épices

*Serves 6. Preparation: 10 min Cooking: 10 min*

*Spiced Sausages*

★

○ **1kg (2¼ lb) flank minced with 100g (4 oz) beef kidney**
○ **2.5ml (½ tsp) mixed spice**
○ **3 pinches thyme**
○ **2 cloves garlic**
○ **100ml (3½ fl oz) beef stock**
○ **salt and freshly ground black pepper**

1. Place the minced meat in a bowl. Peel the garlic and put through a garlic press into the bowl. Add the mixed spice, thyme, salt and pepper to taste. Mix with your hands, then moisten with the stock and mix again until the stock is well absorbed. Divide the mixture into 18 equal parts and form into small sausages 9cm (3½ inches) long, moistening your hands in cold water while you do so.
2. Heat the grill or prepare a barbecue and cook the sausages until they are well browned, about 8-10 minutes.

In Romania, where these sausages (*mititei*) originate, they are served with grilled peppers or marinated cucumbers.

# Bouchées aux Amandes

*Serves 3-4. Preparation: 20 min Cooking: 15 min*

*Almond Meatballs*

★

○ **400g (14 oz) minced steak**
○ **20 blanched almonds**
○ **20ml (4 tsp) very fine semolina**
○ **250g (9 oz) double cream**
○ **1 lemon**
○ **5ml (1 tsp) curry powder**
○ **30ml (2 tbls) flour**
○ **30ml (2 tbls) oil**
○ **50g (2 oz) butter**
○ **salt and pepper**

1. Place the meat in a bowl, season, add 45ml (3 tbls) cream and work mixture until it is well blended.
2. Wash and wipe dry the lemon, grate three-quarters of the rind (only the yellow part, not the white pith) on a fine grater over the dish containing the meat, add the semolina and work everything together well.
3. Put the flour on a plate. Divide the meat into 20 equal parts, dust your hands with flour and roll each portion of meat into a round ball. Place an almond in the centre of each, then roll again to close up.
4. Repeat until all the ingredients have been used up, then heat the oil in frying pan just large enough to hold all the meatballs in one layer. Add the butter and when it is melted add the meatballs.
5. Cook over a low heat for about 10 minutes until the meatballs are well browned. To turn them, shake the pan: the meatballs will roll about and cook uniformly.
6. When the meatballs are cooked, remove from pan with a skimmer, place on a hot dish and keep warm. Discard the cooking fat, squeeze the lemon over the pan, and, over a high flame, scrape the bottom to deglaze. Then add the cream, curry powder, salt and pepper. Boil for 3 minutes until the cream is reduced by half, put the meatballs back in the pan and roll them about in the sauce.
7. When the meatballs are well covered with the sauce, pour the contents of the pan onto a hot serving dish and serve immediately.

Accompany with a rice pilau.

*Salade Suisse (p85)*

# Kefta au Coulis d'Oignons

*Serves 4-5. Preparation and cooking: 1 hr*

## Meatballs with Spiced Onion Sauce

★

- ○ **500g (18 oz) steak minced with 50g (2 oz) beef kidney fat**
- ○ **500g (18 oz) onions**
- ○ **2.5ml (½ tsp) cumin**
- ○ **2.5ml (½ tsp) cinnamon**
- ○ **5ml (1 tsp) chopped mint**
- ○ **2 pinches cayenne pepper**
- ○ **15ml (1 tbls) chopped parsley**
- ○ **15ml (1 tbls) chopped coriander**
- ○ **5ml (1 tsp) grated fresh ginger root**
- ○ **juice of ½ lemon**
- ○ **70g (3 oz) butter**
- ○ **salt**

1. Peel and finely chop or grate the onions. Place 15ml (1 tbls) onion in a bowl. Place the remainder in a saucepan, add ½ litre (18 fl oz) water, ginger, butter, salt and 1 pinch cayenne. Bring to the boil, cover and leave to simmer for 30 minutes.
2. Meanwhile prepare the meatballs: add the meat to the bowl containing the onions and add salt, cinnamon, mint, cumin, 1 pinch cayenne, 7.5ml (½ tbls) each parsley and coriander, and work this mixture with your fingers.
3. Shape into balls, no bigger than billiard balls, by rolling them between the palm of your hands. To make this easier and to prevent them from sticking to your fingers, dip your hands in cold water before making each ball.
4. When the onions are tender, pass them, with their sauce, through a mill and return to the pan, then add the meatballs and cook for 7-8 minutes on a low heat. Shake the pan so that the meatballs roll about in the sauce and cook on all sides.
5. When the meatballs are cooked and the onion sauce is creamy and adheres to the meatballs, add the remainder of the coriander and parsley and the lemon juice, mix and remove from the heat. If there is too much sauce, cook a little longer.

Accompany this Moroccan-inspired dish with saffron rice.

# Feuilleté aux Groseilles

*Serves 6-7. Preparation and cooking: 50 min*

## Minced Steak in Flaky Pastry with Gooseberries

★

- ○ **500g (18 oz) minced steak**
- ○ **200g (7 oz) onions, finely chopped**
- ○ **100g (4 oz) gooseberries, topped and tailed**
- ○ **30ml (2 tbls) pine nuts**
- ○ **5ml (1 tsp) freshly grated ginger root or powdered ginger**
- ○ **2 pinches mixed spice**
- ○ **5ml (1 tsp) sugar**
- ○ **nutmeg**
- ○ **60g (2¼ oz) butter**
- ○ **600g (21 oz) flaky pastry**
- ○ **30ml (2 tbls) flour**
- ○ **1 egg yolk**
- ○ **salt and pepper**

1. Thaw pastry if frozen. Put the onions in a pan with 50g (2 oz) butter, cook over a low heat for 3-4 minutes, then add the meat and cook over high flame for 2 minutes, mashing with a fork, until all trace of pink has disappeared. Remove from the heat, add sugar, salt, pepper and nutmeg to taste, mixed spice and ginger, stir and allow to cool.
2. Meanwhile, toast the pine nuts in a small pan, without fat, shaking the pan to brown them on all sides, then add to the meat.
3. Cut the pastry in two. Roll out the first half on a lightly floured board, making a square of about 30-35cm (12-14 inches).
4. Grease a baking sheet with the remaining butter. Place the pastry square on it, then spread it with the meat, leaving a 2cm (¾ inch) border. Top with gooseberries.
5. Preheat the oven to 220°C (425°F; gas mark 7). Roll out the remainder of the pastry in a similar square and place it on the gooseberries. Dampen the edges of the first square with a brush dipped in water, press together the edges of both squares with your fingers to seal them, then roll up slightly.
6. Brush the pastry with the beaten egg yolk and bake for 20 to 25 minutes, until well browned.

When fresh gooseberries are out of season, use 15ml (1 tbls) gooseberry jelly and omit the sugar.

# Saucisson aux Piments à l'Antillaise

## Sausage with Hot Peppers

*Serves 6. Preparation: 20 min*
*Cooking: 1 hr 30 min Refrigeration: 4 hr*
★ ★

○ **500g (18 oz) minced silverside or chuck**
○ **250g (9 oz) prawns, peeled and chopped**
○ **200g (7 oz) ham, chopped**
○ **1 medium-sized onion**
○ **2 cloves garlic**
○ **2 fresh hot red peppers**
○ **200g (7 oz) shelled peas (petit pois if available)**
○ **90ml (6 tbls) dry breadcrumbs**
○ **2 eggs**
○ **2 bay leaves**
○ **salt**

1. In a bowl, mix the mince, ham and prawns. Peel the garlic and put through a garlic press into the bowl. Peel and grate the onions, chop the peppers and add to the bowl with 30ml (2 tbls) breadcrumbs. Add salt. Break 1 egg into the bowl and work the mixture with your hands until it is well blended and compact, then add the peas and mix carefully.
2. Form the mixture into a sausage 25cm (10 inches) long, moistening your hands with water to make it easier.
3. Beat the second egg in a bowl and brush the sausage with it, then roll in the remaining breadcrumbs. Wrap the sausage tightly in muslin and tie the two ends.
4. Boil some water in a large oval pan, add salt and the bay leaf, and plunge in the sausage, which must be completely immersed. Simmer for 1½ hours.
5. At the end of this time, remove the sausage from the pan and let it cool completely before removing the muslin.

Serve thinly sliced with salads and a cold sweet-and-sour tomato sauce. You can substitute unsweetened cracker or biscuit crumbs for the breadcrumbs.

# Salade Suisse

## Swiss Salad

*Serves 4. Preparation and cooking: 45 min*
★

○ **600g (21 oz) potatoes**
○ **1 cucumber, thinly sliced**
○ **300g (10 oz) fillet**
○ **45ml (3 tbls) mustard**
○ **75ml (2½ fl oz) milk**
○ **2 raw egg yolks**
○ **1 hard-boiled egg**
○ **small handful capers**
○ **salt and pepper**

1. Boil the potatoes, peel and slice while they are still warm. Arrange a layer of potatoes decoratively in a bowl, top with the cucumber slices in a ring, and then with the fillet, cut into small pieces.
2. Blend the mustard with the milk, beating until completely amalgamated, then add the raw egg yolks and crumbled hard-boiled egg.
3. Pour this sauce over the meat and vegetables, sprinkle with capers and add salt and pepper. Mix together at the table.

*When you are cooking a dish to serve cold, or are preparing something in advance which you will be reheating later, cool it quickly at room temperature, then refrigerate it. (Refrigerating hot food is not a good idea – it will eventually damage your refrigerator.)*

# Coquelets aux Trois Poivrons

*Serves 6. Preparation: 20 min Cooking: 1 hr*

## Poussins with Three Peppers

○ **3 good-sized poussins**
○ **3 thin slices smoked streaky bacon**
○ **60ml (4 tbls) olive oil**
○ **2 cloves garlic**
○ **2 medium-sized onions**
○ **45ml (3 tbls) brandy**
○ **1 green pepper**
○ **1 yellow pepper**
○ **1 red pepper**
○ **500g (18 oz) ripe tomatoes**
○ **salt and pepper**

1. Peel and chop the garlic finely. Peel the onions and cut into thin slices.
2. Wash the peppers and cut them into halves. Remove the seeds, then cut into strips 2cm (¾ inch) thick and dice them.
3. Scald the tomatoes in boiling water for 30 seconds, refresh under cold running water, then peel and cut into halves. Squeeze to extract the seeds and chop the tomato pulp roughly.
4. Chop the bacon into small pieces.
5. Heat the oil in a flameproof casserole over a moderate heat and brown the poussins on both sides for about 10 minutes. Pour in the brandy and set alight.
6. Add the bacon, onion, garlic and peppers. Brown over a low heat for 10 minutes, making sure they do not burn, then add the chopped tomato. Season. Cover the casserole and cook for a further 30 minutes over a very low heat. Turn the poussins frequently. Remove the lid and continue cooking for 5 minutes to reduce the sauce until it is a thick consistency.
7. Place the poussins on a serving dish, spoon the peppers around and serve immediately.

# Capon au Kirsch

*Serves 6. Preparation: 15 min Cooking: 1 hr 45 min*

## Capon with Kirsch

★ ★

○ **1 2kg (4½ lb) capon, cut into 20 pieces**
○ **90ml (6 tbls) oil**
○ **100g (4 oz) smoked bacon**
○ **2 medium-sized onions**
○ **100g (4 oz) button mushrooms**
○ **10 sprigs parsley**
○ **2 bay leaves**
○ **125g (5 oz) double cream**
○ **200ml (7 fl oz) dry white wine**
○ **5ml (1 tsp) cornflour**
○ **30ml (2 tbls) water**
○ **1 small bunch chives**
○ **45ml (3 tbls) Kirsch**
○ **salt and pepper**

1. Cut the bacon into strips. Chop the parsley roughly. Cut off the mushroom stalks, wash and drain. Peel and finely slice the onions.
2. Heat the oil in a flameproof casserole and brown the capon joints and bacon over a high heat, turning frequently. Add the sliced onions, bay leaves and wine and season. Cover the casserole and cook over a low heat for 45 minutes.
3. Slice the mushrooms thinly and add to the ingredients in the casserole, together with the parsley. Cook over a very low heat for a further 45 minutes, turning the capon pieces frequently. Then remove the capon pieces and keep warm in the oven.
4. Mix the cornflour with the cold water and add to the cream. Blend the mixture into the casserole and leave to boil for 2 minutes, until the sauce thickens.
5. Chop the chives roughly, add to the sauce and put the capon pieces back in the casserole. Turn the heat off, pour in the Kirsch, and serve immediately.

Serve with fresh buttered pasta or seasonal vegetables.

*A capon is a young cockerel (7 to 10 months old) which is neutered and fattened like a large roaster. Its flesh is firm, tasty and less fatty than that of the large roaster. It can weigh up to 3kg (6½ lb).*

# Coquelets aux Olives

*Braised Poussins with Olives*

*Serves 6. Preparation: 15 min Cooking: 1 hr*

★★

○ **3 poussins**
○ **60g (2½ oz) thin slices of streaky bacon**
○ **60ml (4 tbls) oil**
○ **50g (2 oz) butter**
○ **30ml (2 tbls) anchovy paste**
○ **1 small tin 400g (14 oz) tomatoes**
○ **2ml (½ tsp) oregano**
○ **1 small chilli (or some cayenne pepper)**
○ **150g (6 oz) stoned black olives**
○ **30ml (2 tbls) capers**
○ **15ml (1 tbls) chopped parsley, or fresh chopped basil, or chopped chives**

1. Peel and finely chop the onion. Chop the bacon into small pieces and slice the olives. Drain the capers.
2. Remove the seeds from the tinned tomatoes. Mash roughly with a fork and put into a bowl with the juice.
3. Heat the oil in a large flameproof casserole over a medium heat. Add the onion and bacon and sauté for 5 minutes, then add the butter and brown the poussins on both sides for 10 minutes.
4. Put the anchovy paste into the casserole and blend well with the cooking juices. Turn the poussins in the sauce for two minutes. Then add the tomatoes, oregano, chopped chilli (or cayenne pepper) and cover the casserole. Simmer for 40 minutes, turning the poussins occasionally.
5. Add the capers and olives 10 minutes before the end of the cooking time.
6. When the poussins are cooked place on a serving dish and pour the sauce over them. Sprinkle with herbs and serve at once.

Serve with slices of bread, toasted and rubbed with garlic.

# Poulet à l'Ail Nouveau

*Chicken with Fresh Garlic*

*Serves 4. Preparation: 15 min Cooking: 55 min*

★★

○ **1 1.2kg (2½ lb) chicken, cut into 8 pieces**
○ **50g (2 oz) butter**
○ **15ml (1 tbls) oil**
○ **salt and pepper**
○ **2 heads of fresh garlic, finely chopped**
○ **100ml (3½ fl oz) dry white wine**
○ **½ litre (18 fl oz) warm milk**
○ **5ml (1 tsp) cornflour**
○ **30ml (2 tbls) cold water**
○ **60ml (4 tbls) cream**

1. Heat the oil in a flameproof casserole over a low heat. Add half the butter and brown the chicken pieces on both sides. Season. Remove from the casserole and reserve.
2. Pour off the cooking fat from the casserole and put in the remaining butter and the garlic. Stir continuously with a spatula until it has a creamy consistency. Then pour in the wine and put the chicken pieces back into the casserole. Stir well until the wine has completely evaporated.
3. Pour in the milk and cover the casserole. Simmer for 30 minutes.
4. Remove the chicken and place on a serving dish. Keep warm.
5. Mix the cornflour with the cold water. Blend with the cream and pour into the casserole. Boil the sauce for 2 minutes over a high heat, stirring continuously, then strain through a sieve and pour over the chicken pieces.

Serve with small potato cakes or potato croquettes.

*Pork sausagemeat in France is known as* chair à saucisse, *which is simply pure pork and pork fat minced and seasoned with salt, pepper and herbs. The best substitute in England is fresh, fairly fat pork, minced and well seasoned.*

# Poulet au Sel

*Chicken Baked in Salt*

*Serves 4. Preparation: 10 min  Cooking: 1 hr 30 min*

★ ★

- ○ 1 1.5kg (3½ lb) chicken
- ○ 1 sprig of tarragon
- ○ 10 green peppercorns
- ○ 4kg (9 lb) coarse sea salt

1. Preheat the oven to its maximum setting. Place the peppercorns and the tarragon inside the chicken. Truss the chicken; make sure the neck skin is held in place by the wing tips and that the vent is firmly closed with a skewer or sewn up to prevent the salt getting inside the chicken.
2. Line the bottom and sides of an ovenproof dish, large enough to hold the chicken, with a sheet of foil. Pour 1kg (2¼ lb) of salt into the dish. Spread out well to cover the bottom completely. Place the chicken on top, breast downwards. Pour the remaining salt around and over the chicken. It should be covered by a layer at least 2cm (1 inch) thick.
3. Place the dish, uncovered, in the hot oven for 1 hour 30 minutes.
4. Remove from the oven very carefully, as the dish will be extremely hot. Turn on to a serving dish and remove the foil. The chicken and salt will have formed a solid block.
5. Place the serving dish on the table and break open the salt with a small hammer in front of your guests: the chicken will appear, golden and crusty, tasting delicious.

For this recipe to be a success it is best to use a top-quality fresh chicken.

# Tajine de Poulet

*Chicken Moroccan-Style*

*Serves 4. Preparation: 10 min  Cooking: 1 hr 30 min*

- ○ 1 1.6kg (3½ lb) chicken, cut into 8 pieces
- ○ 2 medium-sized onions
- ○ 1 pinch of saffron
- ○ 5ml (1 tsp) powdered ginger
- ○ 150ml (5 fl oz) oil
- ○ ¼ litre (9 fl oz) water
- ○ 10 sprigs of parsley
- ○ 20 sprigs of coriander
- ○ 5ml (1 tsp) red pepper
- ○ 2.5ml (½ tsp) cumin
- ○ 30ml (2 tbls) lemon juice
- ○ 24 stoned green olives
- ○ 1 pickled lemon
- ○ salt

1. Peel and finely chop the onions. Place in a casserole and add the ginger, saffron, oil and water. Mix well.
2. Place the chicken pieces in the casserole and turn them in the mixture of spices until they are well coated. Add a little more water if necessary and season with salt. Cover and cook for approximately 1 hour 15 minutes, or until the chicken flesh is tender and comes away from the bone easily. While cooking baste the chicken pieces with the sauce so that the meat is well flavoured by the spices.
3. Meanwhile, wash the parsley and coriander. Dry and chop the leaves.
4. 15 minutes before the end of the cooking time add the red pepper, cumin, chopped parsley and coriander to the casserole. Stir well.
5. When the chicken is cooked, dice the pickled lemon and add to the casserole together with the olives and lemon juice. Mix well. Reduce the sauce, with the casserole uncovered, until it is thick and creamy.
6. Pour into a serving dish and serve immediately.

If you cannot get hold of a pickled lemon for this Moroccan recipe, grate the peel of a fresh lemon into the casserole. Pickled lemons or *citrons confits* are small lemons with a strong flavour, preserved in brine.

# Émincés de Poulet au Calvados

*Serves 4. Preparation: 15 min  Cooking: 30 min*

### Slices of Chicken with Calvados

★

- 4 chicken breasts
- 500g (18 oz) button mushrooms
- 24 shallots, or pickling onions
- 50g (2 oz) butter
- 15ml (1 tbls) oil
- 45ml (3 tbls) calvados
- 200g (7 oz) cream
- 5ml (1 tsp) cornflour
- 30ml (2 tbls) cold water
- salt and pepper
- pinch nutmeg

1. Cut each chicken breast into two, then slice lengthways. Peel the onions. Trim the mushrooms. Wash and drain the vegetables and wipe dry.
2. Heat the oil in a frying pan over a medium heat. Add the butter, then the slices of chicken. Brown all over, stirring frequently. Remove and put on one side.
3. Place the onions in the frying pan and gently sauté over a very low heat, stirring frequently.
4. Slice the mushrooms. Add to the onion and cook over a slightly higher heat.
5. When the mushrooms have begun to turn golden and their juices start to run, put the chicken back into the frying pan. Season with salt, pepper and grated nutmeg. Pour in the calvados.
6. Mix the cornflour with the cold water, and then blend in the cream. When the calvados has evaporated pour the cream into the frying pan and mix well. Cook for another 5 minutes, over a medium heat; the cream should take on a lovely golden colour. Serve at once.

Serve with allumettes or sauté potatoes.

# Coq à la Bière

*Serves 4. Preparation: 10 min  Cooking: 1 hr 10 min*

### Cockerel in Beer

★★

- 1  1.3kg (3 lb) oven-ready cockerel
- 6 shallots
- 80g (3 oz) butter
- 30ml (2 tbls) gin
- 1 bottle (½ pint) brown ale
- 200g (7 oz) cream
- 250g (9 oz) button mushrooms
- 30ml (2 tbls) chopped parsley

1. Peel and finely chop the shallots.
2. Trim and wipe the mushrooms. Melt 50g (2 oz) of butter in a flameproof casserole over a low heat. Brown the cockerel all over for 15 minutes; remove from the casserole and put on one side.
3. Place the shallots in the casserole and sauté gently. Return the cockerel to the casserole; pour in the gin and set alight. Add a knob of butter and 45ml (3 tbls) cream. Stir well. Slice the mushrooms and add to the ingredients in the casserole.
4. Pour in the beer. Season and cover with a lid. Simmer for 40 minutes.
5. When the cockerel is cooked place on a serving dish. Cut into 4 large pieces and keep warm. Reduce the sauce to ¼ litre (9 fl oz, slightly less than ½ pint) over a high heat in the uncovered casserole. Then add the remaining cream and leave to reduce for a further 2 minutes.
6. Remove from the heat. Add the remaining knob of butter and pour over the cockerel. Sprinkle with parsley and serve at once.

Serve with allumettes.

*Be careful when using nutmeg. You only need a pinch to flavour stuffings, sautéed dishes, cream sauces and omelettes. Buy it whole if possible, and grate it yourself as required. It retains its flavour better.*

# Coquelets aux Légumes Nouveaux
*Poussins with New Vegetables*

*Serves 4. Preparation: 15 min*
*Cooking: 50 min*
★

- ○ **2 poussins**
- ○ **150g (6 oz) butter**
- ○ **1 bunch of spring onions**
- ○ **500g (1 lb 2 oz) new carrots**
- ○ **15ml (1 tbls) sugar**
- ○ **500g (1 lb 2 oz) new potatoes**
- ○ **3 sprigs tarragon**
- ○ **salt and pepper**

1. Rub the inside of the poussins with salt and pepper. Place a sprig of tarragon inside each bird.
2. Peel the onions, carrots and potatoes. Wash them. Drain and wipe the onions and carrots. Place the potatoes in a saucepan and cover with cold water. Cut the carrots in slices 1cm (½ inch) thick.
3. Melt 50g (2 oz) of butter in a flameproof casserole and brown the poussins all over, over a low heat, for 15 minutes. Continue cooking for a further 25 minutes, adding 30ml (2 tbls) water each time the sauce starts to caramelize. Season.
4. Meanwhile, prepare the vegetables. Boil the potatoes over a medium heat for about 15 minutes. Melt 50g (2 oz) of butter in a saucepan and lightly brown the onions and carrots. Season with salt and sprinkle with sugar. When the sugar has taken on a golden colour, add 200ml (7 fl oz) of water and simmer for about 20 minutes. When cooked, there should be no liquid left in the saucepan.
5. When the potatoes are cooked, strain off the water and replace on the heat with the remaining butter. Season with salt. Brown the potatoes, then sprinkle with the chopped tarragon leaves.
6. When the poussins are cooked, place on a serving dish, and surround with the vegetables. Serve at once.

# Coquelets Fantaisie
*Roast Poussins with Vegetables and Vermouth*

*Serves 4. Preparation: 15 min Cooking: 1 hr*
★★

- ○ **2 poussins**
- ○ **60ml (4 tbls) oil**
- ○ **2 medium-sized onions**
- ○ **100g (4 oz) smoked streaky bacon**
- ○ **500g (1 lb 2 oz) small new potatoes**
- ○ **100g (4 oz) stoneless green olives**
- ○ **250g (9 oz) button mushrooms**
- ○ **4 ripe tomatoes**
- ○ **salt and pepper**
- ○ **150ml (5 fl oz) dry white vermouth**

1. Rub the inside of the poussins with salt and pepper. Brush them with 15ml (1 tbls) of oil. Season the outside with salt.
2. Preheat the oven to 200°C (400°F; gas mark 6). Cut the bacon into strips.
3. Peel and finely slice the onions. Trim the mushrooms and quarter. Peel the potatoes. Wash and wipe them dry.
4. Pour 45ml (3 tbls) of oil into a frying pan. Add the sliced onions, bacon strips and potatoes. Brown all the ingredients for 10 minutes, then add the mushrooms and olives. Season with salt and pepper. Simmer for 5 minutes and then pour all the ingredients into an ovenproof dish.
5. Place the poussins on top. Cut the tomatoes in half and place around the poussins. Pour in the vermouth and cook in the oven for 45 minutes, basting frequently. If at the end of the cooking time the vegetables have dried slightly, add a few tablespoons of water.
6. Serve as soon as you take the dish out of the oven.

*Always try, wherever possible, to obtain the sort of bird from your butcher – poussin, pullet, cockerel or capon – to suit your particular recipe.*

# Poulet Chasseur
## *Chicken Chasseur*

*Serves 4. Preparation: 20 min Cooking: 1 hr*

○ 1  1.2kg (2¾ lb) chicken,
   jointed in 8 pieces
○ 50g (2 oz) butter
○ 15ml (1 tbls) oil
○ 15ml (1 tbls) flour
○ 400g (14 oz) button
   mushrooms
○ 500g (1 lb 2 oz) ripe tomatoes
○ 10 shallots
○ 1 sprig tarragon
○ 250ml (9 fl oz) dry white wine
○ salt and pepper

*Bouquet garni:*
○ 1 sprig thyme
○ 1 bay leaf
○ 3 sprigs parsley

1. Scald the tomatoes in boiling water for 30 seconds. Cool them under a running tap and peel them. Cut in half and squeeze to remove the seeds. Dice the pulp coarsely.
2. Peel and chop the shallots finely.
3. Strip the tarragon leaves. Tie together the herbs for the bouquet garni.
4. Trim, wipe and quarter the mushrooms.
5. Heat the oil in a flameproof casserole. Add the butter and brown the chicken joints all over. Remove from the casserole and leave to drain on a plate.
6. Add the shallots and mushrooms to the casserole. Gently fry, but do not let them colour too much. Then sprinkle on the flour; stir well, and pour in the wine and water.
7. Put the chicken joints back into the casserole. Add the tomatoes, tarragon leaves and the bouquet garni. Season and cover. Simmer for 40 minutes. Serve at once.

Accompany with boiled or steamed potatoes sprinkled with chopped tarragon.

# Poule Bouillie aux Pâtes Fraîches
## *Boiled Chicken with Fresh Noodles*

*Serves 6. Preparation: 10 min*
*Cooking: 1 hr 45 min*
★★

○ 1  1.5kg (3¼ lb) young boiling
   fowl, trussed
○ 3 carrots
○ 2 celery stalks
○ 50g (2 oz) button mushrooms
○ 1 onion
○ 2 cloves
○ 6 peppercorns
○ 2 chicken stock cubes
○ 300g (11 oz) fresh noodles
○ 50g (2 oz) butter
○ grated Gruyère cheese
○ salt and pepper
○ 250ml (9 fl oz) hot water

*Bouquet garni:*
○ 1 sprig thyme
○ 1 bay leaf
○ 4 sprigs parsley

1. Prepare and wash the vegetables. Spike the onion with the cloves. Place the bird in a large saucepan. Add the vegetables, bouquet garni and peppercorns. Season sparingly with salt (the stock cube will already have been salted).
2. Dissolve the stock cubes in 250ml (9 fl oz) hot water. Pour the stock into the saucepan; add enough cold water to cover the bird. Put a lid on the pan and simmer over a low heat for 1 hour 30 minutes.
3. When the bird is cooked, remove from the stock, carve and arrange the pieces in a deep dish. Pour a ladleful of stock over and keep warm.
4. Remove the vegetables from the stock and dice them. Discard the bouquet garni.
5. Cook the noodles in the stock: they should be *al dente* – slightly firm (not soft). Drain and add the vegetables and butter. Mix together well and place on top of the chicken joints. Sprinkle with the grated Gruyère and serve at once.

Rice and peas may be cooked in the stock instead of fresh pasta.

# Coquelets à la Bière

*Poussins in Beer*

*Serves 6. Preparation: 15 min Cooking: 1 hr*

★

○ **3 poussins**
○ **1 medium-sized onion**
○ **30ml (2 tbls) gin**
○ **300g (11 oz) button mushrooms**
○ **50g (2 oz) butter**
○ **125g (4 oz) cream**
○ **1 bottle (½ pint) brown ale**
○ **24 juniper berries**
○ **salt and pepper**
○ **1 small bunch parsley**

1. Rub the inside of the poussins with salt and pepper
2. Peel and finely chop the onion. Trim and wipe the mushrooms. Chop the parsley coarsely.
3. Melt the butter in a heavy pan over a low heat. Brown the poussins on all sides for about 15 minutes. Remove from the heat. Place the onion in the pan and fry gently.
4. Slice the mushrooms thinly. When the onion has begun to turn golden add the mushrooms and fry until the juices run.
5. Place the poussins back in the pan. Season. Moisten with gin and set alight. Pour in the beer and add the juniper berries. Simmer over a medium heat for 25 minutes, turning the poussins frequently. At the end of the cooking time the sauce should be of a thick consistency.
6. When the poussins are cooked remove from the pan and put on a serving dish. With a sharp knife, cut the breasts into two, from the neck to the tail. Place the mushrooms inside the poussins.
7. Blend the cream with the sauce in the pan. Bring to the boil and cook for 1 minute beating with a whisk. Pour over the poussins. Sprinkle with chopped parsley and serve at once.

# Poulet en Papillotes

*Chicken Quarters in Foil*

*Serves 4. Preparation: 20 min Cooking: 1 hr*

★

○ **1 1.2kg (2¾ lb) chicken, cut into quarters**
○ **45ml (3 tbls) olive oil**
○ **1 medium-sized onion**
○ **2 garlic cloves**
○ **500g (1 lb 2 oz) ripe tomatoes**
○ **24 small black olives**
○ **5ml (1 tsp) oregano**
○ **2 bay leaves**
○ **salt and pepper**
○ **coarse salt**

1. Scald the tomatoes in boiling water for 30 seconds. Cool under running water and peel. Cut in half, squeeze to remove seeds, and dice. Mash with a fork.
2. Peel the garlic cloves. Crush, or chop them very finely. Add to the tomato purée.
3. Peel and finely chop the onion. Add to the tomato purée together with the oregano, salt, olives and 30ml (2 tbls) of olive oil. Mix well.
4. Cut four pieces off a large sheet of greaseproof paper or foil. Brush with olive oil. Place a chicken quarter in the centre of each; cover with the sauce and garnish with a half bay leaf. Fold over the foil to enclose the chicken quarter completely.
5. Preheat the oven to 220°C (425°F; gas mark 7). Cover the bottom of a baking tray with coarse salt 1cm (½ inch) thick; place the chicken *en papillotes* on top. The salt will prevent the meat from burning whilst cooking at a very high temperature on a hot baking sheet.
6. Cook for 45 minutes; open the foil, remove the bay leaves and cook for another 15 minutes.

Serve with a green salad.

# Poulet au Vinaigre

*Serves 4. Preparation: 15 min Cooking: 55 min*

## *Chicken in Tarragon Wine Vinegar*

★ ★

- ○ 1  1.2kg (2¾ lb) chicken, jointed in 8 pieces
- ○ 150g (6 oz) butter
- ○ salt and pepper
- ○ 100ml (3½ fl oz) dry white wine
- ○ 100ml (3½ fl oz) tarragon wine vinegar
- ○ 1 tin 400g (14 oz) peeled tomatoes
- ○ 250g (9 oz) button mushrooms
- ○ 1 small bunch parsley

*For the croûtons:*
- ○ 8 slices of French bread
- ○ 50g (2 oz) butter

1. Cut the tinned tomatoes in half and remove the seeds. Mash with a fork and put in a bowl with their juice.
2. In a heavy pan, melt 50g (2 oz) of butter and brown the chicken joints on all sides. Season. Add the vinegar and turn the chicken frequently in the sauce (to moisten the meat well).
3. When the vinegar has completely evaporated, add the wine, reduce by half, then add the tomatoes and cover the pan. Simmer for 30 minutes over a low heat, turning the chicken joints occasionally.
4. Meanwhile, trim and wipe the mushrooms, and slice them thinly. Melt a knob of butter in a frying pan and sauté the mushrooms. When all their juices have run out and they have turned golden, remove from the heat and keep warm.
5. 5 minutes before the end of the cooking time, prepare the croûtons. Melt the butter in a frying pan and briskly fry the slices of bread. Drain on kitchen paper.
6. When the chicken is cooked, remove from the pan and place on a serving dish. Arrange the mushrooms on top and keep warm.
7. Cut the remaining 100g (4 oz) of butter into knobs, and add one by one to the cooking pan, folding them into the sauce a little at a time, using a whisk. Pour the sauce, which should be creamy and frothy, over the chicken joints.
8. Garnish with the croûtons and small sprigs of parsley. Serve at once.

# Poulet en Escabèche

*Serves 4. Preparation: 5 min  Cooking: 20 min  To be served cold*

## *Cold Chicken Breasts in Vinegar Sauce*

★

- ○ 4 chicken breasts
- ○ 90ml (6 tbls) oil
- ○ 4 garlic cloves
- ○ 1 medium-sized onion
- ○ 5ml (1 tsp) rosemary
- ○ 1 small dried chilli
- ○ 200ml (7 fl oz) white wine vinegar
- ○ salt

1. Peel and slice the onion finely. Peel the garlic. Divide each chicken breast into two. Flatten each slice with the blade of a knife.
2. Heat the oil in a frying pan over a medium heat. Fry each chicken breast for 4 to 6 minutes on each side. Season with salt. When cooked, place in a deep ovenproof dish.
3. Add the garlic cloves, sliced onion, rosemary, and flaked chilli to the frying pan. When the garlic and onion are golden, pour in the vinegar and boil for 5 minutes. Add a little more salt, then pour the boiling sauce over the chicken pieces.

This dish is eaten cold. Leave it to stand one or two days in the refrigerator, turning the chicken pieces once or twice so that the sauce penetrates the meat.

*To make sure that chicken joints are well cooked, add them to the casserole or sauté pan 10 minutes before the breast and wings.*

# Cuisses de Poulet aux Épinards

*Serves 4. Preparation and cooking: 1 hr 10 min*

## Chicken Legs with Spinach

★★

- ○ **4 chicken legs**
- ○ **100g (4 oz) butter**
- ○ **30ml (2 tbls) oil**
- ○ **1 medium-sized onion**
- ○ **100ml (3½ fl oz) dry white wine**
- ○ **200ml (7 fl oz) warm water**
- ○ **500g (1 lb 2 oz) spinach**
- ○ **125g (4 oz) cream**
- ○ **5ml (1 tsp) cornflour**
- ○ **30ml (2 tbls) cold water**
- ○ **1 egg yolk**
- ○ **50g (2 oz) grated Parmesan cheese**
- ○ **salt and pepper**

1. Peel and chop the onion finely.
2. Heat the oil in a heavy pan. Add 50g (2 oz) of butter and brown the chicken legs all over. Remove from the pan and put on one side.
3. Pour away half the cooking fat, sauté the onion and put the chicken legs back into the pan. Season. Add the wine and warm water. Cover and simmer for 50 minutes over a low heat, turning the chicken from time to time.
4. 25 minutes before the end of the time, clean, wash and blanch the spinach in a large quantity of boiling salted water for 5 minutes, and strain.
5. Melt the remaining butter in a frying pan over a low heat. Add the spinach and sauté for 5 minutes. Turn off the heat, sprinkle with the grated cheese, mix in well, and cover with a lid to keep warm.
6. In a bowl, beat the egg yolk with the cream, using a fork. Mix the cornflour with cold water and blend with the egg/cream mixture.
7. When the chicken legs are cooked, remove from the pan and arrange on a serving dish. Keep warm.
8. Pour the contents of the bowl into the pan. Mix with the cooking juices, using a whisk, and boil for 1 minute beating all the time. Remove from heat.
9. Place the spinach around the chicken and pour the sauce over. Serve at once.

# Poulet Gratiné

*Serves 4. Preparation and cooking: 1 hr 15 min*

## Chicken Gratin

★★

- ○ **1 1.2kg (2¾ lb) chicken, jointed in 8 pieces**
- ○ **50g (2 oz) butter**
- ○ **15ml (1 tbls) oil**
- ○ **salt**

*For the sauce:*
- ○ **50g (2 oz) butter**
- ○ **50g (2 oz) flour**
- ○ **½ litre (18 fl oz) warm milk**
- ○ **125g (4 oz) cream**
- ○ **100g (4 oz) grated Emmenthal cheese**
- ○ **salt and pepper**
- ○ **pinch nutmeg**

1. In a heavy pan, heat the oil. Add 50g (2 oz) of butter and brown the chicken joints all over. Then add 100ml (3½ fl oz) of water. Season with salt.
2. Cover the pan and simmer for 45 minutes over a low heat, turning the chicken joints occasionally.
3. 15 minutes before the end of cooking time, prepare the sauce. Melt the butter in a saucepan, sprinkle in the flour, and work in. Then add the warm milk a drop at a time, stirring continuously. Season with salt, pepper and grated nutmeg. Add the cream and grated cheese. Remove from the heat and mix everything together well.
4. Preheat the oven to 220°C (425°F; gas mark 7). When the chicken is cooked, remove from the pan and arrange in an ovenproof dish. Pour over the cheese sauce and cook in the oven for 15 minutes, until it browns.
5. Serve in the dish.

Accompany with braised vegetables such as celery or chicory.

# Rôti de Dinde au Céleri

*Serves 4. Preparation: 10 min Cooking: 1 hr 10 min*

★

## Roast Turkey with Celery

○ **800g (1¾ lb) turkey breasts**
○ **2 celery hearts**
○ **4 slices smoked lean bacon**
○ **4 cloves garlic**
○ **2.5ml (½ tsp) powdered cinnamon**
○ **15ml (1 tbls) oil**
○ **salt and pepper**
○ **60ml (4 tbls) cognac**

1. Preheat the oven to 190°C (375°F; gas mark 5).
2. Clean and wash the celery hearts, and cut into thin slices.
3. Grease an ovenproof dish. Put the celery slices and unpeeled garlic cloves into the dish.
4. Roll the turkey breasts together and secure with a piece of string to look like a roast. Place on top of the celery hearts. Lay the bacon slices on top of the turkey.
5. Sprinkle with cinnamon, salt and pepper and cook in the oven for 1 hour 10 minutes, basting frequently with the cooking juices or, if necessary, with a little water.
6. When the turkey roast is cooked, remove from the oven. Sprinkle with cognac, set alight and bring to the table.

# Dindonneau aux Airelles

*Serves 6. Preparation and cooking: 2 hr 15 min*

★★

## Roast Turkey with Bilberry (or Cranberry) Sauce

○ **1 young 2kg (4½ lb) turkey**
○ **100g (4 oz) barding fat, or streaky bacon**
○ **1 carrot**
○ **1 onion**
○ **1 celery stalk**
○ **1 sprig thyme**
○ **1 chicken stock cube**
○ **½ litre (1 pint) warm water**
○ **200ml (7 fl oz) dry white wine**
○ **250g (9 oz) cream**
○ **small punnet of bilberries or cranberries (fresh if possible)**
○ **salt and pepper**

1. Rub the inside of the turkey with salt and pepper. Place the barding fat on the breast and secure with string. Place the turkey in an ovenproof dish.
2. Peel, wash and finely slice the vegetables. Place around the turkey, with the thyme.
3. Preheat the oven to 200°C (400°F; gas mark 6). Dissolve the chicken stock cube in warm water and pour one third into the dish.
4. Cook in the oven for 45 minutes, adding more stock as required. Then reduce the heat to 190°C (375°F; gas mark 5) and cook for another 30 minutes.
5. When the cooking time is over, remove the barding fat and continue cooking for another ½ hour, turning the heat down to 180°C (350°F; gas mark 4). Then place the turkey on a serving dish. Pour the wine into the cooking dish and stir in the cooking juices. Strain the sauce through a sieve and pour into a small saucepan.
6. Discard the vegetables from the cooking dish. Bring the sauce to the boil, and boil until reduced by half. Add the cream, stir well and leave to reduce once more by half.
7. Wash the bilberries or cranberries (if fresh ones) or strain them (if using preserved ones). Add to the sauce and boil for 1 minute. Pour the sauce into a sauceboat.
8. Serve the turkey, handing the sauce separately.

Bilberries or cranberries may be replaced by fresh red or white currants.

*With a jointed chicken or turkey you can prepare two different dishes. You can sauté the chicken or turkey breasts, having cut them into thin slices (or escalopes), or roll them around a savoury filling (they are then known as* paupiettes*).*

*With the remaining joints, prepare a* fricassée *(brown the meat in butter or oil, add some stock, cover, and leave to cook).*

# Rôti de Dindonneau aux Saucisses
*Turkey Roast with Sausages*

*Serves 6.*
*Preparation and cooking: 1 hr 20 min*
★

○ **1 young 1.2kg (2½ lb) turkey**
○ **50g (2 oz) butter**
○ **3 medium-sized onions**
○ **300g (11 oz) button mushrooms**
○ **3 chipolata sausages**
○ **150ml (¼ pint) dry white wine**
○ **125g (4 oz) cream**
○ **salt and pepper**

1. Rub the turkey with salt and pepper. Melt the butter in a flameproof casserole and brown the turkey on both sides. Cover the casserole and continue cooking for 45 minutes over a very low heat. Do not add any water during the cooking unless it sticks.
2. Meanwhile, peel and finely slice the onions. Trim and wash the mushrooms and drain. Remove the skin from the sausages and cut into slices.
3. When the roast is cooked, remove from the casserole and keep warm. Put the onions in the casserole and gently sauté over a low heat, then add the sausage slices and fry until lightly brown.
4. Cut the mushrooms into strips and add to the casserole. Sauté until they have exuded all their juice, then pour in the wine.
5. When the wine has completely evaporated, add the cream, stir well and boil for 1 minute. Turn off the heat.
6. Cut the turkey roast into slices and place on a warm serving dish. Pour the sauce over and serve at once.

Serve with small peas or fresh spinach.

# Dinde au Jus de Grenade
*Turkey with Pomegranate Juice*

*Serves 4. Preparation: 10 min  Cooking: 1 hr 30 min*
★

○ **900g (2 lb) of turkey, legs and breasts, cut into 8 pieces**
○ **8 thin slices of lean bacon**
○ **50g (2 oz) butter**
○ **8 fresh sage leaves**
○ **3 bay leaves**
○ **salt and pepper**
○ **3 ripe pomegranates**

1. Preheat the oven to 200°C (400°F; gas mark 6). Grease an ovenproof dish large enough to contain all the turkey pieces.
2. Place a sage leaf on each piece of turkey. Season with a little salt and pepper. Roll up each piece of turkey in a slice of bacon and secure with a piece of string.
3. Place the rolled turkey pieces in the cooking dish. Cut each bay leaf in half and place in between each turkey roll.
4. Cook in the oven for 45 minutes, basting frequently with the cooking juices.
5. Peel the rind from two pomegranates. Put the seeds into a vegetable mill and pass through the fine mesh of the mill. Pour the juice into the cooking dish.
6. Reduce the heat to 190°C (370°F; gas mark 5) and continue cooking for 45 minutes, basting frequently. When the cooking is over, remove the string and place the turkey pieces on a serving dish. If necessary, add a little water to the sauce in the cooking dish, stir well and pour the sauce over the turkey.
7. Peel the third pomegranate and scoop out the seeds. Garnish the dish with the seeds and serve.

The pomegranate juice may be replaced by the juice of green grapes.

*Why not try one of these turkey recipes as an alternative to the traditional roast at Christmas.*

# Pintade aux Marrons Glacés

*Serves 4. Preparation: 15 min Cooking: 1 hr 15 min*

## Guinea Fowl with Marrons Glacés

★

○ **1 good-sized oven-ready guinea fowl**
○ **300g (11 oz) pieces of marrons glacés (candied chestnuts)**
○ **30ml (2 tbls) double cream**
○ **45ml (3 tbls) armagnac**
○ **4 slices raw ham (eg Parma ham)**
○ **10ml (2 tsp) rosemary**
○ **salt and pepper**
○ **50g (2 oz) butter**
○ **1 chicken stock cube**
○ **150ml (¼ pint) warm water**

1. Mix the pieces of marrons glacés with the cream and 15ml (1 tbls) of armagnac.
2. Rub the inside of the guinea fowl with salt and pepper. Stuff the bird with the chestnut, cream, and armagnac mixture and sew up the vent with a needle and thread.
3. Put the rosemary into a bowl and add 2ml (½ tsp) of salt and the same amount of pepper. Mix well and spread on a board. Roll the guinea fowl in this seasoning and then cover it with the slices of ham, tying them in place with a piece of string.
4. Preheat the oven to 220°C (425°F; gas mark 7). Dissolve the chicken stock cube in a small saucepan.
5. Melt the butter over a low heat in an ovenproof casserole large enough to contain the fowl. Gently brown the guinea fowl for 10 minutes, then pour over 30ml (2 tbls) of armagnac and set alight.
6. Place the casserole in the oven and cook for about 1 hour, basting the guinea fowl with stock every 10 minutes.
7. When the guinea fowl is cooked, remove the string and cut into 4 pieces. Place some stuffing on top of each quarter, with a slice of ham underneath. Serve at once.

To accompany this dish try a green salad, such as chicory, corn salad, or endive, seasoned with French dressing.

# Pintade d'Hiver

*Serves 4. Preparation: 15 min Cooking: 1 hr 30 min*

## Guinea Fowl with Prunes and Chestnuts

★★

○ **1 1.2kg (2½ lb) guinea fowl**
○ **12 chestnuts**
○ **12 prunes**
○ **100g (4 oz) ham**
○ **100g (4 oz) smoked streaky bacon**
○ **50g (2 oz) butter**
○ **1 litre (1¾ pints) milk**
○ **salt**

1. Soak the prunes in warm water for 2 hours before preparing the guinea fowl.
2. After 2 hours drain the prunes, chop the ham and cut the bacon into thin strips.
3. Rub the inside of the guinea fowl with salt, then stuff with the chestnuts, prunes, chopped ham and strips of bacon. Sew the vent with a needle and thread.
4. Generously grease the bottom and sides of a flameproof casserole and put in the guinea fowl. Add the milk, which should just about cover it, and season with salt.
5. Stand the casserole on an asbestos mat and cook over a very low heat for 1 hour 30 minutes, in the simmering milk.
6. Remove the guinea fowl from the casserole and place on a serving dish. Cut it into 4 pieces and put some stuffing on top of each quarter.
7. Reduce the sauce, if necessary, by boiling it for a few minutes. When ready, it should look like golden clotted cream.
8. Pour the sauce over each quarter of guinea fowl and serve at once.

*A fowl with stuffing need not cook any longer than a fowl without stuffing. Ingredients for the stuffing which are not finely chopped require more time to cook; it is therefore necessary to cook (eg fry) onions, strips of bacon, shallots, chestnuts, before they are mixed with the remaining ingredients for the stuffing.*

*A stuffing which is made of a mixture of egg and bread (amongst other ingredients) swells during cooking; therefore you will only need a small amount of stuffing for the fowl.*

# Canard à l'Ananas

### Duck with Pineapple

*Serves 4. Preparation: 10 min Cooking: 1 hr 10 min*

★ ★

○ 1 1.5kg (3½ lb) duck
○ 1 carrot
○ 1 onion
○ 1 celery stalk
○ 1 sprig thyme
○ 1 bay leaf
○ 1 pineapple
○ 60ml (2 fl oz) kirsch
○ 15ml (1 tbls) wine vinegar
○ 100ml (3½ fl oz) dry white wine
○ salt and pepper
○ 15ml (1 tbls) oil

1. Preheat the oven to 220°C (425°F; gas mark 7). Peel the vegetables and cut into thin strips. Rub the duck with oil and grease an ovenproof dish.
2. Rub the inside of the duck with salt and pepper. Place in the oven dish with the vegetable strips around. Add the thyme, bay leaf and 100ml (3½ fl oz) water. Put in the oven and cook for 1 hour, basting the duck frequently. Add more water if the vegetables start to dry up.
3. Meanwhile, prepare the pineapple: slice off the leaf end and cut off the skin, using a sharp knife; then cut into slices 5cm (¼ inch) thick. Place the pineapple slices in a bowl and pour over the kirsch.
4. When the duck is cooked, lift out onto a cooking dish, reserving the cooking liquid. Season the duck with salt, cover with foil and keep warm in the oven (turned off).
5. Place the cooking dish (if flameproof) over a low heat. Add the white wine and reduce the sauce by half, scraping the coagulated cooking juices into the wine. Discard the thyme and bay leaf. Stir in the caramel, vinegar and pineapple slices with the kirsch. Simmer for 2 minutes then turn off the heat.
6. Garnish the duck with pineapple slices and pour the sauce over. Serve at once.

# Canard aux Navets

### Duck with Turnips

*Serves 4. Preparation and cooking: 1 hr 20 min*

★ ★

○ 1 1.4kg (3 lb) duckling
○ 1kg (2½ lb) turnips
○ 12 small onions (or pickling onions)
○ 100g (4 oz) butter
○ 10ml (2 tsp) sugar
○ salt and pepper

1. Peel the onions. Rub the inside of the duck with salt and pepper. Melt 50g (2 oz) of butter in a flameproof casserole and brown the duck on both sides. Add the onions and season. Cover the casserole and simmer over a low heat for 1 hour, turning the duck frequently.
2. Meanwhile, peel and wash the turnips. Drain and wipe them dry. Cut into even-shaped pieces.
3. Melt 60g (2½ oz) of butter in a sauté pan and gently sauté the turnips for 10 minutes, then add 100ml (3½ fl oz) of water. Season with salt and cover the sauté pan with a lid. Simmer over a very low heat for 20 minutes, then sprinkle in the sugar and cook for another 10 minutes, still over a low heat. Let the turnips caramelize on all sides, shaking the pan frequently.
4. When the duck is cooked, add the turnips to the casserole and simmer for 5 minutes. Then arrange the duck on a serving dish, surround with the turnips and onions, pour the cooking liquid over and serve.

*When roasting a fowl, always put some herbs such as rosemary, thyme or tarragon inside the bird. Do not forget to rub the inside with salt and pepper. Instead of stuffing, you can put the liver, heart and gizzard inside it for extra flavour. You may roast it without any fat, but if you want the skin to be golden and crusty, rub it with half a lemon before placing it in the oven.*

# Caneton sur Canapés de Foie

*Duckling on Liver Canapés*

*Serves 2. Preparation and cooking: 1 hr 5 min*

★★

○ **1 800g (1½ lb) duckling**
○ **the duckling liver**
○ **2 finely chopped shallots**
○ **100g (4 oz) butter**
○ **150ml (¼ pint) dry white wine**
○ **salt and pepper**
○ **2 large slices white bread**

1. Rub the inside of the duckling with salt and pepper. Melt 30g (1¼ oz) of butter in a sauté pan and brown the duckling on both sides. Season with salt and pepper, cover and simmer for 45 minutes. The duckling should be well browned on the outside but its flesh should still be slightly pink.
2. 15 minutes before the end of the cooking time, toast the slices of bread. Melt 20g (¾ oz) butter in a small frying pan and gently sauté the shallots. Add the liver and sauté for a few minutes: it should still be pink. Remove the frying pan from the heat, season with salt and pepper and blend the ingredients in an electric blender, or mash well with a fork. Add 30g (1¼ oz) of butter to this purée and mix well. Spread this mixture on to the slices of bread and put in the oven for 5 minutes at 180°C (350°F; gas mark 4).
3. When the duckling is cooked split it in half and place each half on one slice of bread.
4. Skim the fat off the sauté pan, pour in the wine and reduce by half. Remove from the heat and add the 20g (¾ oz) remaining butter. Mix with a fork and pour the sauce over the canapés. Serve immediately.

# Caneton aux Haricots Blancs Frais

*Duckling with Fresh Haricot Beans*

*Serves 4. Preparation: 15 min*
*Cooking: 1 hr 30 min*
★★

○ **1 1.5kg (3¼ lb) duckling, cut into 8 pieces**
○ **1kg (2½ lb) fresh haricot beans**
○ **100g (4 oz) streaky bacon**
○ **1 medium-sized onion**
○ **15ml (1 tbls) tomato purée**
○ **1 bouquet garni: 1 sprig thyme, 1 bay leaf, 6 sprigs parsley**
○ **30ml (2 tbls) goose fat or oil**
○ **2ml (½ tsp) sugar**
○ **salt and pepper**

1. Shell the haricot beans (if fresh ones). Peel and chop the onion. Cut the bacon into strips.
2. Melt the goose fat (or oil) in a flameproof casserole. Quickly sauté the duck pieces over a medium heat, then remove from the casserole and reserve.
3. Put the onion and bacon into the casserole and sauté until slightly golden. Mix the tomato purée with a glass of cold water and pour into the casserole, adding at the same time the sugar and bouquet garni. Add the haricot beans and place the duck pieces on top. Season. Cover with cold water up to the level of the duck.
4. Cover the casserole and simmer over a low heat for 1 hour 10 minutes or more until the haricot beans are tender. Add more water during the cooking if necessary.
5. Serve very hot, in the cooking dish.

*How to roast a fowl well in the oven. First rub the inside of the fowl with salt and pepper. Do not rub the outside with salt, because it would be dissolved into the cooking juices or fat which are used for basting the fowl and would make it too salty. Lightly grease the outside of the fowl (with butter or oil) and cook in a fairly hot oven. When the bird has turned golden reduce the heat progressively until the end of the cooking time. Start basting the fowl only during the last quarter of the cooking time, because basting causes the skin to swell up in large ugly-looking blisters. If you like the skin to be crispy only baste the fowl a little. If you like the flesh to melt in your mouth, baste it frequently.*

*When roasting a large fowl first place some slices of larding fat on the breast or cover with foil or greaseproof paper for the first two thirds of the cooking time. Then remove the larding fat or foil to allow the fowl to brown. If you follow these instructions, the flesh of the fowl should not be too dry.*

# Oie Farcie aux Marrons

*Serves 6-8. Preparation: 50 min Cooking: 2 hr 35 min*

## Goose with Chestnut Stuffing

★★

- ◯ 1 2.5kg (5½ lb) goose
- ◯ 1kg (2¼ lb) chestnuts
- ◯ 1 celeriac
- ◯ 1 carrot
- ◯ 1 large onion
- ◯ 1 celery stalk
- ◯ 1 bay leaf
- ◯ ½ litre (1 pint) dry white wine
- ◯ 15ml (1 tbls) oil
- ◯ salt and pepper

1. Peel the chestnuts. Peel the celeriac and dice it. Put some water in a large saucepan and add the chestnuts. Bring to the boil over a medium heat. After 20 minutes cooking, season with salt and add the celeriac. Boil for another 10 minutes, then drain.
2. Meanwhile, peel the carrot and onion, and cut into thin slices together with the celery stalk. Grease an ovenproof dish and place the vegetables in it, with the bay leaf.
3. Preheat the oven to 200°C (400°F; gas mark 6). Rub the inside of the goose with salt and pepper, and fill it with the chestnuts and celeriac. Sew up the vent with a needle and thread. Place in the cooking dish on the bed of vegetables and cook in the oven for 1 hour.
4. Reduce the heat to 190°C (375°F; gas mark 5) and continue cooking for another 1 hour 30 minutes, adding the wine 100ml (3½ fl oz) at a time to the cooking dish. Baste the goose with this liquid frequently.
5. When the goose is cooked, place on a serving dish. Add a little water (if necessary) to the juices and pass this sauce through a fine sieve. Skim the fat off and pour the sauce into a sauceboat. Carve the goose and place the chestnut and celeriac stuffing around the bird. Serve with the sauce in the sauceboat.

# Oie Rôtie aux Pommes de Terre

*Serves 6. Preparation and cooking: 2 hr*

## Roast Goose with Potatoes

★★

- ◯ 1 2kg (4½ lb) goose
- ◯ 1.5kg (3 lb) potatoes
- ◯ 2 sprigs thyme
- ◯ 1 tin truffles
- ◯ salt and pepper

1. Preheat the oven to 200°C (400°F; gas mark 6). Rub the inside of the goose with salt and pepper and put the thyme inside the bird. Pour 1 glass of water into a meat tin and place the goose in the meat tin sitting on a wire rack. Cook in the oven for 30 minutes.
2. Meanwhile, peel and wash the potatoes, drain and cut them into thin slices.
3. Grease a large ovenproof dish. Arrange the potatoes as tightly as possible in layers. Season and place the strips of truffles in between each layer.
4. After 30 minutes, remove the goose from the oven and place on top of the potatoes. Remove the meat tin from the oven and pour away the water and cooking fat: at this stage, the goose has not rendered any fat. Reduce the heat to 190°C (375°F; gas mark 5) and put the goose back in the oven for 1 hour 30 minutes. The potatoes will cook and be impregnated with the fat and cooking juices from the goose. They should be cooked and flavoured to perfection.
5. When the goose is cooked, remove from the oven. Serve in the cooking dish on the bed of potatoes.

*There are different ways of peeling chestnuts. The two most common are as follows: make a small cut on the flat side of the chestnuts and roast them on a baking tray in a very hot oven for 8 minutes; or, after having made a small cut on each chestnut, plunge them into very hot oil for 8 minutes.*

# Oie Farcie aux Raisins au Rhum

*Goose Stuffed with Sultanas Marinated in Rum*

*Serves 6-8. Preparation: 20 min*
*Cooking: 2 hr 30 min*
★★

○ 1 2.5kg (5½ lb) goose
○ 6 apples (Cox's orange pippins, if possible)
○ 200g (7 oz) sultanas
○ 200ml (7 fl oz) rum
○ 3 chipolata sausages
○ 50g (2 oz) butter
○ 15ml (1 tbls) oil
○ salt and pepper

1. Soak the sultanas in lukewarm water overnight. Drain and put in a large bowl. Heat the rum gently and pour over the sultanas, leave to swell until the next day.
2. The next day, cut the apples into 4, peel and remove the core. Heat the butter in a frying pan and quickly brown the apple quarters over a brisk heat, until they start to caramelize. Turn off the heat.
3. Grill the sausages, but do not let them cook through. Cut into 4 pieces and put aside.
4. Preheat the oven to 200°C (400°F; gas mark 6). Rub the inside of the goose with salt and pepper and stuff with the apples, sausages and sultanas. Sew up the vent with a needle and thread.
5. Grease an ovenproof dish, place the goose in the cooking dish and cook for 1 hour. Then skim the fat off the cooking juices and pour in 200ml (7 fl oz) of water. Turn the heat down to 190°C (375°F; gas mark 5) and cook for a further 1 hour 30 minutes, adding more water as necessary. Baste the goose frequently.
6. When the goose is cooked, place on a serving dish. Deglaze the cooking juices with a little water and pour this sauce into a sauceboat. Serve the goose at once with the sauce in the sauceboat.

Serve with a smooth purée of chestnuts, to which you can add a little of the cooking juices just before serving.

# Oie Farcie aux Reinettes

*Goose with Apple Stuffing*

*Serves 6-8. Preparation: 15 min Cooking: 2 hr 30 min*
★

○ 1 2.5kg (5½ lb) goose
○ 1kg (2½ lb) small apples (Cox's orange pippins, if possible)
○ 2 small sprigs rosemary
○ salt and pepper

1. Rub the inside of the goose with salt and pepper. Wash and wipe the apples. Remove the core using an apple corer, but do not peel them.
2. Preheat the oven to 200°C (400°F; gas mark 6). Fill the goose with the apples and rosemary. Sew up the vent with a needle and thread.
3. Place the goose into a greased ovenproof dish and roast for 1 hour, then reduce the heat to 190°C (375°F; gas mark 5) and cook for a further 1 hour 30 minutes, basting the goose occasionally. From the middle of the cooking time onwards, add a little water whenever the cooking juices start to caramelize.
4. When the goose is cooked, place on a serving dish and carve. Arrange the apples around. Skim the fat off the cooking juices and pour this sauce into a sauceboat.
5. Serve at once, with the sauce in the sauceboat.

You can serve some warm redcurrant jelly, a purée of bilberries or cranberries, or small cherries preserved in vinegar with this dish.

*Up to 4kg (9 lb) a goose may be prepared in the same way as any other fowl. In France, and particularly in the Toulouse area, a goose may weigh up to 10kg (more than 20 lb) but it is used for the* confit *or preserved goose and its liver is used for the famous* foie gras.

*Lapin aux Poivrons (p108)*

# Lapin aux Poivrons

*Serves 4. Preparation: 15 min Cooking: 1 hr 15 min*

## Rabbit with Peppers

★ ★

○ 1 1.2kg (2½ lb) rabbit, cut into 8 pieces
○ 1 large onion
○ 2 cloves garlic, unpeeled
○ 1 green pepper
○ 1 yellow pepper
○ 1 red pepper
○ 1 tin 400g (14 oz) peeled tomatoes
○ 1 sprig thyme
○ 1 bay leaf
○ 15ml (1 tbls) chopped parsley
○ 60ml (4 tbls) oil
○ salt and pepper

1. Peel and chop the onion. Open the tomato tin and pour the tomatoes into a bowl, keeping the juice aside. Cut the tomatoes into halves and remove the seeds. Coarsely mash using a fork. Add the mashed tomatoes to the juice. Wash and cut the peppers into 4. Remove the seeds and cut into strips.
2. Heat the oil in a sauté pan and brown the rabbit pieces over a medium heat, then remove from the pan and sauté the chopped onion until golden. Add the unpeeled cloves of garlic and pepper strips. Lightly sauté all ingredients, then put the rabbit pieces back into the pan.
3. Pour in the tomato purée. Season. Add the thyme and bay leaf. Cover with a lid and simmer over a low heat for 1 hour, turning the rabbit in the sauce occasionally.
4. When the cooking time is over, check whether the rabbit is well done: the meat should come off the bones easily. Reduce the sauce in the uncovered pan and pour all ingredients into a serving dish. Sprinkle with chopped parsley and serve immediately.

Serve with boiled or jacket potatoes.

# Lapin aux Pruneaux

*Serves 4. Preparation and cooking: 2 hr*

## Rabbit with Prunes

★ ★

○ 1 1.2kg (2½ lb) rabbit, cut into 8 pieces
○ 100g (4 oz) streaky, smoked bacon
○ 20 small onions
○ 250g (9 oz) prunes
○ 15ml (1 tbls) Dijon mustard
○ ¼ litre (9 fl oz) dry white wine
○ 15ml (1 tbls) flour
○ 2 pinches thyme
○ 50g (2 oz) butter
○ 30ml (2 tbls) cognac
○ 15ml (1 tbls) liquid caramel
○ salt and pepper

1. The day before cooking the rabbit, or at least 2 hours before, wash and soak the prunes in lukewarm water.
2. Cut the bacon into thin strips and peel the small onions.
3. Melt the butter in a flameproof casserole over a very low heat and gently fry the bacon. Remove from the casserole and brown the rabbit joints; remove from the casserole and put in the onions. Fry until golden, still over a low heat.
4. Meanwhile, rub the rabbit pieces with the mustard. When the onions are golden put the bacon and rabbit back into the casserole. Sprinkle in the flour and stir until it starts to turn golden, then pour in the wine. Season and add the thyme. Cover with a lid and simmer for 1 hour over a low heat.
5. After an hour, add the drained prunes and the cognac. Simmer for a further 30 minutes over a low heat.
6. When the rabbit is cooked, place on a serving dish together with the prunes and onions. Pour the caramel into the casserole and mix well with the cooking juices. Pour this sauce over the rabbit and serve immediately.

Serve with a smooth purée of potatoes or chips.

*The pepper (green, red or yellow) is only the sweet variety of the capsicum. Green peppers are the least sweet of the three kinds, yellow peppers are the sweetest and red peppers are also very sweet but have a nutmeg flavour. When buying peppers, make sure that their skins are smooth, firm and taut: that shows they are fresh.*

# Lapin à l'Espagnole
*Rabbit Spanish-Style*

*Serves 4. Preparation: 10 min Cooking: 1 hr 20 min*

★★

○ 1 1.2kg (2½ lb) rabbit, cut into 8 pieces
○ 250g (9 oz) button mushrooms
○ 100g (4 oz) stuffed green olives
○ ¼ litre (9 fl oz) dry white wine
○ 30ml (2 tbls) chopped parsley
○ 30ml (2 tbls) oil
○ 50g (2 oz) butter
○ salt and pepper
○ 4 medium-sized potatoes
○ the juice of 1 lemon

1. Trim the mushrooms. Wash, drain and cut them into 4 pieces. Sprinkle with the lemon juice.
2. Heat the oil in a sauté pan. Add the butter and brown the rabbit pieces all over. Then add the mushrooms, chopped parsley and white wine. Season, cover the pan and simmer for 1 hour 10 minutes.
3. Meanwhile, wash the potatoes. Put them into a saucepan unpeeled and cover with cold water. When the water starts to boil, cook over a low heat for 15 to 20 minutes. Check whether they are cooked or not by putting the blade of a knife through one. They should still be firm. Remove from the heat and leave to cool. Then peel and cut them into thin slices. Add to the sauté pan together with the olives and cook for 10 minutes (10 minutes before the rabbit should be ready).
4. When the rabbit is cooked, place on a serving dish, arrange the vegetables around and bring to the table.

# Lapin au Lait
*Rabbit in Milk Sauce*

*Serves 4. Preparation and cooking: 1 hr 30 min*

★

○ 1 1.2kg (2½ lb) rabbit, cut into 8 pieces
○ 50g (2 oz) butter
○ 6 fresh sage leaves
○ 2ml (½ tsp) rosemary
○ ½ litre (1 pint) milk
○ salt and pepper
○ nutmeg

1. Melt the butter in a flameproof casserole over a very low heat and brown the rabbit pieces, together with the sage and rosemary. Then pour over the milk. Season with salt, pepper and grated nutmeg. Cover and simmer over a very low heat for 1 hour 15 minutes approximately.
2. At the end of the cooking time the milk will have nearly evaporated and the sauce should be a thick consistency and a golden colour. If not, reduce for a few minutes over a medium heat, turning the rabbit a few times.
3. Serve when the ingredients have taken on a golden colour.

A smooth purée of potatoes is a good accompaniment.

# Lapin à la Crème
*Rabbit in Cream Sauce*

*Serves 4. Preparation and cooking: 1 hr 30 min*

★

○ 1 1.2kg (2½ lb) rabbit, cut into 8 pieces
○ 40g (1½ oz) butter
○ the juice of 1 lemon
○ 250g (9 oz) cream
○ salt and white pepper
○ nutmeg

1. Melt the butter in a flameproof casserole over a very low heat. Brown the rabbit pieces and season with salt and pepper. Pour in the lemon juice, turning the rabbit pieces over a few times, so that the flesh can absorb the lemon juice.
2. When the lemon juice has completely evaporated add the cream and grated nutmeg. Cover the casserole and simmer for 1 hour 15 minutes approximately over a very low heat, until the meat is tender and comes easily off the bones.
3. Arrange the rabbit on a serving dish and pour over the sauce, which should be of a thick consistency and of a golden colour. Serve at once.

Potatoes – steamed, sauté or chips – go very well with this dish.

# Pigeons au Raisin Muscat

*Pigeons with Muscatels*

*Serves 4. Preparation: 10 min Cooking: 45 min*

★★

○ **4 pigeons**
○ **200g (7 oz) larding fat**
○ **30ml (2 tbls) oil**
○ **50g (2 oz) butter**
○ **¼ litre (9 fl oz) dry white wine**
○ **1 sprig thyme**
○ **1 bay leaf**
○ **30ml (2 tbls) cognac**
○ **salt and pepper**
○ **1kg (2½ lb) muscat grapes,
    black or white**

1. Rub the inside of the pigeons with salt and pepper. Put some larding fat on the breast of each pigeon and secure with string. Heat the oil in a flameproof casserole, add the butter and brown the pigeons all over. Season with salt and pepper, add the thyme and bay leaf and pour over the wine. Cover with a lid and simmer over a low heat for 30 minutes.
2. Meanwhile, wash the grapes and remove the pips. Pass 500g (slightly over 1 lb) of the grapes through the fine mesh of a vegetable mill. Strain the juice once more through a fine sieve and reserve.
3. 10 minutes before the end of the cooking time, remove the pigeons from the casserole. Discard the string and larding fat. Put the pigeons back into the casserole breast downwards, so that they can brown.
4. When the pigeons are brown, pour in the grape juice and cognac. When this starts to boil, add the grapes and simmer for 3 minutes, to let them heat up. Then place the pigeons on a serving dish and arrange the rest of the grapes around. Serve immediately.

# Pigeons Chasseur

*Pigeons Chasseur*

*Serves 4. Preparation: 15 min Cooking: 45 min*

○ **4 young pigeons**
○ **12 shallots, finely chopped**
○ **24 button mushrooms**
○ **4 large ripe tomatoes**
○ **½ litre (1 pint) dry white wine**
○ **1 sprig thyme**
○ **½ bay leaf**
○ **10ml (2 tsp) coarsely chopped
    parsley**
○ **30ml (2 tbls) oil**
○ **30g (1 oz) butter**
○ **salt and pepper**

1. Scald the tomatoes in boiling water for 1 minute, then refresh under cold running water. Peel, remove the seeds, mash with a fork and reserve. Trim the mushrooms, wash and drain.
2. Heat the oil in a flameproof casserole, add the butter and brown the pigeons all over, then remove from the heat and fry the shallots.
3. Cut the mushrooms into 4 pieces. Put them into the casserole with the shallots. When they have turned golden, add the tomato purée, simmer for 2 minutes then pour over the wine.
4. When the sauce starts to boil, put the pigeons back into the casserole together with the thyme and bay leaf. Season with salt and pepper, cover with a lid and cook over a low heat for 25 minutes.
5. When the pigeons are cooked, place them on a serving dish and pour over the contents of the casserole. Sprinkle with parsley and serve at once.

Steamed potatoes or rice, lightly buttered, go very well with this dish.

*Basil is a herb which is also known as* pistou *in France, because it is the main ingredient of* pistou *sauce.*

*Do you know how to cook chicken with tarragon* (poulet à l'estragon)? *It is a very simple recipe. First sauté a young chicken, whole or jointed, in a mixture of oil and butter. Cook covered for 40 to 50 minutes. Once cooked, keep the chicken warm and deglaze the cooking juices by adding 100ml (3½ fl oz) of dry white wine into the sauté pan. Reduce the sauce by half, then pour in 100ml (3½ fl oz) of water or stock. Bring to the boil and remove from the heat. Away from the heat, add 5ml (1 tsp) coarsely chopped tarragon and the same amount of chervil. Pour this sauce over the chicken and serve. You can use some cream (instead of the wine) to deglaze the cooking juices.*

# Asperges Lolita
*Asparagus in a Cheese Omelette*

*Serves 4. Preparation and cooking: 1 hr*

★★

- ○ 1kg (2¼ lb) thin green asparagus
- ○ 2 eggs
- ○ 100ml (3½ fl oz) milk
- ○ 100ml (3½ fl oz) fresh double cream
- ○ 100g (4 oz) Emmenthal cheese
- ○ 20ml (4 tsp) oil
- ○ 50g (2 oz) butter
- ○ salt and pepper
- ○ pinch nutmeg
- ○ 15ml (1 tbls) coarse salt

1. Place a large saucepan, three-quarters full of water, over high heat, add coarse salt, and bring to the boil.
2. Scrape or peel and wash the asparagus. Cut into even lengths and tie together. Place the bundle in the boiling water, which should come 1cm (½ inch) below the asparagus tips so that they are not spoiled during cooking. Simmer gently for about 20 minutes. Check cooking by pricking with a knife which should go in easily.
4. Meanwhile, prepare an omelette: beat the eggs with the cream and milk in a bowl. Add salt, pepper, and nutmeg. Divide the mixture to make 4 small omelettes.
5. Add 5ml (1 tsp) of oil to a small frying pan. When the oil is hot, pour one-quarter of the mixture into the pan and cook gently for 3 minutes. Turn the omelette immediately, like a thick pancake. Slide it onto a plate then replace it in the pan to cook on the other side for another 2 minutes. Cook the other 3 omelettes in the same way.
6. When the asparagus is cooked, remove from water, untie and drain on a rack. Divide into 4.
7. Slice the Emmenthal cheese thinly.
8. Set the oven at 220°C (425°F; gas mark 7) and butter a gratin dish.
9. Garnish each omelette with slices of Emmenthal cheese and roll around each portion of asparagus. Place these parcels in a gratin dish and put in the oven for 5 minutes so that the cheese melts. Serve immediately.

Serve ketchups and sauces separately. Garnish with slices of tomato.

# Salade d'Asperges et de Champignons
*Asparagus and Mushroom Salad*

*Serves 4. Preparation: 20 min*
*Cooking: 20 min*

★

- ○ 500g (1 lb 2 oz) blanched asparagus
- ○ 250g (9 oz) fresh button mushrooms
- ○ juice of 1 lemon
- ○ 2 tomatoes
- ○ 30ml (2 tbls) vinegar
- ○ 60ml (4 tbls) oil
- ○ 5ml (1 tsp) mild paprika
- ○ salt and pepper
- ○ 5ml (1 tsp) coarse salt

1. Place large saucepan three-quarters full of water over a high heat, and add coarse salt.
2. Scrape or peel and wash asparagus. Cut into pieces 3cm (1 inch) long – only use top two-thirds of each spear.
3. When the water boils plunge in the asparagus and simmer gently for about 20 minutes.
4. Meanwhile wash, dry and thinly slice the tomatoes. Trim the mushrooms and wipe with a cloth. Slice finely and sprinkle with lemon juice.
5. Strain asparagus in a colander.
6. Prepare vinaigrette with oil and vinegar. Add paprika, salt and pepper.
7. Mix tomatoes and asparagus in the salad bowl. Drain mushrooms and add them. Sprinkle with vinaigrette and put into refrigerator for 30 minutes.

# Ratatouille Sicilienne

*Ratatouille Sicilian-Style*

*Serves 4. Preparation: 20 min  Cooking: 50 min approx*

★★

- 3 aubergines
- 6 ripe tomatoes
- 2 red peppers
- 2 green peppers
- 2 large onions
- 50g (2 oz) pitted green olives
- 50g (2 oz) pitted black olives
- 1 garlic clove
- 75ml (5 tbls) oil
- 15ml (1 tbls) chopped parsley
- salt and pepper

1. Peel the onions and garlic and chop finely. Plunge the tomatoes into boiling water for 30 seconds, strain and hold them under cold running water, then peel. Cut them in half to remove seeds and chop roughly into cubes. Peel the aubergines, wash them and cut into cubes 2cm (1 inch) square. Wash peppers, cut in half lengthways, remove seeds and slice finely.
2. Heat the oil in a saucepan and lightly brown the garlic and onion. Then add the aubergines and peppers and seal them. Then add the tomatoes; season with salt and pepper. Cover the pan tightly and cook for 30 minutes over a low heat.
3. At the end of this time, slice the olives and add to the pan. Leave to simmer for 10 minutes with no lid, then sprinkle with parsley and serve hot or cold.

# Caponata

*Ratatouille with Celery and Olives*

*Serves 4. Preparation and cooking: 40 min*

★

- 4 aubergines
- 1 onion
- 2 sticks of celery
- 100g (4 oz) pitted green olives
- 100ml (3½ fl oz) wine vinegar
- 10ml (2 tsp) tomato concentrate
- 5ml (1 flat tsp) sugar
- 60ml (4 tbls) olive oil
- salt and pepper

1. Wash the aubergines; do not peel but cut into cubes 2cm (1 inch) square. Peel the onion and chop small. Clean and chop the celery. Slice the olives.
2. Heat some oil in a heavy pan and lightly brown the pieces of aubergine over a high heat, turning often. Remove from pan with a slotted spoon and put them on one side.
3. In the oil in which the aubergines were cooked lightly brown the onion and celery. Add the vinegar, sugar, tomato concentrate and olives. Mix well and return the aubergines to the pan. Add salt and pepper. Cook over a low heat for 10 minutes, then remove from heat.

Allow the ratatouille to cool and serve as a main course with slices of bread.

*Jerusalem artichokes, rather neglected nowadays, make a delicious purée. Peel them, wash and cut into cubes, and cook in salted boiling milk. After about 20 minutes, check cooking by piercing with the point of a knife. When cooked, drain and put through a sieve or blender to make a purée. Add salt, pepper and a knob of butter. The same quantity of potato purée may be added to this purée. To accompany game and grilled or roasted white meat, make the purée into rissoles and fry, or else half cook in milk and for the remaining time simmer in cream or a white sauce prepared with milk from the cooking. With cold meats, serve the artichokes cold with a vinaigrette dressing or luke-warm, prepared like potatoes with oil.*

# Barquettes d'Aubergines

*Serves 4. Preparation: 45 min Cooking: 20 min*

*Stuffed Aubergines with Cheese*

★★

- ○ **4 aubergines, not too small**
- ○ **40g (1¾ oz) dried mushrooms (cèpes)**
- ○ **1 egg**
- ○ **2 small sausages**
- ○ **100g (4 oz) soft white cheese: goat's milk or Ricotta**
- ○ **30ml (2 tbls) grated Gruyère or Parmesan cheese**
- ○ **1 garlic clove, finely chopped**
- ○ **45ml (3 tbls) oil**
- ○ **4 slices cheese for grilling**
- ○ **salt and pepper**

1. Wash, but do not peel the aubergines. Cut in two lengthways and arrange in a sieve, sprinkling salt between each layer of aubergines. Leave to drain for 30 minutes. Put mushrooms to soak in warm water.
2. At the end of this time, wash and wipe aubergines. Scoop out pulp and put on one side. Blanch aubergine shells for 5 minutes in salted boiling water. Strain.
3. Strain the mushrooms and chop finely. Skin the sausages and mash with a fork.
4. Mix the mushrooms and aubergine pulp with a fork in a dish. Add the chopped garlic, sausagemeat, soft white cheese and Gruyère cheese and beat in the egg. Add salt and pepper.
5. Set oven at 220°C (425°F; gas mark 7). Grease a gratin dish. Cut the grilling cheese in strips.
6. Stuff the aubergine shells and cover with cheese. Cook in oven for about 20 minutes until the cheese is golden brown. Serve very hot.

# Gâteau de Légumes à l'Origan

*Serves 4-6. Preparation: 10 min*
*Cooking: 1 hr 15 min*

*Vegetable Cake with Marjoram*

★★

- ○ **4 large aubergines**
- ○ **4 large courgettes**
- ○ **5 large ripe tomatoes**
- ○ **12 leaves fresh basil**
- ○ **5ml (1 tsp) marjoram**
- ○ **salt and pepper**
- ○ **200ml (7 fl oz) olive oil for frying**

1. Peel aubergines. Cut them into slices ½cm (⅛ inch) thick, lengthways. Wash courgettes and wipe them. Do not peel. Cut them like the aubergines. Wash tomatoes. Cut into slices ½cm (⅛ inch) thick.
2. Heat 100ml (3½ fl oz) olive oil in large frying pan and fry the slices of courgettes very lightly without allowing to brown, then the slices of aubergines. Let them drain on kitchen paper.
3. Set the oven at 195°C (375°F; gas mark 5). Lightly grease base and sides of a medium-sized casserole about 22cm (10 inches) in diameter. Put a layer of tomatoes on the bottom, then a layer of courgettes, then a layer of aubergines. Continue in this fashion until all the vegetables are used up. Finish with a layer of tomatoes. Put the basil leaves between each layer, sprinkle with marjoram and add salt and pepper.
4. Cover the pan and cook in oven for 1 hour. Then remove, take off lid and wait for 5 minutes before turning the 'cake' out on to a serving dish. Serve either hot or cold.

This delicious savoury dish can be used as a main course or as an accompaniment for roasts, especially roast lamb or roast pork.

*When buying courgettes, avoid those that are very dark green as they will be tasteless. If they are too big, they will have too many seeds. Choose smallish courgettes that are firm and shiny and never, never peel them before cooking or you will lose the best part of the vegetable.*

# Carottes aux Raisins de Smyrne

*Carrots with Sultanas*

*Serves 4. Preparation: 10 min Cooking: 1 hr*

★

○ **600g (1 lb 5 oz) new carrots**
○ **300g (11 oz) small new onions**
○ **150g (6 oz) sultanas**
○ **60g (2½ oz) butter**
○ **250ml (9 fl oz) white wine**
○ **100g (4 oz) cream**
○ **1 bay leaf**
○ **1 sprig thyme**
○ **salt and pepper**
○ **pinch cayenne pepper**

1. Wash the sultanas and leave to soak in cold water.
2. Peel and wash the carrots and onions. Drain the sultanas.
3. Melt the butter in a heavy pan and lightly brown the carrots and onions. Add salt, pepper, a pinch of cayenne pepper, the crushed thyme, bay leaf and sultanas. Cover with white wine and leave to cook covered over a very low heat for 45 minutes. Add fresh cream and mix together well. Cook for a further 10 minutes and serve immediately.

The sultanas may be replaced by muscatels. To give this dish a bitter-sweet flavour, substitute an equal amount of water and cider vinegar for the white wine.

# Purée de Carottes au Lait

*Purée of Carrots with Milk*

*Serves 4. Preparation and cooking: 1 hr*

★

○ **1kg (2¼ lb) carrots**
○ **½ litre (18 fl oz) milk**
○ **6 green peppercorns**
○ **salt and pepper**
○ **pinch nutmeg**

1. Peel, wash and dice the carrots. Put into a saucepan and cover with milk. Add salt, nutmeg and green peppercorns.
2. Cook without a lid for 35 to 40 minutes until all the milk has evaporated. Remove from the heat, leave to cool, and then put the contents of the saucepan through a blender.
3. Reheat the purée over a very low heat, turning with a wooden spoon to prevent the bottom from scorching, and serve.

This purée may be served alone or with other vegetable purées to accompany white meat or poultry.

# Soupe Paysanne

*Peasant-Style Soup*

*Serves 4. Preparation: 15 min Cooking: 40 min*

★ ★

○ **6 large carrots**
○ **4 small potatoes**
○ **2 large onions**
○ **2 turnips**
○ **3 leeks**
○ **1 celeriac**
○ **1 packet frozen peas**
○ **1 stock cube**
○ **¾ litre (27 fl oz) hot water**
○ **15ml (1 tbls) oil**
○ **20g (1 oz) butter**
○ **salt and pepper**

1. Peel and wash the carrots and cut into circles 1cm (½ inch) thick. Peel the onions and chop roughly. Wash and dice the celeriac and turnips.
2. Pour the oil into a large saucepan and add the carrots, onions, celeriac and turnips. Brown lightly.
3. Dissolve the stock cube in hot water. Pour into the pan and bring to the boil.
4. Peel, wash and quarter the potatoes. Peel and wash the leeks, and slice across finely. Place in pan with other vegetables and cook gently for 20 minutes.
5. At the end of this time, add the peas and simmer for another 15 minutes. Add the salt and pepper.
6. Stir in butter and serve hot.

# Cèpes à la Menthe

*Cèpes with Mint*

*Serves 4. Preparation: 10 min Cooking: 45 min*

★ ★

- ○ **500g (1 lb 2 oz) cèpes**
- ○ **2ml (½ tsp) thyme flowers**
- ○ **10 sprigs parsley**
- ○ **4 leaves fresh mint**
- ○ **2 peeled garlic cloves**
- ○ **100ml (3½ fl oz) dry white wine**
- ○ **15ml (1 tbls) fresh cream**
- ○ **45ml (3 tbls) oil**
- ○ **salt and pepper**

1. Clean the mushrooms without washing. Scrape stalks with a small knife and wipe the tops. Slice thinly.
2. Heat some oil in a pan. Add the mushrooms with the garlic cloves. Cook for 5 minutes over a high heat at first, then lower. Season with the salt, pepper and thyme. Sauté for 15 minutes.
3. Meanwhile, wash and wipe the parsley and mint and chop finely.
4. When the mushrooms have cooked for 15 minutes add the white wine and simmer until the liquid has completely evaporated, about 20 minutes.
5. Now sprinkle the parsley and mint over the mushrooms and add the cream. Reduce by cooking further before serving.

Cèpes prepared like this make the perfect accompaniment to roast lamb or game. Other chopped herbs may be used instead of mint.

# Cèpes à la Bordelaise

*Cèpes with Shallots*

*Serves 3-4. Preparation: 15 min Cooking: 20 min approx*

★

- ○ **500g (1 lb 2 oz) cèpes**
- ○ **3 shallots**
- ○ **45ml (3 tbls) olive oil**
- ○ **50g (2 oz) stale bread**
- ○ **15ml (1 tbls) chopped parsley**
- ○ **½ lemon**
- ○ **salt and pepper**

1. Take off mushroom stalks, scrape with a paring knife, and chop into small pieces. Wipe tops and slice thinly. Do not mix.
2. Remove the bread crusts. Grate the bread – you will need 30ml (2 tbls). Peel and chop shallots finely.
3. Heat the oil in a frying pan over a high heat and throw in the sliced mushrooms. Sauté for about 15 minutes, turning frequently until the juices have run and the mushrooms are lightly browned. Then add the chopped stalks, shallots and breadcrumbs. Season with salt and pepper. Sauté together for 5 minutes more and remove from heat.
4. Arrange the mushrooms on a serving dish, sprinkle with parsley, squeeze lemon juice over and serve immediately.

Cèpes prepared in this way (*à la bordelaise*) go perfectly with grills and with braised or roasted game. The shallots may be replaced with garlic cloves, as they do in Provence.

*Fennel, grown in the south of France and in Italy, is available from May to December. It may be eaten raw, finely sliced and dressed with a vinaigrette containing lemon juice. Or it may be added to other salads. Cooked fennel is a delicious accompaniment to all white meat and poultry. Be sure to blanch it first before cooking in butter or cream. Serve it sprinkled with herbs and grated cheese, or place under the grill to turn golden. The leaves of the best fennel are very green, and the bulb should be fleshy, round and very white.*

*Lovers of green vegetables who dislike the bitterness of spinach may like to learn of a ribless variety of seakale which resembles spinach in size and colour but has a sweet, very mild taste. It is becoming increasingly available as its popularity grows since, once tasted, you will want to try it again!*

# Artichauts à la Paysanne

*Artichokes Peasant-Style*

*Serves 4. Preparation: 20 min Cooking: 40 min*

★★

○ **8 artichokes**
○ **300g (11 oz) small onions**
○ **100g (4 oz) pitted green olives**
○ **250g (9 oz) ripe tomatoes**
○ **2 peeled garlic cloves**
○ **15ml (1 tbls) capers**
○ **juice of 1 lemon**
○ **45ml (3 tbls) oil**
○ **salt and pepper**

1. Wash tomatoes, cut into 4, put through sieve or blender. Put on one side. Wash and drain artichokes. Remove tough outer leaves and slice through remaining leaves halfway down. Remove choke. Soak artichokes in water with lemon juice added. Cut into 8. Peel onions. Chop together very finely garlic and one small onion.
2. Heat the oil in a heavy pan. Add to it the garlic and onion mixture, the artichokes, and the whole onions. Season with salt and pepper. Cook for 10 minutes over a low heat, turning often.
3. Pour the tomato purée into the pan. Cover and cook for a further 10 minutes before adding capers and olives. Allow to simmer for 20 minutes. Serve hot or cold.

# Artichauts en Beignets

*Artichoke Fritters*

*Serves 4. Preparation and cooking: 40 min approx*

★★

○ **8 small artichokes**
○ **2 eggs**
○ **200ml (7 fl oz) milk**
○ **80g (3¼ oz) flour**
○ **½ lemon**
○ **salt**
○ **oil for frying**

1. Wash artichokes and remove outer leaves. Slice through remaining leaves halfway down; leave 1cm (½ inch) stalk. Cut artichokes into 4, removing choke, and sprinkle with lemon juice. Blanch for 10 minutes in salted boiling water.
2. Meanwhile, prepare mixture for frying. In a bowl, mix the flour and milk, using a whisk to avoid lumps. Add eggs and salt. Mix again. When artichokes are blanched, strain them and add to the mixture.
3. Heat oil in a large frying pan. When smoke appears, drop in the artichoke fritters and cook until brown, about 3 minutes each. To ensure perfect cooking, do not put too many fritters into pan at the same time.
4. When fritters are well browned, place on absorbent paper and keep warm until ready to serve.

# Artichauts aux Crevettes

*Artichokes with Prawns*

*Serves 4. Preparation and cooking: 30 min*

★

○ **4 artichokes**
○ **200g (7 oz) peeled prawns**
○ **100ml (3½ fl oz) fresh cream**
○ **10ml (2 tsp) mustard**
○ **15ml (1 tbls) oil**
○ **10 sprigs parsley**
○ **6 stalks chives**
○ **1 sprig tarragon**
○ **1 lemon**
○ **salt and pepper**

1. Wash artichokes and remove the tough outer leaves. Slice through remaining leaves one-third from top. Spread centre leaves slightly and remove choke. Cut off stalk near the base. Rub with half a lemon. Cook for 20 minutes in salted boiling water.
2. Chop herbs. Cut prawns into rounds.
3. Put mustard, salt, pepper and juice of ½ lemon into a dish. Mix in oil and cream, beating with fork. Add the prawns and herbs.
4. When artichokes are ready, drain. Allow to cool and stuff with mixture. Serve cold.

# Chou au Vinaigre

*Serves 4. Preparation: 15 min Cooking: 40 min*

*Cabbage in Vinegar*

★

- ○ **1 cabbage or kale about 1kg (2¼ lb)**
- ○ **50g (2 oz) smoked bacon**
- ○ **1 peeled garlic clove**
- ○ **30ml (2 tbls) oil**
- ○ **100ml (3½ fl oz) vinegar**
- ○ **100ml (3½ fl oz) water**
- ○ **salt and pepper**

1. Take off the stem and any damaged leaves and cut the cabbage into four. Wash, then chop finely. Blanch the cabbage for 5 minutes in a large quantity of boiling, salted water and strain.
2. Dice the bacon.
3. Heat the oil in a large pan and lightly brown the whole garlic clove and the bacon. Add the cabbage and cook for 5 minutes, turning often. Pour in the water and vinegar, and season. Cover and cook for 25 minutes over a low heat, turning now and then. At the end of this time if any liquid is left in the pan reduce by cooking uncovered over a high heat for 5 minutes more.

Served very hot, this cabbage can accompany goose, duck, and all kinds of pork dishes, whether grilled or roasted.

# Chou Braisé à la Tomate

*Serves 4. Preparation: 10 min Cooking: 40 min*

*Braised Cabbage with Tomato*

★

- ○ **1 cabbage or kale about 800g (1¾ lb)**
- ○ **100g (4 oz) smoked bacon**
- ○ **6 ripe plum tomatoes**
- ○ **2 peeled garlic cloves**
- ○ **60ml (4 tbls) oil**
- ○ **salt and pepper**

1. Take off the stem and any damaged leaves and cut the cabbage into four. Chop well. Cut the bacon into sticks 0.5cm (¼ inch) thick.
2. Heat the oil in a pan and lightly brown the bacon and garlic. Then remove the garlic and add the cabbage. Mix well with the bacon, add salt and pepper and cover. Leave to cook for 10 minutes over a low heat.
3. Meanwhile, plunge the tomatoes into boiling water for 30 seconds. Drain and cool under a running tap. Peel, cut in half to remove the seeds, and chop roughly.
4. Add the tomatoes to the pan and stir in well. Cover again and leave to cook for a further 25 minutes.

Serve hot to accompany braised or roast pork, frankfurters, or grilled sausages, etc.

# Choux de Bruxelles à la Crème

*Serves 4. Preparation and cooking: 35 min*

*Brussels Sprouts with Cream*

★★

- ○ **800g (1¾ lb) Brussels sprouts**
- ○ **300g (11 oz) fresh cream**
- ○ **1 onion, chopped small**
- ○ **60g (2 oz) flour**
- ○ **15ml (1 tbls) flour**
- ○ **salt and pepper**

1. Wash and drain the sprouts, discarding the outer leaves. Cook for 15 to 20 minutes in boiling, salted water, until they are tender.
2. Melt 50g (2 oz) butter in a pan and lightly brown the chopped onion. Add the sprouts and sauté gently, adding salt and pepper. Pour in half the fresh cream. Stir well and cook for 10 minutes over a low heat.
3. Pour the other half of the cream into a saucepan, together with the remaining butter and flour. Beat with a whisk and cook for 5 minutes. Pour this sauce over the sprouts. Serve.

You may garnish this dish with gherkins and other small pickles.

# Épinards à la Tomate

*Serves 4. Preparation: 30 min Cooking: 10 min*

## Spinach with Tomatoes

★ ★

- ○ **1kg (2¼ lb) spinach**
- ○ **800g (1¾ lb) ripe tomatoes**
- ○ **30ml (2 tbls) oil**
- ○ **60g (2½ oz) grated Gruyère cheese**
- ○ **50g (2 oz) butter**
- ○ **2.5ml (½ tsp) granulated sugar**
- ○ **2.5ml (½ tsp) marjoram**
- ○ **salt and pepper**

1. Cut the stalks off the spinach, wash the leaves but do not drain. Put the leaves in a large saucepan, and cook in their own juice for 5 minutes over a high heat, covered, then strain in a colander, pressing to eliminate all the water. Plunge the tomatoes into boiling water for 30 seconds then drain them and put under cold running water. Peel, cut them in half, press to remove the seeds and chop roughly.
2. Heat the oil in a large frying pan and put in the tomatoes. Add the sugar, salt, pepper and marjoram. Cook for 5 minutes over a high heat, turning continuously, then remove from the heat.
3. Set the oven at 230°C (450°F; gas mark 8). Butter a large gratin dish with 20g (1 oz) butter. Put in the spinach, pour over the tomato sauce, sprinkle with cheese and dot with the rest of the butter. Put the dish in the oven for 10 minutes. Serve very hot from the dish.

# Épinards au Gratin

*Serves 4. Preparation and cooking: 40 min*

## Spinach Gratin

★ ★

- ○ **1kg (2¼ lb) spinach**
- ○ **250ml (9 fl oz) milk**
- ○ **15ml (1 tbls) cornflour**
- ○ **1 egg yolk**
- ○ **100g (4 oz) grated Gruyère cheese**
- ○ **40g (1¾ oz) butter**
- ○ **100ml (3½ fl oz) cold water**
- ○ **salt and pepper**
- ○ **pinch nutmeg**

1. Cut the stalks off the spinach and wash the leaves, then blanch them for 3 minutes in salted boiling water; strain in a colander, pressing on the leaves to eliminate all the water.
2. In a bowl, mix the egg yolk with 15ml (1 tbls) of milk. Mix the cornflour with 100ml (3½ fl oz) cold water.
3. Pour the rest of the milk into a saucepan. Add salt, pepper and nutmeg. Bring to the boil and add the diluted starch. Mix well and allow to boil for 2 minutes, turning continuously. Then remove from the heat, leave to cool and blend in the egg yolk and 70g (3 oz) of grated cheese. Mix again. Check the seasoning.
4. Set the oven at 220°C (425°F; gas mark 7). Grease a gratin dish with 20g (1 oz) butter. Arrange the spinach on it and cover with sauce. Sprinkle with the remaining cheese and dot with knobs of butter.
5. Put the dish in the oven for 15 minutes and serve immediately.

*Legumes (pulses) are beans, lentils and peas picked when ripe, then dried. The best legumes are those which are less than one year old. If they are older than this they will have deteriorated and become indigestible. They should always be soaked for several hours – at most overnight – before cooking to replace the water lost in the drying process. If you soak them for too long they may ferment and become completely uneatable. Unlike fresh vegetables, dried beans and pulses should be put into cold water to cook, which should cover them well as they will continue to swell during cooking. Once they have come to the boil, the heat should be turned very low and they should be left to simmer slowly. When the simmering begins, skim the surface, add a bouquet garni, an onion spiked with cloves, a carrot, and one or more cloves of garlic. Cover the pan and cook until tender. Do not allow to boil, otherwise they will burst. Add salt after 30 minutes of cooking. If the liquid dries up, add more water but it must be boiling, since cold water will arrest the cooking and harden the vegetables.*

*If they are prepared carefully like this, dried beans and pulses can be used as the basis for more elaborate recipes, or they can be served plain with a little butter or puréed. They can be prepared as a salad, served cold or lukewarm.*

# Chou-Fleur Froid aux Langoustines

*Serves 4. Preparation and cooking: 1 hr*

*Cold Cauliflower with Scampi*

★★

○ **1 large cauliflower**
○ **12 scampi**

*For the stock:*
○ **2 litres (3½ pints) cold water**
○ **1 litre (1¾ pints) dry white wine**
○ **100ml (3½ fl oz) vinegar**
○ **40g (2 oz) sea salt**
○ **2 carrots**
○ **1 medium-sized onion**
○ **10 peppercorns**
○ **2 cloves**
○ **1 bouquet garni consisting of: 10 sprigs parsley, 1 sprig thyme and 1 bay leaf**

*For the sauce:*
○ **250ml (9 fl oz) oil**
○ **2 egg yolks**
○ **5ml (1 tsp) mustard**
○ **juice of 1 lemon**
○ **100ml (3½ fl oz) fresh cream**
○ **salt**
○ **pinch curry powder**

1. Wash the cauliflower. Cook for 15 minutes by simmering gently, head downwards, in boiling salted water. Drain.
2. Meanwhile, prepare the court-bouillon. Peel and wash the carrots. Peel onion and spike with cloves. Put the water, wine, vinegar, onion, carrots, bouquet garni and pepper into a large saucepan. Bring to the boil, add salt and boil for 30 minutes. Then add the scampi. Cook for a further 5 minutes, turn off the heat, and allow to cool in the court-bouillon before straining.
3. Prepare the sauce. Put the egg yolks, salt, mustard and lemon juice into a bowl. Beat quickly with a whisk. Dribble the oil in slowly, beating all the time. When the mayonnaise is ready, fold in the fresh cream. Mix. Pour the sauce into a sauceboat and add a pinch of curry powder.
4. Place the cauliflower on a serving dish, and trickle a little sauce over. Surround with the scampi. The remaining sauce should be served separately.

You can enrich this dish with hard-boiled eggs and cold artichoke hearts. The scampi may be replaced by all kinds of shellfish: shrimps, king prawns, or crabs.

# Chou-Fleur aux Deux Paprikas

*Serves 4. Preparation and cooking: 40 min*

*Cauliflower with Two Kinds of Paprika*

★★

○ **1 large cauliflower**
○ **100g (4 oz) bacon**
○ **150g (6 oz) button mushrooms**
○ **150g (6 oz) fresh cream**
○ **60g (2½ oz) butter**
○ **10 chives**
○ **50g (2 oz) grated Gruyère cheese**
○ **5ml (1 tsp) mild paprika**
○ **5ml (1 tsp) strong paprika**
○ **salt and pepper**

1. Wash the cauliflower and separate it into individual flowerets. Cook for about 10 minutes in boiling salted water. Do not let them become mushy. Strain.
2. Meanwhile, cut the bacon into strips. Trim, wipe and slice the mushrooms.
3. Melt 40g (1¾ oz) butter in a heavy pan and sauté the bacon and mushrooms. Season with salt and pepper and the strong paprika. Add the cauliflower flowerets and brown them lightly, turning carefully.
4. Set the oven at 220°C (425°F; gas mark 7). Grease a gratin dish with the remaining butter and pour in the contents of the pan. Cover with fresh cream and the grated cheese and cook in the oven for 10 minutes.
5. Meanwhile, chop the chives. When the dish is cooked, garnish with the chives and the mild paprika. Serve immediately.

The button mushrooms may be replaced by flat-topped mushrooms, or any wild variety.

*To make what the French call potatoes* au diable *you need a special covered dish made of porous clay. Known as a 'devil', it consists of two vessels which fit into each other and is turned over during cooking, which is done over direct heat. The inside of the 'devil' is rubbed with garlic, and the potatoes are baked in their jackets with a sprig of thyme or rosemary and some bay leaves. They are eaten with butter or cream. The variety of potato most suited to this method of cooking is a particularly early kind known as Early Rose.*

# Lentilles à la Paysanne

*Serves 4. Preparation: 20 min Cooking: 1 hr 50 min*

## Lentils Peasant-Style

★★

○ **400g (14 oz) green lentils**
○ **200g (7 oz) smoked bacon**
○ **1 large onion**
○ **2 carrots**
○ **2 turnips**
○ **1 stick celery**
○ **1 bouquet garni consisting of:**
   **10 sprigs parsley, 1 bay leaf,**
   **1 sprig thyme**
○ **1 peeled garlic clove**
○ **40g (1¾ oz) butter**
○ **15ml (1 tbls) flour**
○ **salt and pepper**

1. Sort and wash the lentils. Put them in a large saucepan and cover with cold water. Bring to the boil over a low heat. Boil for 3 minutes then strain.
2. Peel and chop the onion well. Peel the carrots and the turnips, wash them and dice them as small as possible.
3. Melt the butter in a large pan and lightly brown the vegetables, then sprinkle with flour. Mix together with a wooden spoon and pour on 1 litre (1¾ pints) of water. Bring to the boil, then add the lentils, bacon and garlic.
4. Tie together the herbs for the bouquet garni. Clean the celery. Add both to the pan. Season. Pour in 2 litres (3½ pints) of water: this should cover the lentils well to allow them to swell up during cooking. Cover the pan and cook over a low heat for about 1 hour 30 minutes until the lentils are soft. Remove the bouquet garni and serve.

This dish can be enriched by adding braised or grilled pork sausages.

# Lentilles au Lard

*Serves 4. Preparation: 20 min Cooking: 1 hr 30 min*

## Lentils with Bacon

○ **400g (14 oz) green lentils**
○ **150g (6 oz) mild-cured bacon**
○ **1 medium-sized onion**
○ **2 cloves**
○ **1 bouquet garni consisting of:**
   **10 sprigs parsley, 1 bay leaf,**
   **1 sprig thyme**
○ **1 peeled garlic clove**
○ **salt and pepper**

1. Sort the lentils and wash them. Strain and put in a pan, cover well with cold water.
2. Peel the onion and spike it with the cloves. Tie up the bouquet garni. Put both into the pan and add the garlic. Bring to the boil over a very low heat. This will take about 45 minutes.
3. Cut the bacon into sticks about 1cm (½ inch) wide. As soon as the lentils begin to boil, add the bacon, salt, and pepper. Cover the pan and continue cooking over a low heat for about 45 minutes until the lentils are tender and almost all the liquid has evaporated.
4. Before serving, remove the onion and the bouquet garni.

Hot lentils make an excellent accompaniment to roast pork, grilled sausages or boiled salt pork. Hot or cold, seasoned with a vinaigrette dressing and chopped onions, they make a delicious salad.

*Broccoli: the name is Italian in origin and there are at least four different types in France. Two at least are quite common in Great Britain: purple broccoli and calabrese or green broccoli. This has dark green leaves arranged around tight heads or tiny buds on a central stem. Its taste, although sweeter, is like that of green cabbage. It is delicious in a salad, whether hot, warm or cold, seasoned with oil and vinegar or lemon. Purple broccoli is half-leaf, half-flower: smooth leaves, slightly blue-ish in colour, grow round a central stem surrounding one or more heads of the same colour, made up of hundreds of small buds which if allowed to grow would later open into beautiful yellow flowers.*

# Petits Oignons Glacés

*Serves 4. Preparation: 10 min Cooking: 1 hr 10 min*

*Glazed White Onions*

★

○ **1kg (2¼ lb) small white onions**
○ **60g (2½ oz) butter**
○ **45ml (3 tbls) vinegar**
○ **15ml (1 tbls) sugar**
○ **200ml (7 fl oz) water**
○ **salt**

1. Peel the onions and leave them whole. Heat the oil in a frying pan, add the butter and brown the onions lightly. Add salt and sprinkle with sugar. When the onions have caramelized add the vinegar and water.
2. Cover the pan and cook for 1 hour over a low heat, turning the onions now and then. At the end of this time reduce any liquid left in the pan by cooking uncovered over a high heat.

These flavoursome onions should be served as an accompaniment to roast meat, especially pork.

# Feuilleté aux Oignons

*Serves 4. Preparation and cooking: 1 hr*

*Flaky Onion Tart*

★★

○ **1.5kg (3¼ lb) small white onions (in a bunch)**
○ **60ml (4 tbls) oil**
○ **20g (¾ oz) butter**
○ **500g (18 fl oz) frozen flaky pastry**
○ **salt and pepper**

1. Thaw the pastry according to the instructions.
2. Trim and peel the onions, keeping at least 3cm (1 inch) of the green part; slice them very thin. Heat the oil in a frying pan and brown the onions. Season, cover the pan and continue cooking over a very low heat for 15 minutes.
3. Set the oven at 230°C (450°F; gas mark 8). Grease a rectangular oven tray.
4. Roll out the pastry so it is 0.5cm (1/6 inch) thick and place it on the oven tray, trimming the edges. Spread the pastry with the onions.
5. Put the tray in the oven for 20 minutes. Serve hot or warm.

# Oignons Nouveaux Confits

*Serves 6. Preparation: 15 min Cooking: 1 hr approx*

*Pickled Onions*

★

○ **1kg (2¼ lb) small pickling onions (about 50 onions)**
○ **100ml (3½ fl oz) malt vinegar**
○ **30ml (2 tbls) sultanas**
○ **30ml (2 tbls) sugar**
○ **30ml (2 tbls) oil**
○ **30ml (2 tbls) tomato concentrate**
○ **2 cloves**
○ **1 bay leaf**
○ **2ml (½ tsp) salt**

1. Peel the onions and cut off the tails.
2. Put the onions in a large pan and add the sultanas, vinegar, tomato concentrate, sugar, cloves, bay leaf and salt. Cover amply with cold water. Bring to the boil, stirring with a wooden spoon, then lower the heat and cook very gently for about 1 hour, without a lid. At the end of this time nearly all the liquid should have evaporated, leaving only a thick syrup to coat the onions.
3. Allow the onions to cool and place in the refrigerator. They can be eaten several hours later, the following day, or several days later.

These tangy onions may be served with all cold meats, or to start a meal on slices of toasted bread.

*You 'sweat' meat or vegetables by cooking them in a covered pan without any fat: they 'sweat' out all their own liquid. Shallots and onions are treated in this way, which is the opposite of allowing them to brown, without a lid, in butter, oil or some other fat.*

# Courgettes au Gratin
## *Gratin of Courgettes*

*Serves 4. Preparation and cooking: 50 min approx*

- ○ **1kg (2¼ lb) courgettes**
- ○ **500g (1 lb 2 oz) ripe tomatoes**
- ○ **150g (6 oz) grated Parmesan cheese**
- ○ **150g (6 oz) Gruyère cheese**
- ○ **30g (1¼ oz) flour**
- ○ **5ml (1 tsp) marjoram**
- ○ **45ml (3 tbls) olive oil**
- ○ **oil for frying**
- ○ **salt**

1. Cut off both ends of the courgettes. Wash and cut them lengthways into slices 1cm (½ inch) thick. Dip them in flour.
2. Heat oil in frying pan and lightly brown the courgette slices on both sides. Drain them on kitchen paper and add salt.
3. Wash tomatoes and pass them through a fine sieve or purée in the blender. Slice cheese finely.
4. Set oven at 220°C (425°F; gas mark 7).
5. Pour 30ml (2 tbls) olive oil in deep soufflé dish, then put a layer of fried courgettes, a layer of cheese and a layer of tomato purée. Add salt and marjoram. Continue thus until all the vegetables have been used up, finishing with a layer of tomato purée. Sprinkle the top with a spoonful of olive oil, and finish with Parmesan cheese.
6. Put the dish in the oven for 20 minutes and serve very hot.

# Courgettes Farcies au Thon
## *Courgettes Stuffed with Tuna*

*Serves 4. Preparation: 20 min Cooking: 45 min*

★★

- ○ **6 courgettes**
- ○ **1 tin 125g (4 oz) tuna**
- ○ **50g (2 oz) grated Gruyère cheese**
- ○ **15ml (1 tbls) chopped parsley**
- ○ **1 peeled garlic clove**
- ○ **1 egg**
- ○ **15ml (1 tbls) breadcrumbs**
- ○ **15ml (1 tbls) fresh cream**
- ○ **15ml (1 tbls) oil**
- ○ **200ml (7 fl oz) water**
- ○ **20g (1 oz) butter**
- ○ **salt and pepper**
- ○ **pinch nutmeg**

1. Cut off both ends of the courgettes, wash, but do not peel them. Cut in two lengthways. Hollow out the centre. Chop the flesh and put on one side.
2. Prepare the stuffing. Mash the tuna fish with a fork. Chop the garlic finely. Put these in a bowl with the courgette flesh, cheese, garlic and parsley and mix. Add cream and bind everything together with the egg. Season with salt, pepper and nutmeg. Mix again and stuff the courgette shells.
3. Set oven at 205°C (400°F; gas mark 6).
4. Oil an oven dish and arrange the courgettes in it. Scatter with breadcrumbs and dot with knobs of butter. Trickle the water round in the bottom of the dish.
5. Leave in the oven for 45 minutes. Add more water to the bottom of dish if necessary. Serve hot or cold.

*Pepper is the most familiar of all the spices. In various forms – black or white, as whole peppercorns or crushed or milled – it is used as a seasoning to dishes the world over. Peppercorns are the dried fruit of the pepper plant. Black pepper, the unhusked seed, possesses an additional piquancy. White pepper, which has been 'shelled' and washed and has a less subtle flavour, has the advantage of being invisible in white sauces such as béchamel or mayonnaise. Green or fresh pepper is milder, more subtle, and altogether more exotic. It is sold loose and can also be found bottled, tinned, deep frozen or freeze dried. Loose it is rather tasteless, whereas deep frozen it is perhaps at its best, and in its freeze-dried form it can be used like black pepper. It is difficult to mill though, being too light, but is easily crushed with the fingers.*

Mignonnette *or steak pepper is a mixture of black and white pepper ground together. Intended first and foremost for steak, it is also used to season oysters and spicy sauces. Cayenne pepper is derived from the pimento and is extremely piquant.*

# Fèves à la Paysanne
*Broad Beans Peasant-Style*

*Serves 4. Preparation: 20 min  Cooking: 1 hr*

★★

○ **1.5kg (3¼ lb) broad beans**
○ **100g (4 oz) smoked bacon**
○ **1 large onion**
○ **500g (1 lb) small new potatoes**
○ **4 small smoked sausages**
○ **30g (1 oz) butter**
○ **1 chicken stock cube**
○ **250ml (9 fl oz) hot water**
○ **salt and pepper**

1. Shell the beans and slip off the tough skins. Peel and chop the onion. Cut the bacon into sticks.
2. Melt the butter in a pan and lightly brown the onion and the bacon, then add the beans. Dissolve the stock cube in hot water. Pour the stock into the pan and simmer for 30 minutes over a low heat.
3. Meanwhile, scrape the potatoes, wash them, and leave to soak in cold water. After the beans have cooked for 30 minutes, strain the potatoes and put them into the pan. Add salt and pepper, and cook for a further 20 minutes.
4. At the end of this time slice the sausages into rounds across and add to the pan. Cook for another 10 minutes.
5. When the cooking is finished, very little stock should be left in the pan. If too much remains, remove the lid and reduce the liquid by rapid boiling. Serve this dish very hot.

# Fèves à la Romaine
*Broad Beans Roman-Style*

*Serves 4. Preparation: 15 min  Cooking: 50 min approx*

★★

○ **1.5kg (3¼ lb) fresh broad beans**
○ **100g (4 oz) raw ham or mild-cured bacon**
○ **2 lettuce hearts**
○ **1 large onion**
○ **1 chicken stock cube**
○ **250ml (9 fl oz) water**
○ **50g (2 oz) butter**
○ **salt and pepper**

1. Shell the beans and slip off their tough skins. Peel and chop the onion. Cut the ham (or bacon) into fine strips. Separate the lettuce leaves. Wash them and cut into strips 1cm (½ inch) wide.
2. Melt the butter in a heavy pan and lightly brown the onion and the ham. Add the beans. Add very little salt, as the stock will contain salt. Add pepper. Cook for 10 minutes over a low heat, turning the beans often, then add the lettuce. Mix well.
3. Dissolve the stock cube in hot water and pour into the pan. Cover. Leave to simmer for about 30 minutes, until the beans are tender. Serve very hot.

Toast may be served with this dish.

# Fèves aux Poivrons
*Broad Beans with Peppers*

*Serves 4. Preparation: 10 min  Cooking: 55 min*

★

○ **1.5kg (3¼ lb) fresh broad beans**
○ **1 red pepper**
○ **1 large onion**
○ **30g (1¼ oz) butter**
○ **100ml (3½ fl oz) water**
○ **2 pinches sugar**
○ **salt and pepper**

1. Shell the beans and slip off their tough skins. Simmer the beans gently for 30 minutes in boiling, salted water.
2. Meanwhile, wash the peppers, cut them in half lengthways and take out the seeds. Cut them into thin strips. Peel and chop the onion finely.
3. Put the butter into a pan and lightly brown the onions and the peppers over a low heat.
4. Strain the beans and put them into the pan. Add the water and the sugar. Add salt and pepper. Simmer uncovered over a low heat for 15 minutes, adding a little water if necessary. Serve very hot.

# Haricots Frais au Lard

*Serves 4. Preparation and cooking: 1 hr 50 min approx*

## *Fresh Haricot Beans with Bacon*

★ ★

- ○ **1kg (2¼ lb) haricot beans (in pods)**
- ○ **100g (4 oz) smoked bacon**
- ○ **2 medium-sized onions**
- ○ **20g (¾ oz) butter**
- ○ **30ml (2 tbls) oil**
- ○ **1 stock cube**
- ○ **salt and pepper**

1. Shell and wash the haricot beans and put them into a large saucepan, covering with plenty of cold water. Add salt. Cook covered over a low heat for about 1 hour until tender.
2. At the end of this time, peel the onions and cut them into thick circles. Cut the bacon into strips 1cm (½ inch) wide.
3. Heat the oil in a heavy pan, add the butter, then the onions and bacon. Lightly brown over a low heat.
4. Strain the haricot beans, keeping back 250ml (9 fl oz) of the cooking water. Pour this over the stock cube.
5. Put the beans into the dish; mix in the bacon strips and the onions with a wooden spoon, then add the stock. Add salt and pepper, and mix.
6. Cook uncovered over a medium heat for about 20 minutes until the stock has completely evaporated. Serve very hot.

# Haricot Verts au Yaourt

*Serves 4. Preparation: 10 min Cooking: 30 min*

## *French Beans with Yogurt*

- ○ **750g (1 lb 10 oz) French beans**
- ○ **1 large onion**
- ○ **150g (6 oz) cooked ham**
- ○ **2 eggs**
- ○ **1 carton yogurt**
- ○ **50g (2 oz) grated Gruyère cheese**
- ○ **1 garlic clove**
- ○ **15ml (1 tbls) chopped parsley**
- ○ **30ml (2 tbls) oil**
- ○ **20g (¾ oz) butter**
- ○ **5ml (1 tsp) mild paprika**
- ○ **salt and pepper**

1. Top and tail, wash and drain the French beans. Cook the beans in salted, boiling water for 10 minutes; they should remain slightly crunchy. Strain.
2. Meanwhile, peel the garlic and onion and chop them very small. Cut the ham into thin slices.
3. Heat some oil in a frying pan and lightly brown the garlic, onion and ham. Add the French beans and cook for 5 minutes, stirring well, then sprinkle with chopped parsley.
4. Set the oven at 220°C (425°F; gas mark 7).
5. Butter a gratin dish and put the beans in it.
6. Beat the eggs well in a bowl, and add the yogurt, half the cheese, and the paprika. Season. Pour this mixture onto the beans. Sprinkle with the remaining cheese.
7. Put the dish in the oven for 15 minutes and serve immediately.

*Green vegetables cooked in boiling water – French beans, peas, spinach, asparagus – should be cooked only for a short time so that they remain crunchy. To do this, plunge them into a large amount of salted boiling water – 10g-20g (½ oz-¾ oz) sea salt per litre (1¾ pints) water – and boil hard without a lid. Watch the cooking carefully to make sure the vegetables are not overcooked but remain firm. Strain them straight away, season, and serve immediately. Green vegetables prepared in this way, served with a knob of butter and chopped herbs and with no other seasoning, make a delicious dish.*

*If the vegetables are not to be served immediately, strain them just the same, and plunge them into a basin of cold – even iced – water, then strain again. Before serving, plunge the vegetables a second time into boiling water to reheat them without actually re-cooking them. Treated this way, the vegetables will retain their colour and their crunchiness.*

# Petits Pois Frais au Lard

*Serves 4. Preparation: 15 min Cooking: 30 min*

### Fresh Green Peas with Bacon

★

- ○ **1kg (2¼ lb) unshelled peas**
- ○ **100g (4 oz) smoked bacon**
- ○ **1 onion**
- ○ **25g (1 oz) butter**
- ○ **1 stock cube**
- ○ **250ml (9 fl oz) hot water**
- ○ **salt and pepper**
- ○ **1 small red pepper (optional)**

1. Shell the peas. Peel the onion and chop well. Cut the bacon into thin sticks. Wash the red pepper, cut in two to remove the seeds, and slice thinly.
2. Melt the butter in the frying pan and lightly brown the onions and bacon over a very low heat.
3. Dissolve the stock cube in hot water and pour into the pan. Season. Add the peas and the red pepper, and cook for about 20 minutes until the peas are tender. Serve hot.

# Purée de Petits Pois

*Serves 4. Preparation and cooking: 20 min*

### Purée of Peas

★★

- ○ **1 large packet 1kg (2¼ lb) frozen peas**
- ○ **30ml (2 tbls) fresh cream**
- ○ **50g (2 oz) butter**
- ○ **2.5ml (½ tsp) granulated sugar**
- ○ **salt and pepper**

1. Cook the peas according to the instructions.
2. When they are cooked, pass through a sieve or blender to purée, making sure that all the skins are removed.
3. Put the purée into a saucepan over a very low heat, add the butter and the cream, stirring constantly with a wooden spoon to prevent the bottom from burning. Add sugar, salt and pepper and serve immediately.

This delicate purée perfectly accompanies all game birds and roast poultry.

# Jardinière d'Avril

*Serves 4. Preparation: 20 min Cooking: 45 min approx*

### Casserole of Spring Vegetables

★★

- ○ **500g (1 lb 2 oz) unshelled peas**
- ○ **250g (9 oz) small new carrots**
- ○ **250g (9 oz) new turnips**
- ○ **20 small white onions, or large spring onions**
- ○ **1 small lettuce**
- ○ **15ml (1 tbls) oil**
- ○ **80g (3¼ oz) butter**
- ○ **2.5ml (½ tsp) granulated sugar**
- ○ **100ml (3½ fl oz) water**
- ○ **salt**

1. Shell the peas. Peel the onions. Remove the outer leaves of the lettuce, wash and quarter. Scrape the carrots, wash them and cut into 4 lengthways. Peel, wash and dice the turnips into cubes 1cm (¼ inch) square. Put the vegetables on one side, keeping separate.
2. Heat the oil in a thick pan, then add the butter. As soon as it has melted, add the onions and the carrots. Sweat for about 10 minutes over a low heat without allowing them to brown, then add the lettuce and let it cook for 3 minutes before adding the peas and turnips. Season with salt and sugar and mix all together well.
3. Add the water to the pan. Cover, and leave to cook over a low heat without interruption for 30 minutes.
4. At the end of this time, remove the lid. The vegetables should be cooked, but not overcooked – slightly crunchy. If any liquid remains in the pan, increase the heat and reduce it for several minutes, without a lid.

This delicious spring casserole goes with all grilled or roast meat.

*To make Potatoes Savoyard, follow the recipe for Potatoes Dauphinois, but omit the garlic. Replace the milk and cream with chicken stock and sprinkle each layer of potatoes with grated Gruyère cheese.*

*Haricots Frais au Lard (p129)*

# Pois Chiches à la Paysanne

*Serves 4. Preparation: 10 min Cooking: 2 hr 20 min*

## Chickpeas Peasant-Style

★

- ○ **500g (1 lb 2 oz) chickpeas**
- ○ **1 large onion**
- ○ **250g (9 oz) smoked bacon**
- ○ **500g (1 lb 2 oz) potatoes**
- ○ **salt and pepper**

*Bouquet garni:*
- ○ **5 sprigs parsley**
- ○ **1 bay leaf**
- ○ **1 sprig thyme**
- ○ **3 cloves**

1. The day before: put the chickpeas to soak in a large pan of cold water.
2. The next day cut the bacon into sticks, peel the onion and spike it with the cloves. Tie the bouquet garni together.
3. Drain the chickpeas and put them into a heavy pan. Cover well with cold water and add the bouquet garni, the onion and the bacon. Allow to cook, covered, for 2 hours on a low heat.
4. At the end of this time, remove the bouquet garni and the onion. Peel, wash, and quarter the potatoes. Add to the pan and season. Cook for a further 20 minutes and serve very hot.

# Pois Chiches à la Milanaise

*Serves 4. Preparation: 15 min Cooking: 2 hr 20 min*

## Chickpeas Milanese

★ ★

- ○ **300g (11 oz) chickpeas**
- ○ **100g (4 oz) smoked bacon**
- ○ **1 onion**
- ○ **1 carrot**
- ○ **1 celery heart**
- ○ **1 garlic clove**
- ○ **200g (8 oz) pork fat**
- ○ **50g (2 oz) grated Parmesan or Gruyère cheese**
- ○ **12 slices toast**

*Bouquet garni:*
- ○ **1 sprig thyme**
- ○ **1 bay leaf**
- ○ **10 sprigs parsley**

1. The day before: put the chickpeas to soak in a large pan of cold water.
2. The following day cut the bacon into sticks, chop the garlic, cut the pork fat into pieces about 3cm (1 inch) long by 2cm (¾ inch) wide. Peel and wash the carrot, onion and celery.
3. Put the bacon into a heavy pan together with the onion, celery, garlic, bouquet garni and pork fat. Cover with water. Add salt and cook for 30 minutes, then leave to cool.
4. Drain the chickpeas, then add them to the pan. Add 2 litres (3½ pints) of water, and cover.
5. Cook over a low heat for 2 hours. Serve hot with toast and grated cheese.

# Pois Chiches aux Travers de Porc

*Serves 4. Preparation and cooking: 2 hr 10 min*

## Chickpeas with Pork Ribs

★ ★

- ○ **500g (1 lb 2 oz) chickpeas**
- ○ **500g (1 lb 2 oz) ribs of pork**
- ○ **1 thick rasher 50g (2 oz) smoked bacon**
- ○ **2.5ml (½ tsp) rosemary**
- ○ **4 sage leaves**
- ○ **2 peeled garlic cloves**
- ○ **60ml (4 tbls) oil**
- ○ **salt and pepper**

1. The day before: put the chickpeas to soak in a large pan of cold water.
2. The following day drain the chickpeas and put them in a large saucepan with the pork ribs, half the rosemary, 2 sage leaves and 1 garlic clove. Cover with cold water. Add salt and cook for 1 hour 30 minutes by simmering slowly.
3. 15 minutes before the end, cut the rasher of bacon into four. Pour the oil into the pan, add the bacon and brown it lightly. Add the second garlic clove, the rest of the sage and the rosemary, and brown everything lightly.
4. When the chickpeas and pork are cooked, drain them, reserving 200ml (7 fl oz) of the stock.
5. Add the chickpeas and the pork to the pan, pour in stock, and season. Leave to cook for 30 minutes over a low heat. Serve hot.

# Poivrons Farcis au Fromage
## Stuffed Peppers with Cheese Sauce

*Serves 4. Preparation and cooking: 1 hr approx*

★★

- ○ **4 large peppers**
- ○ **5ml (1 tsp) anchovy paste**
- ○ **100g (4 oz) fresh cream**
- ○ **100g (4 oz) grated Gruyère cheese**
- ○ **30ml (2 tbls) vodka, gin or aquavit**
- ○ **30g (1¼ oz) butter**
- ○ **15ml (1 tbls) flour**
- ○ **salt and pepper**
- ○ **pinch nutmeg**

1. Wash the peppers. Slice off the top quarter and remove the seeds.
2. Melt the butter in a saucepan, add the flour, stirring constantly, then the anchovy paste, fresh cream and spirit. Continue to stir for 5 minutes. Blend in the cheese. Season with salt, pepper and nutmeg. Cook over a low heat for 10 minutes, then leave to cool.
3. Set the oven at 205°C (400°F; gas mark 6). Oil a gratin dish.
4. Fill the peppers with the cheese sauce and arrange in the dish. Cook for 40 minutes and serve hot.

# Poivrons Braisés aux Câpres
## Braised Peppers with Capers

*Serves 4. Preparation: 10 min Cooking: 40 min*

- ○ **1.5kg (3¼ lb) red and green peppers**
- ○ **60g (2½ oz) capers**
- ○ **8 anchovy fillets, canned**
- ○ **150ml (5 fl oz) oil**
- ○ **50g (2 oz) stale bread**
- ○ **pepper**

1. Wash and quarter the peppers, removing the seeds and stalk, then cut each quarter into 3 pieces. Drain the capers and chop the anchovies.
2. Heat the oil in a heavy pan and brown the peppers lightly, turning them often. Add the anchovies and capers. Cover and cook for 30 minutes over a very low heat, stirring now and then.
3. When the peppers are cooked, grate the bread and add the breadcrumbs to the peppers. Mix in well and remove from the heat. Season with pepper.
4. Serve hot, warm or cold.

These peppers can be served on their own, or as an accompaniment to roast pork or veal, or grilled or fried fresh tuna fish.

# Poivrons Farcis au Jambon
## Peppers Stuffed with Ham

*Serves 4. Preparation: 20 min Cooking: 40 min*

★★

- ○ **4 red or green peppers**
- ○ **150g (6 oz) cooked ham**
- ○ **100g (4 oz) sausagemeat**
- ○ **2 eggs**
- ○ **2 large ripe tomatoes**
- ○ **50g (2 oz) stale bread**
- ○ **50g (2 oz) grated Gruyère cheese**
- ○ **60ml (4 tbls) breadcrumbs**
- ○ **15ml (1 tbls) oil**
- ○ **salt and pepper**
- ○ **pinch nutmeg**

1. Wash the peppers, and slice off the top quarter, discarding the cap and seeds. Chop the ham. Grate the bread. Plunge the tomatoes into boiling water for 30 seconds, then drain them and hold under cold running water; peel. Cut the tomatoes in half to remove the seeds, and mash roughly with a fork.
2. Mash the sausagemeat in a bowl and add the ham and the tomatoes. Then blend in the eggs and add half the breadcrumbs and 30ml (2 tbls) of grated cheese. Season with salt and a little pepper. Add the nutmeg and stir together well.
3. Set the oven at 205°C (400°F; gas mark 6). Oil a gratin dish.
4. Stuff the peppers with the filling and sprinkle with the rest of the cheese, then the breadcrumbs. Arrange on the dish and cook for 40 minutes. Serve them hot, or very cold.

*To enjoy vegetables* croques-au-sel, *steep them in coarse sea salt with a pinch of paprika added, which gives them a pleasant pink colour. Serve them with thick slices of bread and butter.*

# Pommes de Terre au Lait et à la Crème

*Potatoes with Milk and Cream*

*Serves 4.*
*Preparation: 10 min  Cooking: 1 hr*

★

○ **800g (1¾ lb) potatoes**
○ **½ litre (18 fl oz) milk**
○ **200g (7 oz) fresh cream**
○ **salt and pepper**

1. Choose long potatoes that will remain firm. Peel and wash, and slice across into rounds 3mm (⅛ inch) thick. Wipe them and sprinkle with salt and ground pepper.
2. Boil the milk in a saucepan, throw in the potatoes in small batches and bring to the boil again. Cover and leave to cook for 15 minutes over a very low heat.
3. At the end of this time, the potatoes should have absorbed all the milk. Add the cream and leave to cook over a low heat for 40 minutes more, half-covering the saucepan.

Serve these delicious boiled potatoes as they are or garnish them with herbs to accompany roast or braised meat. If you like you may serve them *au gratin*: pour into a greased dish, sprinkle with grated cheese and put under the grill or in a hot oven for 10 minutes until golden.

# Purée aux Deux Fromages

*Potato Purée with Two Kinds of Cheese*

*Serves 4. Preparation and cooking: 1 hr 10 min*

★★

○ **700g (1½ lb) potatoes**
○ **100g (4 oz) sausagemeat**
○ **150g (6 oz) tomme de Savoie cheese**
○ **50g (2 oz) grated Gruyère cheese**
○ **3 eggs**
○ **15ml (1 tbls) breadcrumbs**
○ **50g (2 oz) butter**
○ **salt and pepper**
○ **pinch nutmeg**

1. Wash the potatoes but do not peel them. Put in a large saucepan and cover with cold water. Bring to the boil, add salt, and simmer gently for about 20 minutes (test with the point of a knife to see if they are cooked).
2. Meanwhile, mash the sausagemeat with a fork. Dice the tomme de Savoie and mix with the sausagemeat. Add the grated Gruyère cheese.
3. When the potatoes are cooked, drain and leave on one side to cool. When you can handle them, peel them and grate them over the dish. Mix everything together very well, and beat in the eggs. Add salt, pepper and nutmeg, and mix again.
4. Set the oven at 205°C (400°F; gas mark 6).
5. Grease a mould or soufflé dish with 20g (¾ oz) butter and scatter it with breadcrumbs. Pour in the mixture and dot with knobs of butter. Cook for 30 minutes and serve hot.

*It is helpful, if cooking chips, to have a deep fryer with a thermostat, or else you can buy a thermometer that you can plunge into the pan while the oil is heating up. Peel, wash and wipe the potatoes, and cut them into sticks 1cm (½ inch) thick for chips or 3mm (⅛ inch) thick for allumettes. Put the potatoes in a frying basket. Heat the oil to 170°C and plunge the basket into the boiling oil. Leave the chips to cook for 5 minutes, then drain and leave to cool. Bring the oil back to a temperature of 170°C (it will have fallen to about 150°C) and plunge the chips in a second time, for 3 to 5 minutes according to their thickness and their quality. When they have browned, drain them, sprinkle with salt and serve immediately.*

*What happens when you cook chips this way? On first coming into contact with the oil an impenetrable skin forms around each chip which seals in almost all the moisture. At the end of this first immersion, the chip is virtually cooked. When it is plunged in the second time, the outside layer becomes crisp and golden; at the same time the chip is puffed up by the water trapped inside. Make sure the oil never smokes and never reaches 180°C. At this temperature even the purest of oils decomposes, smokes and becomes toxic.*

*Petits Pois Frais au Lard (p130)* ▶

# Pommes Dentelle

*Lacy Potato Cakes (Dentelles)*

*Serves 4. Preparation: 15 min Cooking: 20 min*

★★

○ **600g (1 lb 5 oz) potatoes**
○ **50g (2 oz) butter, oil or goose fat**
○ **salt**

1. This recipe really does require firm, waxy potatoes. Peel, wash and wipe the potatoes in a cloth.
2. At the last minute slice the potatoes as finely as possible, as if you were making crisps (use an electric slicer if possible). Put the slices in a bowl.
3. Heat 20g (1 oz) butter, oil or goose fat in a frying pan. With a large spoon add the potato slices, a few at a time, and spread them out into a thin layer so that not more than 3 or 4 are overlapping.
4. Over a moderate heat lightly brown the potato cake on one side, then with a spatula, turn it over to brown on the other; 5 or 6 minutes in all.
5. Place on a plate and keep hot while the next potato cakes are cooking. By using two frying pans you can cook two potato cakes at a time. Add salt at the end of cooking. The potato cakes should be so thin that the pattern on the plate is visible through them. To avoid breaking them, use a small non-stick pan, at most 22cm (8½ inches) in diameter. You can of course make them thicker, but the pan should be covered as soon as the first side is golden to speed up the cooking.

These potato cakes have a very delicate flavour and can be used to accompany any roast meat or casserole.

# Tentation de Jansson

*Jansson's Potatoes with Cream and Anchovies*

*Serves 4. Preparation: 30 min Cooking: 1 hr approx*

★★

○ **1kg (2¼ lb) medium-sized potatoes**
○ **3 large onions**
○ **16 fillets marinated Norwegian anchovies**
○ **150g (6 oz) fresh cream**
○ **100ml (3½ fl oz) milk**
○ **80g (3¼ oz) butter**
○ **30ml (2 tbls) white breadcrumbs**
○ **salt and pepper**

1. Peel the onions and chop them finely.
2. Melt 50g (2 oz) butter in a frying pan and lightly brown the onions over a very low heat.
3. Peel the potatoes, wash and slice.
4. Set the oven at 205°C (400°F; gas mark 6). Grease a gratin dish with 20g (1 oz) butter and put in a layer of potatoes, then a layer of onions, and a layer of anchovies. Continue until all the ingredients are used up, finishing with a layer of potatoes.
5. Heat the milk in a saucepan, add the fresh cream and bring to the boil. Add salt and pepper. Pour this mixture over the potatoes. Sprinkle with breadcrumbs and dot with knobs of butter.
6. Put in the oven for 1 hour. Serve hot.

If no Norwegian anchovies, which are preserved in a slightly sweet brine are available, use salted anchovies instead.

*If you have any vegetable purée to use up, you can always make a gratin or better still, a soufflé or pie, following the recipe for Soufflé of Artichoke Hearts or for Baked Pumpkin. If there is a great deal left over, you can mix with another vegetable. Certain combinations are especially delicious: pumpkin-celery; cauliflower-French beans; peas-spinach.*

# Scaroles Braisées aux Poireaux

*Serves 4. Preparation: 10 min  Cooking: 25 min*

## *Braised Endives with Leeks*

★

○ **2 endives**
○ **6 medium-sized leeks**
○ **60g (2½ oz) butter**
○ **1 stock cube**
○ **100ml (3½ fl oz) hot water**
○ **salt and pepper**

1. Pull apart the leaves of the endives and wash them with plenty of water. Clean the leeks: you should keep most of the green part. Slice both vegetables finely.
2. Melt the butter in a pan, add the vegetables and cook them for 10 minutes over a low heat. Season.
3. Dissolve the stock cube in boiling water and pour into the pan. Cook covered for 15 minutes.
4. At the end of this time, if too much juice remains, reduce over a high heat, stirring all the time. Serve hot.

These braised endives are very good served with boiled or grilled meat.

# Laitues Braisées à la Moelle

*Serves 4. Preparation: 15 min  Cooking: 20 min*

## *Braised Lettuces with Marrow*

★ ★

○ **4 good-sized lettuces**
○ **100g (4 oz) beef marrow**
○ **60g (2½ oz) butter**
○ **salt and pepper**

1. The day before: cut the marrow into slices 0.5cm (⅛ inch) thick, put in a lightly salted bowl of water and leave in the refrigerator overnight.
2. The next day wash the lettuces whole, discarding any withered leaves. Plunge into boiling, salted water for 3 minutes. Drain in a colander, pressing on them lightly to squeeze out all the water.
3. Set the oven at 205°C (400°F; gas mark 6). Grease a gratin dish with 30g (1¼ oz) butter. Drain the slices of marrow.
4. Gently open out the lettuce leaves, without separating, and season the hearts with salt and pepper. Slip a slice of beef marrow between each leaf and close the lettuces up.
5. Arrange the lettuces on the gratin dish and dot with knobs of butter. Cover the dish with a sheet of greaseproof paper or foil.
6. Place in the oven for 20 minutes, remove the cover and serve straight away.

*Fairly difficult to find today are Japanese artichokes, which resemble corkscrews and are covered with a light-brown skin, like a new potato. These roots, originally from Japan, were not cultivated in France until 1882. Their taste is similar to salsify but they are much more tender. If you do manage to get some, wash them and cut off both ends, then put them in a cloth with 2 large handfuls of coarse salt. Roll the cloth round them and twist from left to right and back again. This movement enables the coarse salt grains to rub the peel off. Then wash again, and blanch for 10 minutes in boiling salted water to prevent discoloration during cooking. Strain and sauté in butter in a frying pan for 10 to 15 minutes. Sprinkle with salt, pepper, parsley or chopped herbs before serving. They can also be served with a cream sauce or baked in the oven with a béchamel sauce and grated Gruyère cheese.*

# Tomates Farcies au Riz

*Serves 4. Preparation and cooking: 50 min*

*Tomatoes Stuffed with Rice*

★★

- ○ **8 large tomatoes**
- ○ **40g (1¾ oz) butter**
- ○ **120ml (8 tbls) rice**
- ○ **1 garlic clove, chopped small**
- ○ **15ml (1 tbls) chopped parsley**
- ○ **50g (2 oz) grated Gruyère cheese**
- ○ **15ml (1 tbls) oil**
- ○ **salt and pepper**

1. Wash the tomatoes and slice off across one-quarter of the way from the top. Hollow out the centre with a small spoon and reserve the flesh. Salt the inside of the tomatoes and put them upside down on a plate to 'sweat'.
2. Chop the flesh coarsely.
3. Melt the butter in a saucepan and add the chopped tomato, parsley and garlic. Cook for 15 minutes over a medium heat and purée this sauce in a sieve or blender. Add the rice and half the cheese and mix together. Season and remove from the heat.
4. Set the oven at 220°C (425°F; gas mark 7). Oil an oven dish.
5. Stuff the tomatoes with the mixture and sprinkle with the remaining Gruyère cheese. Arrange the tomatoes in the dish and place in the oven for 20 minutes, the time necessary to cook the rice.
6. Serve this dish hot, or very cold.

# Tomates à la Provencale

*Serves 4. Preparation: 5 min  Cooking: 1 hr 15 min approx*

*Tomatoes with Garlic and Parsley*

★

- ○ **6 good-sized ripe tomatoes**
- ○ **2 garlic cloves**
- ○ **5ml (1 tsp) chopped parsley**
- ○ **200ml (7 fl oz) olive oil**
- ○ **5ml (1 tsp) sugar**
- ○ **salt and pepper**

1. Wash the tomatoes and cut in half, removing the seeds. Heat the oil in a large frying pan and put in the tomatoes, with the cut surface face downwards. Cover the pan and cook for about 15 minutes over a high heat to ensure that the tomatoes give out all their liquid.
2. Meanwhile, peel and chop the garlic. Mix with the chopped parsley.
3. After 15 minutes of cooking, remove the lid and take the pan from the heat. Turn the tomatoes over carefully and sprinkle each one with 2 pinches of sugar, 3 pinches of garlic and parsley, and 1 pinch of salt and pepper.
4. Put the pan back on a very low heat, cover and cook for 1 hour. When the water from the tomatoes has evaporated, add a few spoonfuls of cold water as necessary. If the tomatoes are large, they may need a further 15 minutes' cooking. Traditionally, the tomatoes should be well-cooked and wrinkled.

These tomatoes can also be cooked in a well-oiled dish containing a little water and placed in a hot oven, but this is not the way it is done in Provence. The garlic and parsley mixture may be replaced by butter and chopped parsley, as they do in Lyons. Or you can season the tomatoes with chopped herbs.

*Big round (Marmande) tomatoes can be eaten raw or cooked. The plum variety, which are smaller and longer, are delicious in salads when slightly green, and make wonderful sauces when they are very ripe. To peel them easily, plunge into a saucepan of boiling water for 20 to 30 seconds, then place under cold water: the skin will slide off. Remove the seeds by cutting them in half horizontally, and pressing very gently in the palm of the hand. Do this when preparing tomatoes for salads, stuffings, sauces, casseroles and so on.*

*Poivrons Farci au Fromage (p133)*

# Crème Panachée Chocolat-Orange
## Chocolate and Orange Cream Dessert

*Serves 2. Preparation and cooking: 30 min*
*2 hr before serving* ★

- ○ **400ml (14 fl oz) orange juice**
- ○ **200ml (7 fl oz) milk**
- ○ **15ml (1 tbls) unsweetened cocoa**
- ○ **60ml (4 tbls) cornflour**
- ○ **90ml (6 tbls) sugar**

1. Prepare the orange cream: put 60ml (4 tbls) of sugar together with 45ml (3 tbls) of cornflour in a medium-sized saucepan; mix well and gradually pour in the orange juice, stirring all the time. Place the saucepan over a medium heat and bring to the boil; boil for 1 minute, stirring continuously; then remove from the heat.
2. Prepare the chocolate cream: put the cocoa, 30ml (2 tbls) of sugar and 15ml (1 tbls) of cornflour in a small saucepan. Mix well, then gradually add the cold milk, stirring all the time. Place over a medium heat and bring to the boil. Boil for 1 minute, stirring continuously, and remove from the heat.
3. Pour into two tall, straight glasses in the following manner: first pour the orange cream into the bottom of each glass, which should be held at a slight angle. Leave the glasses in the freezer for 5 minutes, keeping them tilted; then remove, and pour half the chocolate cream into each glass, still at an inclined angle. Put them back in the freezer for 5 minutes. Now set the glasses upright and pour in the rest of the orange cream. Place in the refrigerator for at least 2 hours before serving.

Just before serving, decorate with maraschino cherries. You can make the same dessert with different flavoured creams, such as pineapple, bilberry, tangerine or lemon.

# Crème Soufflée aux Quatre Parfums
## Cream Soufflé with Four Flavourings

*Serves 6. Preparation and cooking: 20 min*
*2 hr before serving* ★★

- ○ **¾ litre (27 fl oz) milk**
- ○ **15ml (1 tbls) good quality instant coffee**
- ○ **30ml (2 tbls) crystallized caramel**
- ○ **45ml (3 tbls) unsweetened cocoa**
- ○ **2.5ml (½ tsp) powdered vanilla**
- ○ **5 eggs**
- ○ **120g (4¾ oz) caster sugar**

1. Put the coffee, cocoa, caramel and vanilla in a saucepan. Mix all the ingredients together and pour the milk in gradually, stirring all the time. Place over a low heat, but do not allow to boil.
2. Break one of the eggs into another saucepan. Separate the other four eggs, putting the whites in a large bowl and adding the yolks to the saucepan. Sprinkle in the sugar and beat well into the egg yolks until the mixture becomes lighter in colour. Then pour in the flavoured milk, stirring continuously.
3. Place the saucepan over a low heat and cook without boiling, stirring all the time. Remove from the heat when the custard has thickened so that it coats the back of a spoon.
4. Strain the custard through a fine sieve. Beat the egg whites until stiff and fold into the warm custard, beating well until the mixture is smooth and light.
5. Leave to cool and place in the refrigerator for at least 1 hour before serving.

Serve with biscuits such as sponge fingers or with slices of sponge cake. This dessert does not keep well, and should be eaten the same day.

# Petits Pots de Crème au Café

*Coffee Ramekins*

*Serves 6. Preparation: 10 min Cooking: 40 min*
*4 hr before serving*
★

○ **200ml (7 fl oz) very strong warm coffee**
○ **600ml (22 fl oz) cream (preferably double cream)**
○ **100g (4 oz) caster sugar**
○ **8 egg yolks**

1. Preheat the oven to 195°C (375°F; gas mark 5). Heat the cream but do not let it boil. Put the egg yolks into a bowl and sprinkle in the sugar. Beat the mixture until it has turned pale and frothy. Then pour in the warm coffee, bit by bit, and the cream, beating in well with a spatula or whisk.
2. Pour the cream mixture into 6 individual ramekins, straining it through a fine sieve.
3. Place the ramekins in a *bain-marie* or large ovenproof dish filled with water, and cook in the oven for 40 minutes. Check whether they are cooked by inserting the blade of a knife into the centre of one of the ramekins. It should come out quite dry and clean. Make sure the water in the *bain-marie* does not boil.
4. When ready, remove the ramekins from the oven and leave to cool. Refrigerate for at least 4 hours before serving.

# Crème Brûlée

*Crème Brûlée (with caramel topping)*

*Serves 6-7. Preparation and cooking: 1 hr*
*the day before serving*
★

○ **1 litre (1¾ pints) double cream**
○ **2 eggs**
○ **10 egg yolks**
○ **100g (4 oz) caster sugar**
○ **5ml (1 tsp) vanilla essence**

*For the caramel:*
○ **60ml (4 tbls) caster sugar**

1. You must make this dessert the day before. Set the oven to 180°C (350°F; gas mark 4). Break 2 eggs into a bowl, and add the 10 egg yolks, then the vanilla and 30ml (2 tbls) of cream. Put the rest of the cream in a saucepan over a low heat, and heat until it 'shivers', but do not let it boil.
2. Meanwhile, sprinkle the sugar on to the eggs in the bowl, beating well until the mixture turns pale and frothy.
3. Pour the warm cream over the egg and sugar mixture, a little at a time, beating continuously. Then strain through a fine sieve into an ovenproof dish 24cm (9½ inches) in diameter.
4. Place the dish in a *bain-marie* and cook in the oven for approximately 45 minutes, or until the blade of a knife comes out clean. Make sure the water in the *bain-marie* does not boil, otherwise the eggs in the mixture may curdle.
5. When it is cooked, remove from the oven and leave to cool. Leave at the top of the refrigerator overnight.
6. The next day, 10 minutes before serving, heat the grill; place some ice cubes in the grill pan. Sprinkle some sugar over the cream and place under the grill. When the sugar has caramelized (after 3 or 4 minutes), remove from the grill and bring to the table.

It is easier to caramelize the cream when it is very cold. You may then replace it in the refrigerator and serve it very well chilled. You should then be able to crack the caramel topping with a spoon, like a pane of glass.

*If you are cooking a cream dessert in individual ramekins or pots in a* bain-marie *over a low heat, place them on a wire rack in a large saucepan or flameproof casserole filled with water and cook covered.*

# Flan
*Baked Custard*

*Serves 6. Preparation: 15 min  Cooking: 40 min*

★

○ ½ litre (18 fl oz) milk
○ 6 eggs
○ 150g (6 oz) caster sugar
○ 1 vanilla pod
○ 1 lemon
○ 100g (4 oz) flour
○ 20g (¾ oz) butter

1. Set the oven at 220°C (425°F; gas mark 7). Split the vanilla pod in two lengthways. Peel the lemon with a sharp knife, leaving the pith. Put the vanilla and spiral of lemon peel in a small saucepan with the milk and bring to the boil. Turn the heat off and leave for about 5 minutes.
2. Meanwhile, grease a mould or sandwich tin 24cm (9½ inches) in diameter. Break the eggs into a bowl, sprinkle in the sugar, and beat until the mixture turns pale and frothy. Then sprinkle in the sifted flour. Continue beating until the mixture is smooth and well blended. Remove the vanilla pod and lemon peel and pour the milk into the bowl, a little at a time, beating continuously. Beat for another 2 minutes so that the flour is completely incorporated in the milk and will not sink to the bottom during cooking.
3. Strain the custard through a fine sieve into the mould, and cook in the oven for 40 minutes. Insert the blade of a knife into the centre to see if it is cooked.
4. Remove the mould from the oven and leave to cool. Serve in the mould, or turn out on to a serving dish.

This simple recipe is always a success with young and old alike. You may replace the lemon peel with some orange flower water for variation.

# Flan de Potiron aux Épices
*Baked Custard with Spiced Pumpkin*

*Serves 6. Preparation: 20 min  Cooking: 1 hr 15 min*
*4 hr before serving*

★

○ 1kg (2¼ lb) slice of pumpkin
○ ⅓ litre (10½ fl oz) milk
○ 100g (4 oz) caster sugar
○ 3 eggs
○ 3 pinches powdered ginger
○ 3 pinches grated nutmeg
○ 1.5ml (¼ tsp) powdered cinnamon
○ 3 pinches ground pepper
○ 3 pinches salt
○ 30ml (2 tbls) flour
○ 20g (¾ oz) butter

1. Peel and cut the pumpkin into large cubes. Place in a saucepan with the milk and salt and simmer over a low heat for approximately 15 minutes, until the pumpkin is tender; then pass through a vegetable mill or blender.
2. Set the oven at 200°C (387°F; gas mark 5½). Break the eggs in a bowl, sprinkle in the sugar and flour, and beat well for 1 minute. Add the pumpkin purée, ginger, nutmeg, cinnamon and pepper. Mix all together well.
3. Grease a mould or sandwich tin 22cm (8½ inches) in diameter. Pour in the custard and place in a *bain-marie*. Cook in the oven for between 45 minutes and 1 hour, until the custard is firm.
4. Remove from the oven and leave to cool completely, then place in the refrigerator for at least 4 hours before serving. Turn out on to a dish and serve.

To shorten the cooking time, you may pour the custard into individual ramekins. Try adding 30ml (2 tbls) of currants or 6 chopped prunes, or even some slices of apple, to the custard before cooking. For even greater flavour, add the finely grated peel of one lemon or half an orange.

*Crème Panachée Chocolat-Orange (p140)* ▶

# Flan de Pommes Caramélisé aux Noix

*Baked Caramel Custard with Apples and Walnuts*

*Serves 6. Preparation: 50 min*
*Cooking: 45 min*
★★

○ **1.5kg (3¼ lb) apples**
○ **180g (7¼ oz) caster sugar**
○ **4 eggs**
○ **1 lemon**
○ **30ml (2 tbls) double cream**
○ **8 walnuts**

1. Preheat the oven to 220°C (425°F; gas mark 7). Quarter the apples, peel and remove the core. Slice them thinly and place in an ovenproof casserole. Cook covered in the oven for 30 minutes.
2. Shell the walnuts and grate them coarsely. Grate the lemon and squeeze the juice.
3. Put 120g (4¾ oz) of the sugar in a saucepan with 30ml (2 tbls) of water and 5ml (1 tsp) of lemon juice. Do not add the lemon peel. Cook over a medium heat until you have a golden syrup. Turn the heat off and add 15ml (1 tbls) of water. Stir in well, then pour the caramel in to a mould or sandwich tin 22cm (8½ inches) in diameter, tilting it so that the caramel coats the bottom and sides evenly. Sprinkle in the coarsely grated walnuts.
4. After the apples have cooked for 30 minutes, remove from the oven and reduce the heat to 195°C (375°F; gas mark 5). Pass the apples through a vegetable mill or blender and put the purée in a saucepan with the remaining sugar and the cream. Cook over a medium heat, stirring with a spatula, until the purée thickens and turns slightly golden.
5. Turn the heat off and add the rest of the lemon juice to the purée with the lemon peel. Stir well and break the eggs in one by one, folding them in with a spatula. Pour the mixture into the mould, smoothing the surface flat with a spatula. Cook in a *bain-marie* in the oven for 45 minutes.
6. After that time, check whether the custard is ready by pressing the centre lightly with your fingertips: if it is firm and springy, it is cooked. Otherwise, leave in the oven for a little longer. Then remove the dish from the oven and leave to cool for 20 minutes; turn out on to a serving dish. This dessert may be eaten slightly warm, cold, or chilled.

# Flan aux Fruits Râpés

*Baked Fruit Custard*

*Serves 6-7. Preparation: 15 min Cooking: 1 hr*
★

○ **⅓ litre (7½ fl oz) milk**
○ **100g (4 oz) single cream**
○ **3 eggs**
○ **45ml (3 tbls) flour**
○ **90ml (6 tbls) caster sugar**
○ **5ml (1 tsp) powdered vanilla**
○ **1 large apple**
○ **1 large pear**
○ **1 large banana**
○ **30ml (2 tbls) currants**
○ **15ml (1 tbls) rum**
○ **1 lemon**
○ **25g (1 oz) butter**

1. Set the oven at 205°C (400°F; gas mark 6). Leave the currants to soak in the rum. Mix the sugar with the vanilla. Break the eggs in to a bowl; stir in the mixed sugar and vanilla, reserving 15ml (1 tbls), and sprinkle in the flour. Stir well until the mixture is smooth and well-blended. Then add the milk and cream, mixing in well.
2. Grease an ovenproof dish or a mould or sandwich tin 24cm (9½ inches) in diameter. Peel the apple, remove the core, and grate it coarsely into the custard. Mix well. Grate the pear and banana in the same way and mix everything together well.
3. Now finely grate the lemon peel over the bowl. Add the currants soaked in rum and mix once more. Pour the mixture into the mould and cook in the oven for 50 minutes to 1 hour, until the fruit custard has turned golden.
4. Remove the dish from the oven and leave to cool before sprinkling with the remaining 15ml (1 tbls) of vanilla sugar. You may serve this dessert straight away, or leave it to cool completely and serve very cold. You should not unmould it.

# Mousse au Chocolat au Lait

*Milk Chocolate Mousse*

*Serves 6-7. Preparation 15 min*
*1 hr before serving*
★

○ **250g (9 oz) milk chocolate**
○ **½ litre (18 fl oz) chilled double cream**
○ **2 egg whites**
○ **75g (3 oz) vanilla sugar**
○ **30ml (2 tbls) unsweetened cocoa powder**

1. Put 30ml (2 tbls) of the cream in a small pan placed in a *bain-marie* (or use a double saucepan); break in the chocolate and leave to melt slowly over a gentle heat.
2. Put the rest of the cream in a large bowl and whisk until stiff. Beat the egg whites until just stiff, gradually adding the vanilla sugar. Fold the egg whites into the whipped cream as carefully as possible, using a spatula.
3. When the chocolate has melted, remove from the heat, stirring with a spatula. Leave to cool for a while, but not completely, otherwise it will harden. Carefully fold into the meringue and cream mixture.
4. When the mixture is well-blended, spoon into individual glasses. Smooth the surface of the mousse and refrigerate for at least one hour before serving.
5. Just before serving, coat with an even sprinkling of cocoa, or make a pattern on the surface by cutting out a paper stencil in whatever design you want. Place this lightly on the mousse and scatter the cocoa over. When you remove the paper, the pattern will appear!

Instead of the cocoa, or as well as, you can use a sprinkling of ground hazelnuts.

# Mousse au Chocolat au Grand Marnier

*Chocolate Mousse with Grand Marnier*

*Serves 8. Preparation: 20 min*
*6 hr before serving*
★ ★

○ **400g (14 oz) bitter chocolate**
○ **200g (7 oz) softened butter**
○ **8 eggs**
○ **45ml (3 tbls) grand marnier**
○ **30ml (2 tbls) caster sugar**
○ **pinch salt**

1. Break the chocolate into pieces and put in to a saucepan placed in a *bain-marie* (or use a double saucepan), and leave over a low heat.
2. Separate the eggs, keeping the yolks on one side and putting the whites into a large bowl; sprinkle the salt over.
3. When the chocolate has melted, remove the saucepan from the heat and stir well with a spatula until it is smooth. Stir in the softened butter. When the mixture is well-blended, beat in the egg yolks, one at a time, and then add the liqueur, still beating briskly.
4. Beat the egg whites until stiff, gradually adding the sugar a little at a time. Gently fold in the chocolate mixture, using a spatula.
5. Pour the mousse in to a large glass bowl and leave to set in the refrigerator for at least 6 hours before serving.

Serve with small almond biscuits or macaroons. You may use an orange liqueur or a coffee liqueur such as Tia Maria instead of the grand marnier if you prefer.

# Oeufs à la Neige Caramélisés

*Snow Eggs with Caramel*

*Serves 6. Preparation and cooking: 45 min*
*1 hr before serving*
★★

○ **1 litre (1¾ pints) milk**
○ **1 vanilla pod**
○ **8 eggs**
○ **150g (6 oz) caster sugar**
○ **2 pinches salt**

*For the caramel:*
○ **100g (4 oz) caster sugar**

1. With a sharp knife, split the vanilla pod in half lengthways. Put with the milk in a saucepan and bring to the boil. Turn the heat off, cover with a lid, and leave to infuse.
2. Separate the eggs, putting the whites in a large bowl and sprinkling with salt. Put the yolks in a saucepan (enamelled or stainless steel) and sprinkle in the sugar (keeping back 30ml (2 tbls) which will be added to the egg whites). Beat the yolks and sugar together until they turn pale and frothy. Slowly pour in some of the milk, stirring continuously, and when the ingredients are well blended, pour in the rest quickly. Place the saucepan over a low heat. Cook, stirring all the time, until the custard thickens and coats the back of a spoon evenly. Strain through a sieve into a bowl, and leave to cool, placing the bowl in cold water and stirring the custard from time to time.
3. Beat the egg whites until very stiff, then whisk in 30ml (2 tbls) of sugar and continue beating for 1 minute. Meanwhile, fill a large pan three-quarters full of water and bring to the boil. Reduce the heat and let the surface of the water just shiver.
4. Plunge a long-handled ladle into cold water, then pick up a spoonful of the meringue mixture and slide into the water, hitting the handle of the ladle sharply on the edge of the pan to release the mixture. Plunge the ladle into cold water before picking up another spoonful – this will make it much easier to slip off into the water. Spoon out 3 to 6 spoonfuls of the meringue mixture as quickly as possible. After 30 seconds, turn over each little 'island' or ball, using a slotted spoon, and cook for another 30 seconds. Then lift them out and place on a wire rack covered with muslin. Make sure that each 'island' does not come into contact with the others in the water, and when cooked, arrange them wide apart.
5. When the custard has cooked, pour it into a glass bowl and delicately place the meringue balls or 'snow eggs' on top. Prepare the caramel. Put 100g (4 oz) caster sugar with 30ml (2 tbls) of water in a small saucepan. Cook until it turns golden and slowly trickle the caramel over the meringues. Serve at once.

Unless the kitchen is very warm, it should not be necessary to refrigerate this dish. The caramel should always be prepared at the last moment, so that it does not have time to melt the meringue.

*Because icing sugar is extremely fine and light, it tends to settle in the packet and become lumpy – and so you must always sift it before giving soufflés, pancakes, and fritters a light dusting of sugar. The best way is to use a cylindrical metal sifter with a pierced lid which will ensure that the icing sugar is spread evenly and lightly.*

# Blanche-Neige aux Fruits Rouges

*Snow-white Dessert with Red Soft Fruits*

*Serves 6. Preparation: 45 min*
*3 hr before serving*
★

○ **400ml (14 fl oz) milk**
○ **400ml (14 fl oz) chilled double cream**
○ **150g (6 oz) caster sugar**
○ **4 drops vanilla essence**
○ **2 drops bitter almond essence**
○ **6 gelatine sheets**

*For the garnish:*
○ **300g (11 oz) raspberries**
○ **300g (11 oz) wild strawberries**
○ **400g (14 oz) redcurrants**
○ **150g (6 oz) caster sugar**
○ **30ml (2 tbls) kirsch**

*For the mould:*
○ **15ml (1 tbls) caster sugar**

1. Soak the gelatine in cold water. Put the milk and sugar in a saucepan and bring to the boil over a medium heat. Then add the drained gelatine (it should melt immediately). Stir in well and leave to cool, standing the saucepan in cold water.
2. Meanwhile, whip the cream. When the milk starts to set, stir in the vanilla and bitter almond essence and beat for 5 minutes to let as much air in as possible. Then fold the whipped cream in gently.
3. Wet a mould, sprinkle in the sugar and fill. Chill in the refrigerator for 3 hours.
4. Make the garnish. Put 150g (6 oz) caster sugar in a saucepan with 100ml (3½ fl oz) of water over a low heat. When the sugar has melted, turn off the heat. Wash the redcurrants and pass through a sieve or mill, over a bowl. Stir in the cold syrup and kirsch. Wash and hull the strawberries and raspberries, and stir into the puréed fruit. Chill in the refrigerator.
5. Turn out the bavaroise on to a deep serving dish. Pour over the red fruit purée and serve at once.

# Blanc-Manger

*Blancmange*

*Serves 8. Preparation: 30 min*
*4 hr before serving*
★ ★

○ **1 litre (1¾ pints) double cream**
○ **110g (4½ oz) caster sugar**
○ **25g (1 oz) vanilla sugar**
○ **7 gelatine sheets**
○ **250g (9 oz) sweet almonds**
○ **3 bitter almonds or 3 drops of bitter almond essence**

*For the mould:*
○ **15ml (1 tbls) caster sugar**

1. Put half the cream in the refrigerator to use later. Soak the gelatine in cold water. Plunge the sweet and bitter almonds in boiling water, drain immediately and rinse under running water. Skin them between your fingers and place in a blender with 45ml (3 tbls) of cream. Blend until the almonds are finely ground, then add the remaining cream a little at a time. Sieve the almond purée through a muslin cloth into a bowl, squeezing the cloth as tightly as possible to extract all the juice. If you are not using bitter almonds, add the bitter almond essence to the purée. Sprinkle in the sugar and stir in well.
2. Put a quarter of the almond purée in a small saucepan and cook over a low heat. Do not let it boil. Then add the drained gelatine (it will melt immediately). Stir well. Add a quarter of what is left in the bowl to the saucepan, stirring continuously with a spatula. Then pour the contents of the saucepan back into the bowl, still stirring. Blend all together well.
3. When the almond cream is starting to set, whip the reserved cream until stiff and sprinkle in the vanilla sugar. Fold into the almond cream in the bowl as gently as possible. Pour the blancmange into a wetted mould sprinkled with sugar and chill for at least 4 hours before turning out.

Accompany this delicious and traditional dessert (the true ancestor of all bavaroises and utterly unlike nursery blancmanges remembered from childhood) with whole or puréed red fruit, or with a compote of black cherries stewed in red wine.

# Soufflé Minute au Cacao

*Serves 3. Preparation: 10 min Cooking: 20 min*

*Quick Cocoa Soufflé*

★

○ **3 eggs**
○ **45ml (3 tbls) caster sugar**
○ **15ml (1 tbls) unsweetened cocoa powder**
○ **20g (¾ oz) butter**
○ **pinch salt**

1. Preheat the oven to 200°C (387°F; gas mark 5½). Butter the bottom and sides of a soufflé dish 16cm (6½ inches) in diameter and 6cm (2½ inches) high, and sprinkle in 15ml (1 tbls) of sugar. Tilt the mould in your hands to spread the sugar evenly, then shake out the excess. Always take care not to smear the butter and sugar coating with your fingers – this may prevent the soufflé from rising properly.
2. Prepare the soufflé. Separate the eggs, and sprinkle the whites with salt. Put the yolks into a bowl, sprinkle in the sugar and beat until the mixture turns pale and frothy. Then beat in the cocoa powder. Whisk the egg whites until just stiff and fold into the yolks, lifting the mixture carefully with a spatula.
3. Turn the mixture into the soufflé mould and cook for 20 minutes in the oven until the soufflé has risen and turned golden – and it should smell quite delicious!

For extra flavour, add the grated peel of half a lemon or orange with a pinch of powdered vanilla to the soufflé mixture.

*Even some famous chefs have failed to achieve the perfect soufflé. And yet it is not a miracle – so long as you follow the rules of the game. A soufflé must satisfy two requirements to be counted a success: it must look good, and it must taste good. Sometimes a good-looking soufflé may turn out to contain too much flour and will be disappointingly heavy; and a delicious-tasting soufflé may be flawed by its undistinguished appearance.*

*There are three basic rules which must be respected. First the egg whites must be beaten only until just stiff and they must be added to the other ingredients in two stages. A little of the beaten egg whites should first be incorporated with the rest, and this mixture should then be returned to the other egg whites. The tricky part comes now! Turning the bowl clockwise, gently fold the mixture in, dividing it into triangular sections with your spatula and lifting from the bottom to the top so that all is smooth and well-blended. You must do it quickly.*

*Secondly, the soufflé mixture must fill the mould three-quarters full. If you put in too much it will puff up over the rim of the mould, and if you don't use enough it will look as if it has failed to rise properly at all and won't turn an attractive golden colour. The best soufflé moulds are of fireproof porcelain. They should be 5cm (2 inches) high and not more than 18cm (7 inches) in diameter. Small soufflés usually look better. The mould should be generously greased with butter and the bottom and sides evenly coated with sugar. Don't smear the coating with your fingers – you'll prevent the soufflé from rising properly in that spot.*

*Thirdly, the oven must not be too hot, otherwise the soufflé will cook quickly on the outside and remain liquid at the centre. Nor should it be too cold, as then it will not rise. You need a medium heat to be sure of a well-risen and properly cooked soufflé.*

# Charlotte Doigts de Fée au Caramel
*Caramel Charlotte with Meringue Fingers*

○ **4 egg yolks**
○ **150g (6 oz) caster sugar**
○ **250ml (9 fl oz) very strong coffee**
○ **6 gelatine sheets**
○ **250ml (9 fl oz) chilled double cream**
○ **25g (1 oz) vanilla sugar**
○ **100g (4 oz) doigts de fée (chocolate- or coffee-coated meringue fingers)**

*To decorate:*
○ **15 to 20 coffee beans coated in chocolate, or steeped in liqueur.**

1. Soak the gelatine in cold water. Put the sugar in a saucepan with 60ml (4 tbls) of water over a low heat until it forms a golden syrup. Remove from the heat and slowly pour in the coffee, stirring continuously.
2. Put the egg yolks in a saucepan. Beat, slowly pouring in the coffee-flavoured caramel. Place the saucepan in a *bain-marie* over a low heat (the water should just shiver). Continue beating until the mixture has thickened and is three times the volume, then add the drained gelatine. Beat for another minute, then remove from the heat and leave to cool.
3. Whip the cream, sprinkle in the vanilla sugar, and continue whipping until very stiff. Put about 30ml (2 tbls) in the refrigerator.
4. When the mousse is cold and is starting to set, fold in the rest of the whipped cream. Wet a mould or sandwich tin and fill with the mousse to a height of 4-5cm (1¾-2 inches). Smooth the top with a spatula and chill for 3 hours or more.
5. Just before serving, dip the mould in warm water for 10 seconds and turn out on to a serving dish. Surround with the meringue fingers placed edge-to-edge like a wall. Pipe on the reserved whipped cream to decorate attractively and dot with the coffee beans.

# Charlotte aux Fruits Rouges
*Strawberry and Raspberry Charlotte*

○ **500g (1 lb 2 oz) mixed soft fruit: strawberries, wild strawberries, raspberries**
○ **150g (6 oz) redcurrant jelly**
○ **250ml (9 fl oz) milk**
○ **125g (5 oz) caster sugar**
○ **4 egg yolks**
○ **4 gelatine sheets**
○ **250ml (9 fl oz) chilled double cream**
○ **25g (1 oz) vanilla sugar**
○ **60ml (4 tbls) kirsch**
○ **24 sponge fingers**

1. Soak the gelatine in cold water. Melt the redcurrant jelly over a low heat. Bring the milk to the boil.
2. In a saucepan, beat the egg yolks with the sugar and vanilla sugar, then pour in the milk. Cook over a low heat until the custard is thick enough to coat the back of a spoon evenly. Add the drained gelatine, stir in well and strain through a fine sieve in to a bowl standing in cold water.
3. Put 45ml (3 tbls) of kirsch in a deep dish with 90ml (6 tbls) of water. Dip the sponge fingers in this one by one, and line the bottom and sides of a charlotte mould 18cm (7 inches) in diameter with them. Brush with a little melted jelly. Add the remaining kirsch to the rest of the jelly and dip the fruit into it, gently turning the fruit over to coat thoroughly. Place a layer of fruit in the mould.
4. Whip the cream and gently fold in to the custard which should be starting to set. Pour a layer of this mixture on to the fruit, then add alternate layers of the remaining fruit and the custard. Cover with sponge fingers and chill for at least 3 hours. Turn out on to a serving dish.

A purée of red soft fruits, with lemon juice and sugar, will go very well with this summer charlotte. Instead of mixing the fruit, you can use either raspberries or strawberries on their own.

# Hérisson aux Marrons

*Serves 6. Preparation: 30 min (15 min the day before)*

## Marron and Chocolate Hedgehog

★

- ○ **500g (18 oz) unsweetened marron purée**
- ○ **100g (4 oz) fondant chocolate**
- ○ **60ml (4 tbls) caster sugar**
- ○ **100ml (3½ fl oz) single cream**
- ○ **50g (2 oz) butter**
- ○ **25g (1 oz) vanilla sugar**
- ○ **30ml (2 tbls) rum**

*To decorate:*
- ○ **200ml (7 fl oz) chilled double cream**
- ○ **15ml (1 tbls) icing sugar**
- ○ **25g (1 oz) vanilla sugar**

1. Beat the marron purée until creamy, using a spatula. Put the sugar, vanilla sugar and cream in a small saucepan and place in a *bain-marie*. Break in the chocolate and leave to melt over a low heat without stirring. Then add the butter, mixing in with a spatula until the mixture is smooth, and next the marron purée and rum. Mix all together well.
2. Wet a cylindrical (deep cake tin) or domed mould, such as a glass cheese cover. Sprinkle in the sugar evenly and fill with the mixture. Smooth the surface with a spatula and chill in the refrigerator until the next day (or even longer).
3. Just before serving, dip the mould in warm water for 10 seconds and turn out on to a serving dish. Whip the cream until stiff, beat in the caster and vanilla sugar and put into an icing bag with a 1cm (½ inch) diameter plain nozzle. Pipe on small raised dots or cones, very close together, to look like the prickles on a hedgehog. Serve at once.

Serve this dessert with a warm chocolate sauce made from 100g (4 oz) bitter chocolate melted in 200ml (7 fl oz) double cream or milk and mixed with 25g (1 oz) butter.

# Crème de Patates Douces au Chocolat

*Serves 6. Preparation and cooking: 55 min (1 hr before serving)*

## Sweet Potato Gâteau with Chocolate Sauce

★

- ○ **1.2kg (2¾ lb) sweet potatoes**
- ○ **50g (2 oz) vanilla sugar**
- ○ **250g (9 oz) plain chocolate**
- ○ **400ml (14 fl oz) milk**

1. Wash the sweet potatoes. Put in a large saucepan, cover generously with cold water, and cook over a medium heat for about 30 minutes. Check whether they are cooked by piercing with a knife. (You can also steam the sweet potatoes.)
2. Drain in a colander and leave to cool for 5 minutes. Then peel, while they are still warm, and sieve into a bowl.
3. Heat 150ml (5 fl oz) of milk with the vanilla sugar. When the sugar has melted, pour the milk on to the sweet potatoes, stirring in vigorously with a spatula.
4. Pour the purée into a deep dish and mould in to the shape of a volcano (or you can use a kugelhopf mould). Leave to cool.
5. Meanwhile, break the chocolate into pieces in a saucepan with the remaining milk and stand in a *bain-marie* (or use a double saucepan) to melt slowly over a low heat. Smooth the surface of the chocolate with a spatula, then remove from the heat and leave to cool for 5 minutes, if necessary by standing in cold water.
6. When it has cooled to lukewarm, pour the chocolate into the crater of the volcano so that it overflows and runs down the outside of the cake, and spreads around the bottom. Leave in a cool place or refrigerator for at least one hour before serving. It should be cold, but not chilled.

You may, if you choose, add more sugar to the purée of sweet potatoes . . . or else a knob of butter, some cinnamon, or some grated nutmeg. The milk can be replaced by single cream or coconut milk.

# Semoule aux Poires Sauce Chocolat
*Serves 6. Preparation and cooking: 50 min*
*(3 hr before serving)*
★
## Semolina and Pears with Chocolate Sauce

○ **900g (2 lb) pears (6 small ones or 3 large ones)**
○ **150g (6 oz) very fine semolina**
○ **150g (6 oz) caster sugar**
○ **50g (2 oz) vanilla sugar**
○ **250g (9 oz) single cream**
○ **30ml (2 tbls) rum (optional)**

*For the sauce:*
○ **150g (6 oz) fondant chocolate**
○ **200ml (7 fl oz) milk**
○ **30g (1 oz) butter**

1. If the pears are small, peel them, leaving the stalks on. If they are large, cut in half, peel and remove the stalk and core.
2. Bring 1 litre (1¾ pints) of water to the boil over a medium heat with the caster and vanilla sugar. Cook the pears in this syrup for 15 to 30 minutes. When the tip of a knife pierces them easily, drain them and place in a bowl, moistened with a little of the syrup they cooked in.
3. You will need about three-quarters of a litre (1¼ pints) of this syrup to make the semolina. Make up the rest with water. Bring the syrup to the boil, sprinkle in the semolina, stirring with a spatula, and cook over a low heat for 15 minutes, still stirring all the time. After 12 minutes, slowly pour in the cream. Add the rum away from the heat and mix well.
4. Wet a savarin or ring mould, and fill with the warm semolina; smooth the surface with a spatula and leave to cool. Put the pears and the semolina pudding in the refrigerator for 3 hours.
5. 10 minutes before serving, turn the semolina pudding out on to a serving dish and place the pears in the centre. Make the sauce by adding the chocolate pieces to the boiling milk in a saucepan and leaving to melt over a low heat. Then stir the butter in quickly with a spatula. When the sauce is smooth, remove from the heat and pour a little over the pears. Serve the rest in a sauceboat.

# Gâteau de Semoule aux Raisins
*Serves 6-8. Preparation and cooking: 50 min*
*1 hr before serving*
★
## Semolina Pudding with Sultanas

○ **1½ litres (barely 2½ pints) milk**
○ **1 vanilla pod split in half**
○ **4 eggs**
○ **90ml (6 tbls) fine semolina**
○ **115ml (9 tbls) sugar**
○ **100g (4 oz) sultanas**
○ **45ml (3 tbls) rum or kirsch**

*For the caramel:*
○ **60ml (4 tbls) sugar**

1. The day before, wash the sultanas and leave to soak in the rum or kirsch.
2. The next day, bring the milk to the boil together with the vanilla and sugar. Then remove from the heat and leave to infuse.
3. Prepare the caramel. Put the sugar and 30ml (2 tbls) of water in a small saucepan and cook over a medium heat until a golden syrup is formed. Pour this into a brioche or charlotte mould of 1½ litre (2½ pints) capacity. Tilt the mould in your hands to coat the bottom and sides of the mould evenly with the caramel.
4. Separate the eggs, putting the whites in a large bowl. Whisk until stiff.
5. Put 1 litre (1¾ pints) of the flavoured and sweetened milk in a saucepan and bring to the boil. Sprinkle in the semolina and cook for approximately 8 minutes, stirring continuously. Then fold in the beaten egg whites and cook for another 2 minutes, still stirring. Add the sultanas, mix well and remove from heat.
Turn the rice pudding into the caramelized mould. Pat firmly down, and smooth the top of the pudding with a spatula. Leave to cool.
6. Meanwhile, prepare a custard sauce with the egg yolks and remaining milk, following the instructions given on page 9. Leave to cool.
7. When the pudding and custard are cold, serve together; or chill in the refrigerator for a few hours more.

# Crêpes Classiques
## Traditional Pancakes

*20-24 pancakes. Preparation: 10 min (1 hr before cooking)*
*Cooking: 40 min*
★

○ **250g (9 oz) flour**
○ **3 eggs**
○ **½ litre (18 fl oz) milk**
○ **2.5ml (½ tsp) salt**
○ **15ml (1 tbls) caster sugar**
○ **30ml (2 tbls) oil (optional)**

*For flavouring:*
○ **15ml (1 tbls) rum or 15ml**
   **(1 tbls) orange flower water**

*For cooking:*
○ **50g (2 oz) butter**

1. Sift the flour into a bowl. Make a well in the centre and break in the eggs. Add the oil, salt and sugar, with the flavouring and a little milk. Blend all together well, working from the centre out round and round in a circle. Pour the milk in slowly, stirring continuously. When the batter is smooth and well-blended, strain through a sieve into a bowl. Leave to rest for at least one hour.
2. Cook the pancakes. Melt the butter in a frying pan kept only for cooking pancakes; it should be 20cm (8 inches) in diameter. When it has melted, pour off the butter into a bowl; grease the pan with a little of the butter each time before cooking the pancake. When the pan is really hot ladle out a little of the batter into it, and tilt it to spread the batter in an even circle. Cook the pancake on one side and then toss it (or flip it over with a spatula) to cook the other side. The cooking should take about one minute in all.
3. Keep the pancakes warm by piling them on a dish placed over a saucepan filled with boiling water.

Serve with various kinds of jams, or with marron purée, honey, or sugar. You can fill them with slices of apple that have been sugared and sautéed in butter. To make sure of really crisp pancakes, add another egg to the batter and replace half the amount of milk with water. For a lighter pancake, use half milk and half beer; or just water on its own. If the batter is too thick, add a little water just before cooking. Never add more milk – it makes the pancakes heavy.

# Crêpes à la Minute
## Quick Pancakes

*18-24 pancakes. Preparation: 5 min Cooking: 25 min*

★

○ **125g (5 oz) flour**
○ **3 eggs**
○ **30ml (2 tbls) oil**
○ **50g (2 oz) melted butter**
○ **1ml (¼ tsp) salt**
○ **15ml (1 tbls) caster sugar**
○ **25g (1 oz) vanilla sugar**
○ **15ml (1 tbls) rum**
○ **350ml (12½ fl oz) milk**
○ **grated peel of ½ orange or**
   **lemon (optional)**

*For cooking:*
○ **25g (1 oz) butter approx**

1. For this recipe it is best to use an electric blender or beater. Put the flour, eggs, salt, sugar, vanilla sugar, oil, melted butter, rum, milk and grated peel into a large bowl or in the blender. Beat at the fast speed with the electric beater for 1 minute, then strain the batter through a sieve. This batter does not need to rest because it is so rich in eggs and fats, and so it can be used immediately.
2. Melt the butter in the frying pan. Pour in a little batter, using a small ladle, and tilt the pan all round in a circular movement. After a few seconds of cooking, flip the pancake over with a palette knife or spatula (these pancakes are too thin to be tossed) and cook on the other side for 10 to 12 seconds. In between making each pancake, lightly grease the pan with a cloth or piece of kitchen paper dipped in the melted butter.
3. Stack the pancakes in a pile on a dish placed over a pan of boiling water to keep warm.

Serve the pancakes sprinkled with a little sugar, mixed with vanilla sugar if you like, and with more grated peel. They are also excellent served cold with jam, honey or sugar.

*Semoule aux Poires Sauce Chocolat (p153)* ▶

# Couronne de Pommes

*Apple Crown Pudding*

*Serves 6-8. Preparation 30 min Cooking: 1 hr 30 min*
*the day before*
★

○ **1.5kg (3¼ lb) apples**
○ **500g (18 oz) caster sugar**
○ **1 lemon**
○ **1 vanilla pod**

1. Peel and core the apples, and put the peel and core in a saucepan with ½ litre (18 fl oz) of water. Cut the lemon in half and rub over the quarters of peeled apple, so that they do not discolour. Bring the contents of the saucepan to the boil over a high heat, and cook for 15 minutes, covered, then sieve the contents into another saucepan. This juice, rich in pectin, will set the apples, once cooked.
2. Split the vanilla pod lengthways in half. Put in to the juice, add the sugar as well, and place the saucepan over a high heat. When the syrup has turned nearly golden, throw in the apple quarters, shaking the saucepan to make sure the fruit is coated all over. Reduce the heat. Cook, uncovered, shaking the saucepan from time to time, until the apples become transparent. Do not stir, or else the fruit will disintegrate. It will take from 1 hour to 1 hour 30 minutes to cook them, depending on the quality of the apples.
3. Fill a wetted savarin or ring mould 24cm (9½ inches) in diameter with the cooked apples; remove the vanilla pod, and leave to cool. Then chill in the refrigerator until next day.
4. The next day, turn out on to a serving dish and serve at once.

This apple crown pudding is delicious served with an egg custard sauce, or simply with some double cream.

# Pommes en Papillottes

*Baked Apples with Redcurrant Jelly*

*Serves 6. Preparation: 15 min cooking: 45 min*
★

○ **6 apples**
○ **30ml (2 tbls) caster sugar**
○ **30ml (2 tbls) redcurrant (or quince) jelly**
○ **6 pinches cinnamon**

1. Set the oven to 220°C (425°F; gas mark 7). Wash and wipe the apples. Cut a small slice off the bottom of each so that they do not roll. Remove the core with a sharp knife, making sure at least 1cm (½ inch) is left at the bottom (if you use an apple corer you are liable to go right through).
2. Put 5ml (1 tsp) of the jelly, with 5ml (1 tsp) of sugar and a pinch of cinnamon inside each apple. Wrap each one up as tightly as possible in foil or greaseproof paper.
3. Arrange the apples in foil on a wire rack in a baking tin and cook in the oven for 45 minutes.
4. When cooked, remove from the oven and bring to the table as they are. Let your guests unwrap their own apples so they can savour the delicious smell themselves!

You may prefer to fill the apples with blossom honey mixed with chopped walnuts and sultanas, instead of the jelly and cinnamon.

*If you add a few drops of lemon juice or vinegar to the sugar when making caramel, it will prevent the syrup from crystallizing during cooking – otherwise this will occur whenever you dip a spoon into the caramel or add the nuts – walnuts, hazelnuts, or almonds – to make praline.*

# Pommes de Pin

*Apple Pinecones*

*Serves 6. Preparation: 20 min  Cooking: 30 min*

★

○ **6 apples**
○ **60g (2½ oz) butter**
○ **30ml (6 tsp) sultanas**
○ **30ml (6 tsp) caster sugar**
○ **120g (4¾ oz) flaked almonds**

1. Set the oven to 205°C (400°F; gas mark 6). Peel the apples in a spiral, making sure they are as well shaped as possible. Cut a small slice off the bottom of each to stop them from rolling. Remove the core with a sharp knife, leaving at least 1cm (½ inch) at the bottom. (If you use an apple corer you will go right through.)
2. Butter a baking dish large enough to fit all the apples with plenty of room between them. Place them in the dish, and put a little knob of butter inside each, followed in turn by 5ml (1 tsp) of sultanas, 5ml (1 tsp) of sugar, and then another knob of butter. Pour 60ml (4 tbls) of water into the dish.
3. Place in the oven and cook for 30 minutes or more. Check to see if the apples are cooked by piercing with a knife or skewer. It should go in quite easily.
4. While the apples are cooking, put the almonds in a large frying pan over a medium heat. Brown, shaking the pan all the time. Then remove from the heat and put on one side.
5. Remove the apples from the oven and transfer to a serving dish, using a spatula or slice. Spike each apple with the best-looking almonds set closely together so that they look like pinecones. Sprinkle the remaining almonds over, and serve.

Serve these apples lukewarm, if you prefer, accompanied by a crème pâtissière flavoured with rum, or by a sabayon.

# Poires-Hérissons

*Pear Hedgehogs*

*Serves 6. Preparation: 15 min  Cooking: 20 min*

○ **6 large pears**
○ **100g (4 oz) flaked almonds**
○ **24 currants**
○ **1 lemon**
○ **30g (1¼ oz) butter**
○ **30ml (2 tbls) caster sugar**

1. Set the oven to 220°C (425°F; gas mark 7). Cut the lemon in half. Slice the pears lengthways into equal halves. Peel and remove the core, and rub each half with the lemon.
2. Butter a baking dish large enough to hold all the fruit easily. Arrange the pears, flat side down, in it and squeeze the lemon juice over. Sprinkle with sugar. Add 90ml (6 tbls) of water to the dish and cook in the oven for 20 minutes, until the pears are cooked (a knife should pierce them easily). Baste the pears with the cooking juice while they are cooking.
3. Meanwhile, brown the almonds in a frying pan over a medium heat, shaking the pan frequently, to prevent them from burning. Put on one side.
4. Lift the cooked pears carefully on to a serving dish, using a spatula or slice. If any juice is left in the dish, pour it over the pears to glaze them.
5. Spike the pears all over with the almonds, starting from the stalk end: they should look like hedgehogs. Use the currants for eyes. Serve at once, or leave to cool for a while.

Serve with a hot chocolate sauce: 150g (6 oz) chocolate melted with 45ml (3 tbls) of water. Or you can accompany this dessert with an egg custard flavoured with kirsch.

# Beignets de Bananes au Citron Vert

*Banana Fritters with Lime*

*Serves 6. Preparation: 15 min
(30 min before cooking) Cooking: 15 min*
★★

○ **2 medium-sized bananas**
○ **30ml (2 tbls) lime juice**
○ **45ml (3 tbls) white rum**
○ **45ml (3 tbls) caster sugar**
○ **250g (9 oz) flour**
○ **1 egg**
○ **200ml (7 fl oz) butter**
○ **25g (1 oz) butter**
○ **2.5ml (½ tsp) baking powder**
○ **2 pinches salt**
○ **oil for deep frying**

*To serve:*
○ **caster sugar to taste**

1. Peel and cut the bananas across into rounds or lengthways in half. Put in a bowl and moisten with the lime juice and 30ml (2 tbls) of rum; mix together and sprinkle with 30ml (2 tbls) of sugar. Mix once more and leave to stand, turning the banana slices over from time to time.
2. 10 minutes before cooking the fritters, prepare the batter. Melt the butter in a small saucepan over a low heat; then leave to cool. Beat the egg with the milk in a bowl; put the flour in another bowl, stir in the salt, 15ml (1 tbls) of sugar and the baking powder. Then slowly pour in the egg and milk mixture, stirring continuously with a spatula. Add the melted butter and the remaining 15ml (1 tbls) of rum. Mix well until the batter is smooth.
3. Heat the oil in a deep fryer: it should be at least 5cm (2 inches) high. Wipe the banana slices, and dip them in the batter, 6 at a time. When the oil is very hot but not smoking, put in the banana fritters and fry on both sides. Remove from the oil with a slotted spoon and drain on kitchen paper.
4. When the fritters are ready, stack them in a pile and serve at once, sprinkled with sugar, or not – as you wish.

This dessert is a speciality of Martinique.

# Beignets d'Ananas au Rhum

*Pineapple Fritters with Rum*

*Serves 5. Preparation: 15 min (1 hr before cooking)
Cooking: 15 min*
★

○ **10 slices of pineapple (tinned in syrup)**
○ **150g (6 oz) flour**
○ **100ml (3½ fl oz) beer**
○ **25g (1 oz) butter**
○ **pinch salt**
○ **30ml (2 tbls) caster sugar**
○ **30ml (2 tbls) white rum**
○ **2 egg whites**
○ **oil for deep frying**

*To serve:*
○ **icing sugar**

1. One hour before cooking the fritters, drain the pineapple slices well, wipe dry, and put on a plate, moistened with rum and sprinkled with sugar on both sides.
2. Melt the butter in a small saucepan over a low heat. In a bowl, mix the flour, salt, and melted butter. Slowly pour in the beer, together with an equal amount of water, working the flour in with a spatula. When the batter is smooth, leave to stand for one hour.
3. Just before cooking the fritters, heat the oil in a deep fryer: it should be at least 5cm (2 inches) high. Drain the pineapple slices on kitchen paper. Keep the juice. Beat the egg whites until they form soft peaks, and fold in to the batter with the pineapple juice, using a whisk.
4. When the oil is very hot but not smoking, dip the pineapple slices in the batter, then put in the oil. When the fritters are golden on one side, turn over and fry on the other side. Remove from the oil with a slotted spoon and drain on kitchen paper.
5. Arrange the fritters in a serving dish and sprinkle with icing sugar. Eat at once.

*Beignets de Bananes au Citron Vert* ❯

# Wines: the Finishing Touch

Nowadays excellent quality table wines are within the reach of everyone, though you should expect to pay more for a good vintage wine from one of the famous vineyards, such as Nuits-St-Georges or Schloss Johannisberg Riesling. When buying French wine, look for the *Appellation Contrôlée* label, which is a guarantee of quality.

Below is a guide to the wines that go best with certain foods, but there are no absolute *rules* about which wine to serve with what food – in the end it is your palate that must decide. For a large, formal meal, certain wines traditionally follow each other through the menu and you could serve three or even four wines at one meal. In this case, it is usual to serve dry sherry with the soup, dry white wine with the fish course, claret or burgundy with the meat or game and a white dessert wine or medium sweet champagne with the dessert. For cheese, your guests would return to the claret or burgundy. Certain foods kill the flavour of wine and should therefore be avoided if you are planning to serve wine with the meal. Mint sauce, for example, or any salad with a strong vinaigrette dressing, will destroy the taste of the wine.

Remember that red wines are generally served *chambré*, or at room temperature, to bring out the flavour. Draw the cork at least three or four hours before you plan to drink the wine and let the bottle stand in the kitchen or a warm room. (Never be tempted into putting the bottle in hot water or in front of the fire – the flavour will be ruined.) The exception to the *chambré* rule is Beaujolais, which can be served cool – some people even serve it chilled. White or rosé wines are usually served chilled – the easiest way is to put them in the fridge an hour before serving, or plunge them into an ice bucket, if you have one. Champagne should also be served well chilled and is generally brought to the table in an ice bucket.

| **Wines to Serve with Food** | |
|---|---|
| *Oysters, shellfish* | Chablis, dry Moselle, Champagne |
| *Fried or grilled fish* | Dry Graves, Moselle, Hock, Rosé, Blanc de Blanc |
| *Fish with sauces* | Riesling, Pouilly-Fuissé, Chablis |
| *Veal, pork or chicken dishes (served simply)* | Rosé, Riesling, a light red wine such as Beaujolais |
| *Chicken or pork served with a rich sauce* | Claret, Côte de Rhône, Médoc |
| *Rich meat dishes, steaks, game* | Red Burgundy, Rioja, Red Chianti |
| *Lamb or duck* | Claret, Beaujolais |
| *Desserts and puddings* | White Bordeaux, Sauternes, Entre Deux Mers |
| *Cheese* | Burgundy, Rioja, Cabernet Sauvignon |